Overruling
Democracy

Overruling
Democracy

The Supreme Court vs. The American People

Jamin B. Raskin

NEW YORK AND LONDON

Published in 2003 by
Routledge
29 West 35th Street
New York, NY 10001
www.routledge-ny.com

Published in Great Britain by
Routledge
11 New Fetter Lane
London EC4P 4EE
www.routledge.co.uk

Routledge is an imprint of the Taylor & Francis Group.
Printed in the United States of America on acid-free paper.
Design and typography: Jack Donner

10 9 8 7 6 5 4 3 2 1

Library of Congress Cataloging-in-Publication Data

Raskin, Jamin B.
   Overruling democracy : the Supreme Court versus the American people /
By Jamin B. Raskin.
     p. cm.
Includes bibliographical references and index.
   ISBN 0–415–93439–7 (hbk.)
1. United States. Supreme Court. 2. Political questions and judicial power—
United States. I. Title.
  KF8748 .R33 2002
  347.73'26—dc21

                                          2002011222

To my mother and father

CONTENTS

ACKNOWLEDGMENTS

In my journey toward becoming a scholar of constitutional democracy, I have had the benefit of extraordinary teachers along the way. None was more powerful in her influence over me than the late Professor Judith N. Shklar (1928–1992), with whom I studied from my first semester as a freshman at Harvard College in 1979 until I graduated in 1983. I then taught with her as a teaching fellow in political theory courses between 1984 and 1987 when I was a student at Harvard Law School. I learned much from a masterful English teacher named Missy Holland and the brilliant scholar of international affairs, Stanley Hoffmann. But, for my purposes, Mrs. Shklar was simply in a class by herself.

Mrs. Shklar embodied the best that American radicalism, liberalism and conservatism have to offer. The radical side of Mrs. Shklar linked the possibility of justice on earth to the strength of political democracy. She argued that, in the struggle for justice against power, people must be given the democratic right and space to speak for themselves. She rejected the conservative argument that law-obeying people should be presumed to be content with traditional hierarchies and inequalities. As she put it in a book called *The Faces of Injustice* (1990, p. 124): "Tradition is often nothing but the evidence of silence." It is political democracy and the struggle for it that give voice in history to popular aspirations for greater justice.

But Mrs. Shklar did not glorify the victims of injustice. In this sense, she articulated with much greater subtlety the point that contemporary conservatives have been trying to make in the ongoing backlash against "political correctness." Her point was that the experience of being discriminated against or oppressed does not necessarily instill moral virtue in victims. Many victims turn into bitter and tyrannical people. Some turn around and become oppressors themselves. (Think of victims of child abuse who become child abusers.) The reason that we oppose official tyranny and cruelty is not that the victims are more virtuous than everyone else but that everyone has a right to be free, no one has a right to oppress other people, and tyranny generates a paralyzing fear that undermines the capacity for good citizenship and collective social progress.

At the heart of things, Mrs. Shklar was a liberal, and hers was a liberalism born of the appalling catastrophes of the twentieth century, which were all too personal for her. She believed in what she called a "liberalism of fear." The freedom and security of citizens must be guarded against injustice, arbitrary action and cruelty. Sovereign power must be divided up and controlled through the checking and balancing of powers, as James Madison argued. The structural accomplishments of the American Framers were profoundly important, Mrs. Shklar thought, and she castigated snobbish scholars who treated European political theorists as inherently superior to American theorists even though our democratic institutions have been far more resilient and successful than many of their European counterparts.

As a liberal, Mrs. Shklar understood that the requirements of justice are a moving target in history since we must listen to the victims of injustice to determine what justice requires. We can keep faith with justice only by way of a supple and open democracy that grants people rights of effective political representation and self-presentation. Democracy without liberalism will undermine freedom, it is well understood, but liberalism without democracy will undermine justice. No democracy without liberalism, no liberalism without democracy.

A day does not go by when I do not think of Mrs. Shklar, who died in 1992, but I hope that this book stands up for progressive liberal democracy in a way that would have made her happy (even if she would have, no doubt, argued with every page).

At Harvard Law School, where I turned my attention to how the American Constitution structures American democracy, I studied with some of the great legal minds of the age: the towering Laurence Tribe, my constitutional law professor who continues to have a profound effect on my thinking about the Supreme Court; Duncan Kennedy, the intellectual leader of critical legal studies, who taught me to train a piercing skepticism on claims of logical necessity in law; the great legal historian Morton Horwitz; Randall Kennedy, a scholar of surpassing moral and political insight; Daniel Meltzer, whose work on federal courts was brilliantly illuminating; the irrepressible Alan Dershowitz; Susan Estrich, whose class on labor law ignited an abiding interest in the subject; and Gerald Frug, who brought a passionate democratic intensity to the study of local government law. They are obviously responsible for nothing in this book, but I will always cherish their intellectual examples and their support over the years.

Before reentering academia, I practiced law as an assistant attorney general in Massachusetts and then as general counsel of the National Rainbow Coalition. In the former post, I handled a number of cases relating to constitutional law and election law and learned much from my boss, Attorney General James Shannon, Alice Daniel, who headed the Government Bureau, and Assistant Attorney Generals Tom Barnico, Richard Brunell, and Reed Witherby. Then, as the lawyer for the Rainbow Coalition, I became fascinated with the way that election law structures political conflict. I learned much about how American politics works from Rev. Jesse Jackson, Jr., Minyon Moore, Steve Cobble and Frank Watkins, and became friends with my contemporary, Jesse L. Jackson, Jr., now a congressman from the Second Congressional District of Illinois, whose wonderful book, *A More Perfect Union* (2001), is far more sweeping than this one in calling for constitutional changes as ambitious as a right to housing, a right to employment, and a right to progressive income taxation. May his career flourish.

I became a law professor at American University's Washington College of Law (WCL) in 1990 and also had the pleasure of serving as associate dean for several years under two great and inspiring deans, Elliott Milstein and Claudio Grossman, who have both been indispensably supportive of my work. All of my colleagues have been helpful. Some have been integrally involved in the development of my ideas about democracy and the Constitution and have in some cases read drafts of these chapters. I want to thank Muneer Ahmad, Padideh Ala'i, Kenneth Anderson, Jonathan Baker, Susan Bennett, Pamela Bridgewater, Susan Carle, Angela Davis, Robert Dinerstein, Darren Hutchinson, Peter Jaszi, Candace Kovacic-Fleischer, Jim May, Mark Niles, Diane Orentlicher, Nancy Polikoff, Andrew Popper, Paul Rice, Jim Salzman, Herman Schwartz, Ann Shalleck, Brenda Smith, Michael Tigar, Robert Vaughn, Leti Volpp, and Rick Wilson. I owe a special debt to my colleague and codirector of WCL's Program on Law and Government, Tom Sargentich; to my friend and codirector of the Marshall-Brennan Fellowship Program, Steve Wermiel; to my unflappable assistant, Leslie Scott; and to Michelle Carhart, Maryam Ahranjani, Moira Lee, Fahryn Hoffmann and Catherine Beane, the team of people who kept the Marshall-Brennan Fellowship Program humming even when my office door was locked.

As a law professor, I have been able to represent, consult and work with many causes and people who have been important to me, including the Service Employees International Union, Greenpeace, Ross Perot, Clay

Mulford, Russ Verney, Global Exchange, Students United Against Sweat-shops, Ralph Nader, the American Civil Liberties Union, students at Blair High School in Montgomery County and many other high school students across the country. I have learned an extraordinary amount from Sue Schurman, David Merkowitz, Leo Gant, and Harriet Cooperman, my colleagues on the State Higher Education Relations Board in Maryland, as well as Karl Pence and Erika Lell.

I profited from delivering several of these chapters as workshop talks at Georgetown University Law Center, Rutgers Law School in Camden, the University of North Carolina School of Law and Florida Coastal School of Law.

Although I wrote it in two years, *Overruling Democracy* represents many years of thinking, advocacy and discussion. Readers interested in a more formal and systematic doctrinal treatment of the main issues raised in this book should consult law review articles I wrote over the last decade, published in the *Texas Law Review*, the *University of Pennsylvania Law Review*, the *Columbia Law Review*, the *Harvard Civil Rights–Civil Liberties Law Review*, the *American University Law Review*, the *University of Maryland Law Review*, the *American University Journal of Gender, Social Policy & the Law*, the *Administrative Law Review*, the *University of Virginia Journal of Law and Politics*, *Human Rights Brief*, the *Harvard Journal of Law and Public Policy*, the *Howard Law Journal*, the *Yale Law and Policy Review*, and the *Hastings Law Journal*. I benefited from the help of many student law review editors along the way.

There are many people in legal academia whose work on the Constitution or democracy I have treasured, including Carl Bogus at Roger Williams; Richard Briffault, Kendall Thomas and Patricia Williams at Columbia; David Kairys at Temple; James Boyle, Walter Dellinger and Stanley Fish at Duke; David Luban, Gary Peller, David Cole and Nina Pillard at Georgetown; Paul Butler, Peter Raven-Hansen and Jeffrey Rosen at George Washington; Lani Guinier at Harvard; Tim Canova at the University of New Mexico; Burt Neuborne at New York University; Erwin Chemerinsky at the University of California, Los Angeles; William P. Marshall and Dean Gene Nichol at the University of North Carolina; Karl Klare, James Hackney and Lucy Williams at Northeastern; Pam Karlan at Stanford; and Jed Rubenfeld at Yale.

My constitutional thinking has been sharpened by coming into contact with several strong conservative thinkers, including Judge Richard

Posner, Charles Krauthammer and Judge Kenneth Starr, and the lucid libertarian Doug Bandow. My analysis of the proposed flag desecration amendment and constitutional patriotism was markedly improved by a series of electrifying debates I had with Harvard law professor Richard Parker and the leader of the Citizens' Flag Alliance, Dan Wheeler.

Many good friends have (knowingly or not) been important influences on my thinking in this book, including Congresswoman Eleanor Holmes Norton, Christopher Hitchens and Carol Blue, Douglas and Laura Gansler, Mary Houghton and Kevin Barr, Dar Williams, Jonathan Soros, John Peter and Dina Sarbanes, Ali Nathan, Kevin Chavous, Jay Spievack, Kate Bennis, Reed Thompson, and Julia Sweig, Ivanhoe Donaldson, Daniel Solomon, Danny Weiss, Rob Richie, Mike Subin, Judy Minor, Mary Beth Tinker, Mark Plotkin, and my best friend from college and law school, Michael Anderson, a magnificent lawyer whose powerful insights on labor law and the First Amendment were indispensable to me.

I have been blessed over the years with brilliant and hardworking student research assistants. I want to recognize Brian Holland, Justin Antonipillai, Danielle Fagre, Eric Lerum, Sheila Moreira, Tali Neuwirth, Christopher Capel, Om Gillette, Adam Wilczewski, Ben Sigel, Josh Krintzman, David Maloney, Ryan Borho, Rena Sheinkman and Jeannette Manning.

Above all, my love and gratitude go to all of the members of my family for their infinite patience and solidarity. My children, Hannah, Tommy and Tabitha, asked ridiculously precocious questions and have recently taken to challenging what they call the "Dadocracy" in our household. My beloved wife Sarah always believed in the project and put up with my late–night writing habits, which are something out of *The Shining*. I have been bolstered by the love and support of other family members, including Erika, Keith, Emily, Zachary and Maggie; Noah, Mina, Mariah and Boman; Eden and Lynn; Bobbi, Dick and Jedd; Herb and Arlene; Kenneth, Abby, Phoebe and Lily; Rasheed, Myrna, Shammy, Khalid and Zina; Mel and Roberta; Keith and Patty and their families.

The book is dedicated to my beloved late mother, Barbara Raskin (1935–1999), whose best-selling literary voice I have tried in vain to channel here, and my father, the philosopher Marcus G. Raskin, whose surpassing intellectual integrity and luminous humanism have been a daily inspiration to me for as long as I can remember.

—Jamin B. Raskin, June 6, 2002

CHAPTER ONE

The Supreme Court
and America's Democracy Deficit

*The trouble . . . is that we have taken democracy for granted; we have
thought and acted as if our forefathers had founded it once and for all.
We have forgotten that it has to be enacted anew in every generation, in
every year and day, in the living relations of person to person in all
social forms and institutions.*

—John Dewey, *Education Today*[1]

When you enter the United States Supreme Court, you pass under a motto
engraved over the front entrance that reads "Equal Justice Under Law."

It is an attractive promise that the Court holds out to those of us on
street level: that parties coming before the Court will be treated fairly and
equally without regard to race, ethnicity, wealth, political party, ideology
or other arbitrary factors. All that matters inside these marbled walls is the
law itself.

This promise evokes what Professor Judith N. Shklar used to call *passive justice.* All the Court must do to render "equal justice under law" is
decide cases and controversies neutrally within the existing scheme of rights,
powers, and entitlements. This promise of judicial neutrality under the rule
of law is essential. As we shall see, it is also easily broken.

But justice also has another meaning, more dynamic than mere neutrality in adjudication. *Active justice* appears when we test the existing
distribution of power, wealth and rights in society against our sense of justice and morality. Thus, even if the Court fairly resolves conflicts under the
current legal regime, profound injustices may still be embedded in the deep
structure and functions of society. For example, American wealth was built
on the slave labor and exploitation of African Americans, but the present
legal regime offers no way of articulating, much less quantifying and rectifying, the historical injuries visited on African Americans. To take another

example, children born into different circumstances in American society, great wealth or great poverty, have radically different chances for success in life. The Court does not address these kinds of background injustices and inequalities.

We cannot really expect the Court to render active justice for us. Many liberals, still starstruck by the Warren Court, have forgotten this point. The Court's job, by definition in a democracy, is to respond to litigants by enforcing the commands of written law. Its work involves methodical interpretation of our Constitution, treaties and federal statutes. It is up to us, the sovereign people, and our representatives in Congress and the legislatures, to make the constitutional amendments, write the laws and develop the policies that will render life in our society more just for all. The Court can enforce the law fairly, but the people must articulate and define justice and push its meanings forward.

But to promote justice actively in this way, we—the people—need to use the channels of constitutional democracy. And this is the first place where the Supreme Court does play a critical role in making active justice possible. It must guard zealously the people's constitutional rights of democratic participation. In elections, it must be a scrupulously fair umpire to keep the channels of political change open. Citizens must always be able to exercise our political rights freely in order to promote political agendas of justice and progress. The Court must grant us democratic breathing space.

Equally important, when we the people do successfully mobilize for progressive laws promoting justice, the Court's obligation is to not strike them down unless they violate some other explicit constitutional boundary. The Court should never invalidate laws just because they offend the political sensibilities of a majority of the justices; if this is the only problem with our laws, the Court should stand aside. If we can agree that the Court should not go beyond the bounds of law to pursue active justice, surely we can agree that the Court should not go beyond the bounds of law to *defeat* active justice. As Justice Stephen Breyer has recently argued in an important article trying to restore democratic self-government to the heart of the constitutional enterprise, our democratically enacted laws and policies should have presumptive legitimacy unless they clearly violate other constitutional rights or boundaries.[2]

But the current conservative majority on the Supreme Court has failed to live up to both its neutrality obligations under passive justice and its defense-of-political-democracy obligations under the theory of active justice. In terms of rendering formally neutral and unbiased decisions in particular cases, protecting the basic democratic rights of the people to participate, and refraining from aggressive judicial activism based on the political preferences of the justices, the Supreme Court has proven to be an historic disappointment and, in some respects, a nightmare.

The Rehnquist Court's shocking majority decision in *Bush v. Gore*,[3] which clinched the 2000 presidential election for the Republican Party, embodied all of the Court's relevant faults: it departed from neutrality, trampled the democratic rights of the people and actively carried out a partisan agenda. *Bush v. Gore* was no fluke but a trademark judicial intervention against popular democracy: deeply partisan, racially inflected and wholly unmoored from well-established legal doctrine. It is the paradigm illustration of the Court's betrayal of principles of legal neutrality to accomplish partisan and ideological goals. But behind *Bush v. Gore* lies a thick and unprincipled jurisprudence, hostile to popular democracy and protective of race privilege and corporate power.

Far from rendering neutral justice, the conservative Court has developed racial and partisan double standards to govern democratic politics. Under the five-to-four holdings in *Shaw v. Reno*[4] (1993) and *Miller v. Johnson*[5] (1995), white citizens have acquired a presumptive right under the Equal Protection Clause not to live in majority African-American and Hispanic districts that have an odd-looking perimeter. Yet, African-Americans and Hispanics have no corresponding right under Equal Protection not to live in majority white districts that have an odd perimeter. In *Forbes v. Arkansas Education Television Commission*[6] (1998), the Court's majority upheld the right of government media outlets to exclude Independent candidates for Congress from taxpayer-funded debates that stations sponsor between Democratic and Republican candidates.

Dramatic departures from judicial neutrality like these have turned Equal Protection and First Amendment principles on their head. There are Justices on the Court—Antonin Scalia and Clarence Thomas—who, to my knowledge, have never found that the government has violated the Equal Protection rights of racial minorities (other than in the creation of majority-minority districts!), but frequently vote to uphold Equal Protection attacks by whites on progressive affirmative action policies or legislative redistrictings that produce non-white majorities. Similarly, large corporations that want to spend money from their treasuries to influence public referenda campaigns are treated with far more constitutional solicitude and respect than actual live citizens who want to participate in politics outside of the "two-party system."

Furthermore, in fits of judicial activism evocative of the infamous *Lochner* era, the Court's majority reaches out to strike down progressive rights-expanding legislation at both the federal and state levels. Its justifications vary but the Court often invokes the vacillating and inscrutable requirements of "federalism," a word that appears nowhere in the Constitution but that has often proved handy for negating federal protection of the rights of the people. Chief Justice William Rehnquist and Justices Anthony Kennedy, Sandra Day O'Connor, Scalia, and Thomas have thus struck down a steady flow of laws passed by Congress, especially laws expanding the rights of the people or advancing progressive social and environmental agendas.

In the past several years, the Court's conservative majority has invalidated, in whole or in part, the Violence Against Women Act,[7] which gave women the right to bring federal suit against gender-based attackers; the Gun-Free School Zones Act,[8] which made it a crime to possess a firearm near a school; the Religious Freedom Restoration Act,[9] which prevented government from trampling individual religious rights without a compelling interest; the Brady Handgun Violence Prevention Act,[10] which tried to improve public safety by imposing waiting periods on handgun purchasers; parts of the Fair Labor Standards Act[11] that gave state employees the right to sue their employers in state court; the Low-Level Radioactive Waste Policy Act,[12] which tried to develop a national policy for states to follow in the disposal of radioactive waste; parts of the Age Discrimination in Employment Act dealing with state employees;[13] the standing of environmental groups under the Endangered Species Act;[14] and application of Title I of the Americans With Disabilities Act to state employers,[15] to name some of the more readily recognizable progressive laws that have been chopped down of late.

In 1819, Chief Justice John Marshall articulated what he hoped would become a habit of judicial deference to the expansive exercise of congressional powers in *McCulloch v. Maryland*.[16] He rejected the argument that the national government was the product of the states (rather than the people as a whole) and that it must remain beholden to the states for their approval of federal policies: "The government of the Union ... is emphatically and truly a government of the people. In form and in substance it emanates from them, its powers are granted by them, and are to be exercised directly on them, and for their benefit."[17] An original American conservative, Chief Justice Marshall found that, under the Necessary and Proper Clause, the Court must give Congress sufficient space to use its enumerated powers to develop a vibrant national economy and society. In his famous words, "we must never forget, that it is *a constitution* we are expounding."[18]

The motto of the current conservative Court may as well be: "we must never forget, that it is a constitution we are *shrinking*." For at the same moment that it is curtailing the constitutional rights of the people, it is dismantling the powers of Congress to act in pursuit of nation public purposes. In the entire first two centuries of the Constitution's existence, the Court struck down just 127 federal laws, but between 1987, when William Rehnquist took over as Chief Justice, and 2002, the Court has invalidated a remarkable 33 federal enactments.[19]

You can get a good perspective on the pace of current judicial activism by comparing it to the *Lochner* period when the Court struck down 184 progressive federal or state laws between 1899 and 1937, for an average of about five per year. The current Court overturns federal and state laws at a much faster clip. In the 1999 Term, for example, it toppled eighteen federal and state laws and policies, and in 2000, it eliminated another seventeen.

To be sure, certain decisions nullifying state or federal laws get the constitutional issues right. For example, *Santa Fe v. Doe*,[20] which struck down organized student prayers at public high school football games, was clearly compelled by Establishment Clause jurisprudence (notwithstanding the fact that Justices Rehnquist, Scalia, and Thomas dissented!). Other decisions, like those overruling the Violence against Women Act or the Gun-Free School Zones Act, invoke the dubious new federalism which has stretched the Eleventh Amendment beyond recognition and is glaringly hostile to congressional power under the Commerce Clause and section five of the Fourteenth Amendment.[21] Meantime, the Court has frequently disregarded its solemnly proclaimed devotion to the states by casually toppling local affirmative action policies,[22] state-drawn majority-minority legislative districts, and state purchasing and contracting decisions based on human rights considerations,[23] to name just a few important counterexamples.

However one judges the merits of this or that decision, the Justices who pose as champions of judicial restraint and enemies of the despised "judicial activism" have indisputably become some of American history's judicial activists *par excellence*. This is true regardless of your definition of activism. Professor William P. Marshall of the University of North Carolina School of Law has worked out the different possible meanings of judicial activism and argued decisively that the Rehnquist Court majority passes the test for each one with flying colors.[24]

As Professor Marshall shows, the conservative justices have failed to defer to the decisions of elected branches, repeatedly betrayed a doctrine of strict textualism or Framers' "original intent," have not even pretended to defer to case precedent, refused to conform to jurisdictional limitations on the Court's power, spontaneously invented new constitutional rights and theories, imposed continuing affirmative obligations on the other branches, and used judicial power to accomplish partisan objectives. Each of these deployments of judicial activism collides with the right of the people to practice democratic self-government.

To see the conservative Justices as judicial activists may be disorienting for many Americans since the white-hot rhetoric of "judicial activism" has been the signature gripe and rallying cry of conservatives for fifty years. After the *Brown* decision in 1954, white racial conservatives in the South vilified the Court[25] and pasted "Impeach Earl Warren" bumper stickers on their cars.[26] Cultural conservatives attacked the Court's 1973 decision in *Roe v. Wade*, which upheld abortion rights. They still denounce the majority's lingering defense of the right to choose in the *Casey* decision as the political handiwork of an "Imperial Judiciary,"[27] in the accusing words of Justice Scalia. Quite amazingly, in the face of the hyperactivism of the conservative Justices themselves, President Bush and Senate Republicans continue to beat the drums against "judicial activism" and call for the approval of judges committed to judicial restraint.[28] A constitutionally illiterate nation falls for this brazen trick.

But progressives have almost always had more cause than conservatives to assail the activism of the Supreme Court, which has been a force of ferocious political reaction for most of its existence. President Lincoln denounced the *Dred Scott* decision, which many Radical Republicans saw as the product of a sectional judicial conspiracy to protect slavery against the Radical Republicans in Congress.[29] During the New Deal, progressives challenged the Court's manic *Lochner*-era jurisprudence, which wiped out major pieces of progressive legislation and inscribed "laissez-faire" economics and a sharp class bias into constitutional law.[30] Before his dramatic "Court-packing" plan finally succeeded in changing the Court's direction, President Franklin D. Roosevelt and other progressives portrayed the conservative justices as old men out-of-touch with society and bent on imposing their policy preferences through judicial legislation.[31]

Today again we face relentless judicial activism against democracy. The unifying philosophy of the Rehnquist Court is not federalism, judicial restraint, strict textualism, or original intent but hostility to popular democracy, especially when it involves empowerment of racial and political minorities. This stance is opposite to the Court's proper role, which should be to faithfully interpret the Constitution through the lens of participatory self-government and render universal justice in defense of the rights and liberties of all Americans. Justice Stephen Breyer has recently articulated a fine understanding of our Constitution as a project in democratic self-government.[32]

But the Court's majority, far from acting as the protector of democracy, validates undemocratic arrangements and invalidates any move to open up the system. The Court has openly declared that citizens have no constitutional right to vote in presidential elections. It has struck down many of the first majority-African-American districts to come into being since Reconstruction in Southern States and simultaneously approved the outrageous practice of states drawing districts with the aim of reelecting specific incumbents. It has helped prop up the "two-party system," despite the fact that it is wholly imaginary in a constitutional sense. It has constitutionalized the political free speech rights of private corporations. In 2000, after overturning the state law judgments of a state supreme court, it became the first Court in our history to decide a presidential election, essentially naming the president who, in turn, will name new justices. It has declared that education is no constitutional right and that distributing educational resources on the basis of the wealth of neighborhoods is legitimate. The current Supreme Court takes an already democratically imperfect document—the Constitution of the United States—and grants it indefensibly restrictive and elitist constructions.

The conservative majority on the Court has never told us its overarching theory of political democracy in the Constitution. We do get a sense of it though, through its bottom-line results and tantalizing hints dropped along the way. In the eyes of the Court, democracy is rooted not in the right of the American people to vote and govern but in a set of state-based institutional arrangements for selecting leaders. These localized operations involve a carefully controlled "two-party system," in which incumbent officeholders may entrench themselves through redistricting and other election laws that stifle competition from new parties. This system has an unmistakably white complexion, since the Court fully expects race to play a role in map drawing decisions but finds many majority-African-American and Hispanic districts to be unlawful violations of "color blindness." Democratic politics are treated in the final analysis as an irredeemably grubby business whose elected actors can be displaced at will by the Court, which is free to improvise new one-time-only rules to settle election conflicts and strike down bad laws.

We have a window into the mind of American judicial conservatism in the irrepressibly honest writing of Judge Richard Posner, who is not only a delightful snob and misanthrope but a vigorous opponent of "pure democracy," which he describes as "an extremely dangerous system of government."[33] His book on the 2000 presidential election, *Breaking the Deadlock*, sides with the five-justice majority in *Bush v. Gore* and crackles with contempt for the disorder of democratic political institutions.[34] Significantly, however, Judge Posner quite joyfully makes mincemeat of the majority's silly doctrinal rationales for its decision in *Bush v. Gore*. Yet, he but still maintains that the Court correctly intervened to maintain stability, the cherished conservative value. This is a profoundly extraconstitutional, indeed unconstitutional, defense of the Court's actions, but Judge Posner calls it "pragmatic" and contends that it is the only plausible justification for the Court's opinion. Pragmatism here does not mean the progressive democratic experimentalism of John Dewey but rather prudential calculations and policy guesses made by those who have state power. The impulse that explicitly motivates Judge Posner, and unifies the Court's treatment of American politics, is fear of popular democracy and the "philistine"[35] attitudes of the public. Judge Posner captures the spirit of the Rehnquist Court when he writes: "Limited democracy is best."[36]

With precisely this fear of democracy (and the Democratic Party) animating its work, the Court now actively subverts political principles and rights for which the people have been fighting during the past two centuries of civilizing struggle: the right to vote, the right to participate, the right to political equality in legislative redistricting, the right of access to the ballot, the equal rights of political parties, and the right of equal liberty to speak. These rights are necessary to ground American democracy in the "Consent of the Governed," the principle that Thomas Jefferson declared essential to protect both equality and our "unalienable Rights" to "Life, Liberty, and the Pursuit of Happiness."[37]

Though imperfect, the Constitution, including the Bill of Rights and later amendments, can be read, and has been as recently as the Warren Court, to establish a far more participatory democracy. The original document was loaded down with structures, such as indirect selection of senators and the electoral college, institutionalizing fear of what conservatives like Justice Story would come to call "King Mob."[38] Yet the Court came to understand the First Amendment as the bulwark of free political expression and thought. The Fourteenth Amendment supplied the central ideal of Equal Protection. Political struggle by outsider groups produced the suffrage-enlarging Fifteenth, Seventeenth, Nineteenth, Twenty-third, Twenty-fourth and Twenty-sixth amendments. These provisions establish the structure of a democratic Constitution.

However, the Rehnquist majority still interprets the Constitution as an essentially anti-democratic document. It refuses to perceive even the most *minimal* political rights as being grounded in the document. It remains certain, as it stated calmly in *Bush v. Gore*, that "the individual citizen has no federal constitutional right to vote" in presidential elections.[39] It took the same position with respect to voting in congressional elections when it dismissed a voting rights lawsuit brought by the people of the District of Columbia against their disenfranchisement and lack of representation in the Senate and House of Representatives.[40]

Without the organizing principle of the right to vote—the gold standard of democracy now taken for granted all over the civilized world[41]— the Court casually fashions anti-democratic approaches to the significant structural problems that arise in the sphere of politics. What infuses the Court's response to problems with legislative redistricting, ballot access, discrimination against new parties, debate exclusion, corporate money and power in elections, and educational inequality is never a belief in strong and universal participatory democracy but a stubborn and elitist resistance to it.

Of all of its grandiose adventures in judicial activism, the Court's stifling of political democracy at the source is its greatest offense. For judicial activism is restricting democracy just when we need the Court to be protecting it. America faces a structural democracy deficit. Millions of people remain wholly or partially disenfranchised: hundreds of thousands of citizens living in Washington, D.C., one and a half million former felons who have paid their debt to society but are prevented from voting by their states, several million people living in Puerto Rico and other federal territories, and the random millions of people all over America whose ballots are lost, miscounted or destroyed in every federal election—the reserve army of the disenfranchised that potentially includes us all.

In elections, the all-powerful background rules of the game are stacked.[42] Incumbent officials from the "two-party system" draw their own legislative districts with the unabashed goal of getting themselves reelected. The insider parties have declared themselves "major" and have used law to suppress the emergence of competitive "minor" parties. They restrict access to the ballot, gerrymander candidate debates, and selectively hand themselves hundreds of millions of dollars in public subsidies for their presidential campaigns and to carry the triumphal message of two-party American political democracy to foreign countries.[43] Even after passage of the legally imperiled McCain-Feingold legislation, the meaning of our votes is degraded by an exclusionary "wealth primary" system,[44] where private campaign financing often becomes critical to electoral success and crucial to the making of public policy. And our public schools, which should be the pride of democracy, not only remain separate and radically unequal along the lines of class, geography and race, but leave young people unprepared for participation in even the shrunken down and hollowed out democracy we maintain.

This book tells the story of the Court's anti-democratic constitutional politics. It begins, as it must, with the debacle of the December 2000 decision in *Bush v. Gore*, which astonished tens of millions of people but actually marked the convergence of several long-running counter-democratic tendencies in the Court's jurisprudence. In subsequent chapters I describe how these judicial tendencies have been undermining the possibilities of democratic self-government. In politics, a little interference with democratic rights goes a long way.

The Court that curbs popular democracy in the electoral sphere naturally refuses to embed democratic values in society's other main institutions. Thus, in subsequent chapters, I show also how the Court's jurisprudence helps to deform two institutions that are critically related to the daily health of political democracy: public schools and private corporations.

The answer to the Court's counter-democratic impulses, of course, lies in returning to democracy itself, the pragmatic principle that joins the people with the power in all things. The urgent project of our time is to free popular democratic politics from the stranglehold of the Court. This means overcoming liberal fears about constitutional change and promoting progressive constitutional amendments to establish the citizen's right to vote, majority rule in presidential elections, the equal rights of all political parties, and the young person's right to an equal education for democratic citizenship. We should confront head-on the cosmetic patriotism of the proposed Flag Desecration Amendment and other proposed right-wing amendments. We need to replace these diversions with a democratic constitutional patriotism that will provide the center of gravity for progressive politics in the new century.

We Americans must have the courage to step outside the conservative force field of the Supreme Court and reclaim our right to be the authors of America.

CHAPTER TWO

The Court Supreme

Bush v. Gore
and the Judicial Assault on Democracy

Our consideration is limited to the present circumstances, for the problem of equal protection in election processes generally presents many complexities.

—*Bush v. Gore*, majority opinion

What need we fear who knows it, when none can call our power to account?

—Lady MacBeth in *MacBeth*

Although it remained obscure for most of the 1990s, the Supreme Court's assault on democracy crashed onto the public stage just after 10:00 P.M. on December 12, 2000. America woke up the next morning to reckon with the new age of conservative judicial supremacy.

In a bitterly divided five-to-four decision, the Court's ruling faction gave America its first judicially settled presidential election. The decision to halt vote-counting in Florida amazed at least the 52 percent majority of voting Americans who cast ballots for the Democratic Party nominee, Vice President Al Gore, or the Green Party candidate, Ralph Nader. However, the Court's decision expressed perfectly its paramount commitment to the political rights of conservative majority-white factions in each state, its hostility to potential electoral majorities comprised of African Americans and Hispanics, its perplexing eagerness to show favoritism towards certain political parties over others, and its readiness in the crunch to substitute its political will for that of the people.

The *Bush v. Gore* decision nullified the Florida Supreme Court's order of a statewide manual recount of thousands of ballots in the state's 2000 presidential election.[1] These were mostly "undervote" punch-card ballots that, for various reasons, including mechanical error and lack of manual strength in the voter, failed to register a presidential choice in the mechanical vote-tabulation process. The Florida Supreme Court's order of a statewide recount of all such "pregnant," "dimpled" or "hanging chad" ballots answered Republican complaints that it would be unfair (even if perfectly lawful in the state) to recount ballots manually in only the few counties where Vice President Gore had asked for such action.[2]

The Court majority, however, determined that the Florida Supreme Court erred when it directed election officials to enforce the state law standard of following "the will of the voter" in the manual counting of these ballots.[3] The U.S. Supreme Court worried that "standards for accepting or rejecting contested ballots might vary not only from county to county but indeed within a single county from one recount team to another."[4] Thus, it found that the Florida Supreme Court's order violated the Equal Protection Clause.

The proper remedy for this Equal Protection violation, according to the majority, would have been for the Florida Supreme Court to engage in the "substantial additional work" of specifying the substandards governing different kinds of ballots.[5] The problem, according to the majority, and the reason why, alas, it had to blow the whistle on the vote-counting, was because the Florida Supreme Court said that the legislature intended the state's electors to be chosen by December 12. The Court found that this

> date is upon us, and there is no recount procedure in place under the State Supreme Court's order that comports with minimal constitutional standards. Because it is evident that any recount seeking to meet the December 12 date will be unconstitutional for the reasons we have discussed, we reverse the judgment of the Supreme Court of Florida ordering a recount to proceed.[6]

On this reasoning, the U.S. Supreme Count terminated all further vote-counting and became the first Court in American history to determine the outcome of a presidential election.

Before I analyze the integrity and logic of this decision, it is important to say that the point here is not to prove that Vice President Gore really won the election or that it was stolen from him on the ground in Florida. My analysis does not depend on Gore actually having collected a popular vote majority (which he did) or an electoral college majority (which he may or may not have). Rather, I want to show that, without reference to who "really" won, the Rehnquist Court's decision in *Bush v.*

Gore was utterly result-oriented and unprincipled, in a way that we will soon recognize as familiar from its other decisions governing democratic politics.

A Political Question Raised by a Candidate with no Standing

Released a remarkable 34 hours after oral argment, the majority's decision was a hundred-yard dash. Five sprinting Justices raced past every familiar principle of constitutional law to reach a political finish line. At the starting lineup, the Rehnquist majority disregarded several of its traditionally cherished tenets. At the beginning, it never paused to consider whether the whole case was a nonjusticiable "political question" constitutionally assigned to Congress. This is a serious problem since the initial justification for judicial intervention was that the Florida Supreme Court, in interpreting state law, was somehow disrespecting the state legislature's primary control over the electoral process under Article II of the Constitution. But if this was the case, there is a powerful argument that the Court should have stayed out and allowed Congress to resolve the issue. After all, Article II and the Twelfth Amendment give Congress the central structural role in the counting and consideration of electoral college votes. The Twelfth Amendment tells us that the presidential electors:

> shall make distinct lists of all persons voted for as President, and of all persons voted for as Vice President, and of the number of votes for each, which lists they shall sign and certify, and transmit sealed to the seat of the government of the United States, directed to the President of the Senate;—The President of the Senate shall, in the presence of the Senate and House of Representatives, open all the certificates, and the votes shall then be counted.

If no presidential candidate collects a majority in the electoral college, then the president is chosen by the House of Representatives. Nowhere is the Supreme Court given any formal role at all in choosing the president or resolving competing interpretations of the electoral college provisions. The Court's complete textual absence from the Electoral College provisions makes its failure to consider the "political question" doctrine before forging ahead deeply troubling. In *Nixon v. United States,*[7] the Court dismissed on "political question" grounds a complaint by an impeached federal judge who claimed that he was not properly "tried" by the Senate, as called for by Article I, Section 3, since the full Senate gave the preliminary evidence-gathering function to a committee before receiving a report and hearing final arguments in the case. Chief Justice Rehnquist found for the Court that impeachment process is exclusively for the Senate to work out since there is a "textually demonstrable constitutional commitment of the issue" to that body.[8] Significantly, Chief Justice Rehnquist noted that the Court had not been offered "evidence of a single word in the history of the Constitutional Convention or in contemporary commentary that even alludes to the possibility of judicial review in the context of impeachment powers."[9] This same lack of historical evidence for a contemplated role for judicial review exists with respect to the Electoral College. Chief Justice Rehnquist also noted the decisive checks-and-balances concerns where the Court was invited to overturn the impeachment and conviction of one of the federal judiciary's own judges. The same kind of structural conflict of interest looms where the justices help put into office a president who will have power to appoint their new colleagues on the bench.

The "political question" character of the electoral college issue is reinforced by compelling "prudential" political question considerations. Nothing could be more perilous for the Court's legitimacy than to pick the popular vote loser as the Electoral College winner in a razor-close presidential election on novel and controversial grounds that the Court declares non-binding in other cases.

Even if we pull ourselves over the political question hurdle, the Court's approach to the Equal Protection problem was even more hasty and objectionable. The majority declined to ask whether Governor Bush, a Texas voter, had constitutional standing to raise an Equal Protection claim against Florida regarding the ballots of certain unidentified Florida voters. In Equal Protection cases involving racial minorities, the Court has always held that plaintiffs may assert neither the rights of other people nor abstract principles of fairness. As the Court found in *Allen v. Wright*, civil-rights plaintiffs must establish their own standing by showing that they suffered a concrete *personal* injury, traceable to the government and redressable by the courts.[10] In that 1984 case, Justice O'Connor wrote a majority opinion that denied standing to African-American parents who sought to compel the Internal Revenue Service to enforce the law by withdrawing tax exemptions from private schools that racially discriminated.[11] She stated that citizens have no general right to make government comply with the law and found that the African-American plaintiffs were not personally harmed by the "abstract stigmatic injury" associated with white flight allegedly facilitated by the IRS's failure to enforce the law.[12]

But in *Bush v. Gore*, the Rehnquist majority did not question whether, much less explain how, the appellant Bush was personally injured by the order of a manual recount. Assuming that there was a threatened injury to a subclass of pregnant-chad voters, it would have been an injury visited upon *them*, not upon Bush, Gore, or anyone else.[13] If Bush's claim is that he would have been personally injured as a candidate because all ballots were not in fact *counted*, then this might have been a plausible argument. Perhaps a candidate could act as a proxy for a group of anonymous voters in danger of having their ballots discarded. The problem is that the relief Bush sought, and the relief ordered, was not the counting of *all* the pregnant and dimpled chad ballots but the counting of *none* of them. Thus had the Court conducted a normal standing analysis, Bush would have had to allege a hypothetical injury arising out of the *counting* of a class of ballots. But these are ballots that the Court ultimately determined *should have been counted!*

Even if we assume, bizarrely, that Bush was going to be prospectively injured by the hypothetical possibility that anonymous third-party citizens not in the case might have their pregnant-chad ballots counted differently in one part of Florida than in another, how could *stopping the vote count* sufficiently redress these third-party injuries? If your vote is in danger of not counting, how does it help you for the Supreme Court to make sure that someone else's vote is not counted along with it? The Court skipped merrily over this insoluble contradiction and simply assumed Bush's standing.[14] In the Rehnquist Court, we shall see, white citizens in election cases are automatically assumed to have standing, especially if they have a racially charged complaint.

This standing problem mirrors the outrageous character of the Rehnquist Court's emergency stay of the manual recount on December 7, 2000. Dissenting Justices Stevens, Souter, Ginsburg and Breyer pointed out that the injunction against the "counting of legal votes" offended traditions of federalism, judicial respect for the highest courts of the states, separation of powers and judicial restraint.[15] The dissenters hit the nail on the head when they wrote: "Counting every legally cast vote cannot constitute irreparable harm."[16] Although we do not know what the majority had in mind at this point other than freezing the result, Justice Scalia offered his own spirited defense of the stay: "The counting of votes that are of questionable legality does in my view threaten irreparable harm to petitioner, and to the country, by casting a cloud upon what he claims to be the legitimacy of his election."[17]

What an amazing claim this is. To begin with, Justice Scalia's suggestion that the pregnant-chad ballots were of "questionable legality" directly
opposes the Court's eventual holding. The ultimate decision found not that
these ballots were suspicious but that the people who cast them had an
Equal Protection right to get them counted in a fair process. Thus, the
majority *temporarily* halted vote-counting because the ballots were of "questionable legality," at least according to Justice Scalia, and then *permanently*
halted vote-counting because the same ballots deserved a system of perfect standards and it was too late to craft one.

Leaving the "heads we win, tails you lose" cleverness aside, can "casting
a cloud" on an election by means of vote-counting constitute "irreparable
harm"?[18] In *Allen v. Wright*, the Court held generally that purely reputa-
tional or stigmatic harms are not sufficient to give rise to constitutional
standing against the government.[19] In *New York Times v. Sullivan*, the
Court held specifically that public officials can bring defamation actions
only if there are defamatory lies told about them with "actual malice."[20]
It is hard to see how government counting ballots—even ballots that may
later be invalidated—can be likened to private individuals telling defamatory lies about public officials. Indeed, under Justice Scalia's reasoning,
it should be unlawful for an election board to release election totals in
any close race before a final recount because an early false impression
that the winner actually lost would presumably irreparably harm him. Furthermore, Justice Scalia voted with the majority in *Clinton v. Jones* to allow
civil suits against the president to proceed even while he was in office.[21]
Doesn't this decision establish that "casting a cloud" on a president in office
is not legally cognizable harm but indeed a citizen's basic constitutional
right?

Even if we agree to treat condensation gathering over candidates as
actionable harm, can a candidate's interest in running away from dark
clouds outweigh the interest that the people (and other candidates) have
in seeing all of the votes counted? Consider the equities. If the moving
party (Bush) was right but the vote-counting proceeded, the worst that
could happen is that some people would say he was not really elected. But
this is something that was bound to—and did—happen anyway. However, if the moving party was wrong and the vote-counting was terminated,
the worst that could happen would be that the actual winner of the presidential election would be denied his office! In weighing the harms, the
two sides of the scale are not even close. In any event, the majority, if it
had really been serious about both the harm issue and a semblance of

democracy, could have simply ordered that the vote-counting proceed but that the results in all counties be embargoed until the Court could reach its final decision.

Before any briefing or oral arguments ever took place on the merits, the emergency stay actually decided the case. By cutting off the vote counting in December, the Court set the stage for its final judgment holding that insufficient time existed to proceed with what it saw as a *constitutionally required* recount. But the reason there was (allegedly) not enough time to count ballots was that the Court had itself halted counting on grounds that the truth might constitute irreparable harm.

Vote-Counting as Injury; Disenfranchisement as Remedy

By the time they reached the merits of Bush's substantive Equal Protection claim on the evening of Tuesday, December 12, the Justices in the majority had thrown caution to the wind and were hell-bent on protecting the Bush victory. When the Bush lawyers had presented their original petition to the Court on November 22, 2000, the Equal Protection theory they had presented was so weak in terms of traditional doctrinal understandings that the Court refused even to certify it for consideration. This was before three Justices in the majority realized that the Equal Protection theory was the only available hook upon which to hang their hats. So what was a throwaway argument scoffed at by constitutional experts across the spectrum became the foundation of the Court's opinion.

The *Bush* majority was foggy about which standard of review it was applying. Clearly strict scrutiny did not apply because there was no "suspect class" targeted for adverse treatment based on race or ethnicity. Nor was there any invidious *purpose* to discriminate against anyone. This is the kind of showing the Court demands that minorities make in Equal Protection suits when challenging ostensibly race-neutral classifications.[22] Nor was there any fundamental burden on the citizen's right to vote that could trigger strict scrutiny. What was at issue was the kind of run-of-the-mill electoral regulation that the Court ordinarily treats on the most deferential minimum-rationality basis.

Thus Florida's system should have had to pass only low-level "rational basis" scrutiny—and, in truth, this scrutiny belonged under procedural Due Process standards, not Equal Protection. After all, the issue was the procedures and standards by which specific ballots could be adjudicated valid or invalid.

It is plainly the case that Florida's "intent of the voter" standard would have easily passed a "rational basis" Due Process examination. Almost every state in the union, including Texas, uses the identical "intent of the voter" standard for manual recounts, which are made available everywhere. No state specifies a more precise pregnant-chad substandard, and the Court never before dreamed of nationalizing vote-count standards as a Due Process mandate. Even if minor problems in varying methods of vote-counting existed, it is perfectly rational for election judges to make a frontline determination on whether a ballot reflects an intention to cast a vote. Furthermore, if substantially different standards emerge requiring more specific resolution, it is completely rational and normal to have the high court of the state reconcile the different standards and pass upon the handful of close calls.

The potential variation among Florida counties in treatment of ballots was trivial compared to the actual and sweeping disparities that exist among counties with respect to voting machinery and counting procedures. In Florida, the number of discredited "undercount" ballots varied widely depending on the state and quality of the machinery used in the county, a kind of variation that often corresponds closely to race and wealth.[23] Justice Breyer remarked in *Bush v. Gore* that "the ballots of voters in counties that use punch-card systems are more likely to be disqualified than those in counties using optical-scanning systems,"[24] which translates into a situation in which voters already arrive at the polls with an unequal chance that their votes will be counted.

Above all, it is impossible to see how the Court could remedy the potential disenfranchisement of voters by forbidding the counting of their ballots. If voters are threatened with constitutional injury by possibly not having their votes counted, the injury becomes certain if the Court's relief is to *order* that they not be counted. How can the rights of pregnant-chad voters be vindicated by relief compelling exclusion of their ballots? The paradoxical holding reflects the fact that no injured plaintiffs as parties were present in *Bush v. Gore* to complain about the absurdity of disenfranchisement as the remedy for voting rights violations. The plaintiff was not a voter at all but a candidate desperately looking for ways to *prevent* the counting of the ballots.

The majority not only ordered disenfranchisement as the remedy for hypothetical disenfranchisement but also invoked voting rights cases to justify it. The Court cited *Harper v. Virginia Board of Elections*, which struck down the poll tax in Virginia state elections in 1966 as discrimination against the poor.[25] In states such as Florida, however, where many of the poor have the worst voting machines and the highest rates of ballot spoiling, a statewide manual recount would have given poor voters *more* equal treatment, not less. Indeed, the voting technology problems that disproportionately harmed the poor and minorities act as a kind of diffuse poll tax, but the Court made sure these effects would not be corrected by the Florida Supreme Court. If there was an Equal Protection violation in *Bush v. Gore*, it is not found in anything the Florida Supreme Court did but in the bizarre "relief" the Court ordered.

The pretext for the decision to shut down the manual vote recount on December 12 was that there was no time left for the Florida Supreme Court to articulate an acceptable and uniform vote-counting substandard. But why not simply allow the recount? The state electors did not meet until December 18, six days later. Surely the hand counts of several thousand "undercount" ballots could be completed in that time. Why not remand the case to the Florida Supreme Court with the instruction to get the job done? This was the quite sensible and honorable position of Justice Breyer, who wrote that, "there is no justification for the majority's remedy...."[26] The majority took the position that, under the Electoral Count Act of 1887, 3 U.S.C. sec. 5, controversies over the electors need to be resolved "six days prior to the meeting of the Electoral College" and—what do you know—that very day, December 12 "is upon us." Indeed, with the Court's release of the decision at 10:00 P.M., December 12th, alas, would actually be over in two hours. How melancholy!

In reality, as the majority understood perfectly well, 3 U.S.C. sec. 5 simply extends a statutory "safe harbor" to states appointing their electoral-college votes. It imposes no absolute requirement or deadline, and many states have appointed their electors long after this date without any problem in getting Congress to accept them. Justice Stevens pointed out in dissent that in the 1960 presidential election, Congress accepted Hawaii's electoral votes, which were appointed on January 4, 1961, *several weeks* after the safe harbor period ended.[27]

In any event, the question of when Florida must complete the counting of its ballots is a paradigmatic *state-law* issue. Indeed, in a federal law sense, as the majority itself recognized, a state could constitutionally decide not to appoint any electors at all. Thus, whether Florida law actually converts the federal "safe harbor" timetable into an absolute statutory requirement, or whether it favors the "will of the people" above this other value is a state law question that only the Florida Supreme Court can answer by interpreting the Florida Constitution and state law. Yet the Court's majority, without analysis or explanation, not only raised but decided this fundamental state law issue, calling off a state's counting of ballots in a presidential election for the first time in the nation's history.[28] Furthermore, while it disregarded and disrespected almost everything else that the Florida high court did, the Supreme Court magnified and distorted a passing statement by the Florida Court about December 12 to determine the state's own law, the award of its presidential electors and the political future of the American people. Yet nowhere did Florida law mention December 12, much less as some kind of compulsory statutory deadline.

Of course, if the Rehnquist majority had been serious about creating exact equality and parity across America's different voting districts, it would have caused something like a revolution in our decentralized electoral system, where thousands of jurisdictions use widely differing kinds of machines, ballots, counting procedures, registration procedures, redistricting processes and voting systems. But the Court obviously saw the danger here and hurried to stuff the genie back in the bottle: "Our consideration is limited to the present circumstances," the majority wrote without a trace of shame, "for the problem of equal protection in election processes generally presents many complexities."[29] The Court took a case that was not ripe and gave us a decision that was a dead letter on arrival.

In a slapdash job of interpretation, the conservatives upended four foundational relationships in our constitutional system. They usurped the role of the Florida Supreme Court in interpreting state law. They nullified the putative role of the American people by halting the counting of ballots in a presidential election and effectively choosing the president. They preempted Congress's powers under Article II to accept or reject the states' electoral college votes.[30] And they reversed the proper distribution of powers in national government by having Supreme Court Justices appoint the president, rather than the other way around. John Kenneth Galbraith shrewdly likened the new mode of presidential election to the cozy dynamics of American corporate governance, where the board appoints the president of the company, and the president in turn recommends new members of the board. The Republic now awaits President Bush's Supreme Court nominees, who will presumably be cut from the same ideological cloth as his favorite Justices, Scalia and Thomas, loyal members of the *Bush v. Gore* majority.

What If It Had Been *Gore v. Bush*?

Had Gore and Bush been in each other's places, the conservative justices surely would have dismissed the suit. Had Gore sought the Court's intervention to overturn the Florida Supreme Court's decision to order a statewide manual recount at Bush's request, the *Bush* five would have voted to *decline* jurisdiction on federalism, political question, standing and separation-of-powers grounds. If somehow, miraculously, jurisdiction had been granted, they would have scoffed at the substantive claim that there was some kind of anticipatory Equal Protection violation afoot in Florida threatening the rights of pregnant chads to be treated equally across county lines. If by some fluke they found that Equal Protection was even implicated by the manual recount order, they would not have dreamed of usurping the Florida Supreme Court by deciding the state law question of whether there was sufficient time and statutory authority to develop a new substandard and complete the statewide recount.

Indeed, if Gore had made these daring claims, the Rehnquist majority would have fallen back on its ordinary lethargic indifference to the denial of the right to vote. There is no shortage of evidence of this apathy. On October 16, less than two months before deciding *Bush*, the Court dismissed, without even scheduling oral argument, an Equal Protection attack on the disenfranchisement of more than half a million American citizens living in the District of Columbia who have had no representation in the U.S. House or U.S. Senate for two centuries.[31] Unlike *Bush v. Gore*, this was not an abstract claim about a hypothetical future harm relating to a couple of anonymous voters. The plaintiffs in *Alexander v. Daley* were named citizens drawn from all eight wards of the District of Columbia, including university presidents, teachers, doctors, football players, firefighters, businesspeople, the retired and numerous veterans of foreign wars. Their lead counsel, the D.C. corporation counsel, alleged that they and all Washingtonians would continue to be denied congressional representation absent intervention by the Court.[32]

The Court's cavalier decision not even to hear this voting-rights suit fairly exemplifies its stony indifference to the trampling of political rights, especially where African-American majorities are concerned. The Rehnquist majority has insisted that it will find no Equal Protection violations against minorities in the arrangement of ostensibly race-neutral voting processes unless plaintiffs can first show a governmental *purpose* to discriminate. In *City of Mobile v. Bolden*, for example, the Court rejected both

Equal Protection and Fifteenth Amendment attacks on an at-large system
of municipal elections in a majority-white city that had reliably produced
an all-white city council for decades.[33] The Court emphasized that such
at-large elections would only "violate the Fourteenth Amendment if their
purpose were invidiously to minimize or cancel out the voting potential of
racial or ethnic minorities...."[34]

Yet in *Bush*, this purpose test vanished. The plaintiffs never argued—
and the Court never found—that the Florida legislature's purpose in not
specifying a vote-counting substandard was to minimize or cancel out anyone's vote. Indeed, the Court never found that minimizing or canceling
out votes was even the *effect* of the standard. The Court simply discovered
to its horror that different legal substandards potentially might be used
for vote-counting in different Florida counties. Why this commonplace
situation suddenly troubled a Court that has no problem with radically differing rates of use of the death penalty for murderers of whites and
murderers of minorities[35] is puzzling. Moreover, the Court also accepts
radically differing levels of spending on public school students in rich and
poor school districts.[36] Thus, dimpled chads now have more constitutional
rights than dimpled children.

Now, is not the obverse also true—that the dissenting liberal justices in
Bush would have voted in favor of vacating the Florida Supreme Court and
preventing a recount if Gore had won? I do not believe so. The majority
decision in *Bush* was so brazen a departure for the conservatives and so ferocious an assault on both conventional conservative and liberal doctrinal
understandings that the liberals would not have dared to invent a dramatic
new Equal Protection right in those circumstances to favor a Democratic
candidate. They almost certainly never would have taken the case and, if
they had, almost certainly would have left the case to the Florida Supreme
Court to resolve.

Liberals on the court tend to have an abstract commitment to principles of fairness and freedom that makes them better (though far from
perfect) upholders of the rule of law in times of crisis. This is, in fact,
the classic conservative complaint about liberals: their minds are filled
with hopelessly abstract and universal principles that they would impose
on social institutions without proper deference to the time-honored habits
and working mechanisms of tradition and authority. Conservative theorist Jerry Muller observes: "Whether termed 'the abuse of reason' (by
Burke), 'rationalism in politics' (by Oakeshott), or 'constructivism' (by
Hayek), the conservative accusation against liberal and radical thought

is fundamentally the same: liberals and radicals are said to depend upon a systematic, deductivist, universalistic form of reasoning. . . ."[37]

Conservatives are more politically astute, more alert to the concrete political effects of legal arguments and constitutional propositions. How will deployment of this or that principle affect the people whom we care most about? Their heads are not in the clouds of high principle. Edmund Burke stated this disposition succinctly in what could be the very motto of the conservative majority in *Bush v. Gore*: "The practical consequences of any political tenet go a great way in deciding upon its value. Political problems do not primarily concern truth or falsehood. They relate to good or evil. What in the result is likely to produce evil, is politically false: that which is productive of good, politically is true."[38] Did the conservatives reason backward, consciously or subconsciously, from the result they wanted to reach (the political good)? There can be little doubt about it.

There is, of course, no way to prove this to be the case, history not being falsifiable, and the point is not a crucial one. I am not invested in demonstrating the superior moral virtue of the more liberal justices—Justice John Paul Stevens, Justice David Souter, Justice Stephen Breyer, and Justice Ruth Bader Ginsburg, two Republican and two Democratic appointees. But it is certainly worth noting that, in the bewildering maze of litigation that took place in the 2000 election, every judge described in the press as conservative decided in favor of Bush while a number of liberal Democratic appointees decided against Gore.

Perhaps the best example is Judge Nikki Clark, who presided over the case of *Jacobs v. Seminole County Canvassing Board*, which concerned the Republican voter registrar in Seminole County inviting a Republican party official to work in her office to add missing voter identification numbers to Republican voters' requests for absentee ballots.[39] Despite the fact that there was convincing proof that this invitation was unlawful and a lopsided partisan tampering with the electoral process, Judge Clark nonetheless found that disqualifying hundreds of absentee ballots would not be a fair remedy for the statutory violation.[40] Amazingly, in an act of characteristic psychological projection, the Republicans had sought to remove Judge Clark, a liberal Democrat, from the case on grounds of partisan bias. Yet the value system that Judge Clark actually brought to the case was one favoring constitutional democracy and vindicating, come what may, the much-maligned and trampled "will of the people." This outlook, born of the hard-won twentieth-century struggle for the right to vote in the Deep South, required not the invalidation of ballots, whatever may have been

the eye-popping shenanigans of county and party officials, but the counting of all ballots. Too bad she was not the Chief Justice of the U.S. Supreme
Court.

Bush v. Gore and the Dred Scott Decision: Which One's Worse?

Bush v. Gore is quite demonstrably the least defensible Supreme Court decision in history. Many people do not want to believe that, and I earned a
solid rebuke from the Wall Street Journal for making the point in print.[41]
Many conservatives clearly wish the title of "Worst Case" to belong for all
time to the infamous Dred Scott decision.[42] But Dred Scott was, by comparison to Bush v. Gore, a well-reasoned and logically coherent decision. It
was, in fact, a masterpiece of "original intent" analysis that forcefully demonstrated that the original Constitution was designed as a white man's compact
and that the Framers never contemplated that slaves or their descendants
could sue in federal court.[43]

Dred Scott was a jurisdictional decision, turning principally on whether
an African American could be a federally recognized "citizen" of a state
for the purpose of establishing diversity jurisdiction in federal court.[44] Dred
Scott, a slave in Missouri, brought suit in federal court against his owner,
a New York citizen, asserting his legal emancipation when a prior owner
brought him to Illinois and parts of the Louisiana Territory, which were
free.[45] Chief Justice Taney disposed of the suit by holding that there was
no diversity jurisdiction in the case because no African American could
ever be a "citizen" within the meaning of the Constitution.[46] To support
this proposition, Taney assembled a mountain of textual, statutory and historical evidence that neither the Framers nor the states ever considered
"Africans" as potential citizens.[47] "On the contrary," he wrote:

> they were at that time considered as a subordinate and inferior class of beings,
> who had been subjugated by the dominant race, and, whether emanci-
> pated or not, yet remained subject to their authority, and had no rights or
> privileges but such as those who held the power and the Government might
> choose to grant them.[48]

We like to pretend that the Court erred grievously in Dred Scott because
we want to believe that the Civil War might have been averted by some
other decision. But this is fooling ourselves. The Court engaged in unnecessary and unwarranted activism when it struck down the Missouri

Compromise, but in interpreting the meaning of the word "citizen," it articulated well the social consensus about the meaning of the Constitution. It would take a Civil War, Reconstruction and the lives of hundreds of thousands of Americans to remake the Constitution. Of course, the type of originalism that Justice Taney practiced (and that is embraced by conservatives today) is not the only theory of constitutional interpretation. This decision was not necessarily "right." Indeed, there were even originalist-type arguments on the other side, since the text of the Constitution did not *foreclose* the possibility of African-American freedmen becoming citizens of states. After all, several states had extended to freedmen their civil and political rights. This was essentially the position adopted by Justice Curtis in dissent.[49] Yet, if we look at the original understanding of the Constitution and the *traditions* of the time of its writing, which is certainly Justice Scalia's methodology, it seems certain the majority was right. But whatever its final merits, at least the *Dred Scott* majority decision *had* a coherent theory rooted in the history and text of the Constitution.

By contrast, *Bush v. Gore* is an affront to rule-of-law principles. The majority decision has no grounding in textualism or originalism, the interpretive strategies normally celebrated by conservatives. Nor does it have any connection to a progressive constitutionalism, whose focus in politics is on the democratic will of the people and the intent of the voter. These are the very concepts defeated by the Court's reasoning. In order to stop the vote-counting, the majority briefly inflated to blimp-sized dimensions the Equal Protection Clause, the part of the Constitution these Justices have done everything in their power to shrink as it applies to the rights of racial minorities. All of the air has, of course, gone out of Equal Protection since the decision.

Hypocrisy or Reaction?

Many critics of the *Bush v. Gore* decision have assailed the five majority Justices for acting in bad faith—that is, hypocritically, with the knowledge that they were betraying their own principles for partisan purposes. In his book, *Supreme Injustice*, Harvard Law Professor Alan Dershowitz took pains to describe his argument as "*ad hominem*": "I am accusing them of partisan favoritism—bias—toward one litigant and against another. I am also accusing them of dishonesty, of trying to hide their bias behind plausible legal arguments that they never would have put forward had the shoe been on the other foot."[50] His colleague, Professor Randall Kennedy, said that they "acted in bad faith and with partisan prejudice."[51] Former prosecutor Vincent Bugliosi denounced the "brazen, shameless majority" for its "fraudulent" jurisprudence and called the five Justices "criminals in the truest sense of the word."[52] George Washington Law Professor Jeffrey Rosen titled his *New Republic* essay "Disgrace: The Supreme Court Commits Suicide" and referred to the "Republican larcenists, in and out of robes, who arranged to suppress the truth about the vote in Florida and thereby to make off with the election of 2000...."[53] New York University law professor Anthony Amsterdam charged the Court with "sickening hypocrisy."[54]

The *Bush* five and their supporters indignantly deny these charges and protest their innocence. It was only a matter of days after the decision that Justice Thomas and Chief Justice Rehnquist were reassuring the public that partisanship never enters into their reasoning.[55] And they seem honestly to believe this. Their conviction on this point teaches us something about the character of human reasoning and our infinite powers of self-justification and rationalization. Would it ever really be possible for any of us, much less a Justice whose entire career is based on the idea of independent and unbiased rationality, to step outside of our situation and judge our own actions hypocritical?

It is, no doubt, comforting to think that the justices acted hypocritically. For if they knew that there was no valid basis for stopping the vote-counting but chose to do it anyway, we would at least preserve the consoling comfort that there is a natural and agreed-upon rational order in the legal universe. But doesn't it seem more likely, after Legal Realism and Critical Legal Studies, that there is no such order and that the five Justices actually believed, in their heart of hearts, that theirs was the right decision? We resist this conclusion because we then face the disturbing possibility that the underlying premises of constitutional law are not ultimately the discovery of an empirical science but a kind of political rhetoric by other means. We would have nothing solid to fall back upon other than our ability to forge consensus out of our values.

It is thus tempting for us to call conservative Justices hypocrites and to judge their souls rather than describe what they indisputably are: reactionary judicial activists. Hypocrisy is a moral charge that indirectly flatters our own integrity and objectivity. Reaction is a political charge that invites us to think and act politically to change the balance of power in favor of the values we champion.

Intriguingly, most of the Court's harshest critics never called for the impeachment of the offending Justices for knowingly subverting the Constitution. Why not? The Republicans brought impeachment charges against President Clinton for acts far less damaging to American democracy and the rule of law. Perhaps it is because they regard *Bush v. Gore* as a freakish moral lapse rather than a logical entry in an ongoing political project.

Progressives certainly can understand the appeal of a political analysis that "put[s] hypocrisy first,"[56] in the words of Judith N. Shklar. But we have special reason to reject excessive reliance on that approach to understanding law. As Thomas Paine wrote in his preface to *Common Sense*, "the Object for Attention" must be "the *Doctrine itself*, not the *Man*."[57] However, Paine also later remarked that "the political characters, political dependencies, and political Connections of men, being of a public nature, differ exceedingly from the circumstances of private life: And they are in many instances so nearly related to the measures they propose, that, to prevent our being deceived by the last, we *must* be acquainted with the first."[58]

In this sense, it is fair for critics of *Bush v. Gore*, such as Professor Dershowitz, to point out the dense network of political connections and conflicts that entangled the Justices with the parties and lawyers before the Court. The five Justices in the majority were appointed by Presidents Nixon, Reagan and the first Bush. Justice Scalia's son worked for Gibson Dunn, one of the law firms representing Bush in the case. Justice Thomas's wife was collecting résumés at the time to staff the prospective Bush administration from her perch at the Heritage Foundation. Justice Thomas maintained a busy schedule speaking to conservative groups like the Federalist Society. Chief Justice Rehnquist allegedly had a desire to retire and a corresponding strong preference to be replaced by a Republican appointee. Reportedly, he also had a personal history of challenging African-American and Hispanic Democratic voters at Arizona polling places in 1962.[59] As the Republican nominee, Governor George W. Bush hailed Justices Thomas and Scalia as his ideal jurists. One could spend pages on these kinds of connections and overlaps.

But these apparent conflicts of interest (*confluence* of interests is actually more like it) take us only so far in our juridical analysis. In reality, we all are compromised and defined by partisan beliefs and values, not necessarily in the narrow sense of attachment to a political party, we hope, but certainly in the larger sense of commitments to ideas and values. The particular entanglements that catch public attention—Justice Scalia's son, Justice Thomas's wife—reflect life circumstances and associations that simply open a little window into the underlying structures of feeling

and belief that motivate us. But does anyone really think that the case
would have come out any differently had Justice Scalia's son not been
working at Gibson Dunn or had Virginia Thomas not been preparing for
the presidential transition at the Heritage Foundation? Even without these
charged personal associations, the conservatives on the Court would have
been motivated sufficiently to secure a halt in the vote-counting and a
Bush victory.

To shift the discussion from hypocrisy to reaction is not to rehabilitate
the majority. I yield nothing to Dershowitz, Kennedy, Bugliosi, Rosen
and Amsterdam (each of whose work I admire) in my contempt for that
egregious decision. To charge bad faith, however, requires us to assume that
the Justices in the majority knew that what they were doing was wrong and
acted in conscious disregard of its unfairness. This is questionable psychological speculation that distracts us from the *ideological and
jurisprudential system* that produced and excused this outrageous assault on
democracy.

In fact, although no precise doctrinal foundation existed for what the
conservative Justices did, their unprincipled treatment of the issues is perfectly congruent with their reactionary approach to other key cases
structuring political democracy. This case was the natural successor to decisions dismantling majority-African-American and Hispanic legislative
districts and replacing them with majority-white districts, cases upholding discriminatory ballot-access laws and establishing the "two-party
system," and cases upholding the exclusion of third-party candidates from
government-sponsored or corporate-sponsored candidate debates.

Judges must try to be fair-minded in interpreting the grammar of constitutional law. But when push comes to shove, there are no "neutral
principles of constitutional law,"[60] as Herbert Wechsler famously promised.
There are principles that advance particular norms and values and, once
developed, they should be applied in a scrupulously neutral way. But their
content is never neutral; it is, by definition, motivated and partial to particular values.

In *Bush v. Gore*, five conservative Republican-appointed Justices exam-
ined the same facts and same body of law as four moderate-to-liberal
Justices—two Republican appointees and two Democratic appointees—
but came up with, for the most part, completely different judgments about
how to analyze, resolve and dispose of the case. This division reflected
not the stupidity, venality or moral obtuseness of one group or the other
but the fact that adjudication requires, above all, interpretive judgment.

Legal interpretation occurs inescapably through the filter of political attitudes, beliefs, and values that shape all human perception and judgment.
Judges and Justices are human beings, part of the genus mammal, and in
humans, "emotion is integral to the processes of reasoning and decision
making, for worse and for better."[61]

We clearly need more Justices with a commitment to democratic reading of the Consitution. This is an urgent imperative. But, in the meantime,
the pressing issue for citizens is different. We cannot always control what
a Court will do in a given situation, but we can supply written principles
to guide its deliberations. Why was our constitutional language so pliable
and malleable that the *Bush* majority could arrive at this profoundly anti-
democratic resolution? Why is democracy such a weakly embodied
constitutional value? The Court's entire analysis in *Bush v. Gore* depends
on a single statement in its decision denying the existence of a right that
most Americans assume to be the very foundation of the whole constitutional structure: the right to vote.

CHAPTER THREE

Reading Democracy Out
The Citizen Has No Right to Vote
and the Majority Doesn't Rule

It's a long road from law to justice.
—Dar Williams, *I Had No Right*, on "Green World"
(BMG/Razor & Tie Entertainment 2000)

The key sentence in *Bush v. Gore* makes an early and ominous cameo appearance early on in the decision, like Alfred Hitchcock slipping himself into one of his murder mysteries. Almost in passing, the majority writes: "The individual citizen has no federal constitutional right to vote for electors for the President of the United States....[1]"

Read it again: we, the people, have no constitutional right to vote for president or for the electors who choose the president. This dazzling declaration creates the karma—the logical sequence of cause and effect— that permits the Court to disenfranchise thousands of people as a remedy for hypothetical problems in the counting of a few ballots.

The Court's assumption that there is no right to vote for president is not logically or historically compelled. True, the Constitution nowhere explicitly states that all citizens have a right to vote. But there is a powerful argument that the "one person, one vote" decisions in the 1960s established the states' duty to include citizens in all elections.[2] Indeed, the "one person, one vote" cases replaced the geographically based system of state power brokers with the powerful nationalizing ideal of universal democratic participation by everyone in American society. Thus, it is hard to see in the twenty-first century why the textual silence around the right to vote in presidential elections should be more controlling than the textual silence around other rights or powers that have been found in the Constitution, such as the right to choose an abortion,[3] the right to marry,[4] or the power of government to disregard normal search-warrant and probable cause requirements in public schools[5] and at borders.[6]

The Constitution heavily favors voting, including amendments specifically protecting "the right of citizens of the United States to vote" in cases of
discrimination on the basis of race[7] or sex,[8] residency in the District of
Columbia (in presidential elections),[9] failure to pay poll taxes,[10] or age once
a citizen is eighteen years old.[11] If you combine this overwhelming constitutional preference for suffrage with the Ninth Amendment, which states
that the "enumeration in the Constitution, of certain rights, shall not be
construed to deny or disparage others retained by the people," it seems logically irresistible that the people have a democratic right to vote.

But the current Court reads the Constitution as establishing the state
legislatures' absolute power to choose presidential electors without public
participation if they so desire. Although the states presently hold popular
elections to choose the electors, the Court was emphatic that any legislature could decide to bypass the voters and appoint electors of its choosing:
"the State legislature's power to select the manner for appointing electors
is plenary; it may, if it so chooses, select the electors itself . . ."[12]

The constitutional silence where the right to vote should be explains
an awful lot about the chaotic 2000 election. Because we have not grounded
voting in the constitutional architecture, it becomes a political plaything
vulnerable to the ploys and whims of local elites. The NAACP's hearings
into what went wrong in Florida found time-honored tricks and ploys: poll
workers illegally insisting that African Americans produce two forms of
identification, including one photo ID; mysteriously changed polling places
and painfully incompetent poll attendants; eight thousand Floridians being
wrongly purged as ex-felons by a state-hired private consultant who did
not even give them notice; punch card ballots being marred and thrown
away; and misleading ballot designs, such as the infamous "butterfly ballot" that produced the anomaly of Jewish Holocaust survivors voting *en
masse* for Patrick Buchanan.[13]

Without a national constitutional structure supporting the act of voting, the bottom easily falls out of democratic participation. The 2000
election was ultimately decided not by the people, a majority of whom
clearly opposed the victor,[14] but by a sequence of deliberate and accidental disenfranchising events, a hell-bent five-Justice bloc on the Supreme
Court, and the state-legislature-controlled and party-dominated electoral
college.

The strategic machinations and negligence of our election managers are
predictable where suffrage is not a bedrock constitutional right enforceable
in federal court but a political right struggling to stay afloat in the sea of con-

test. Local manipulators of public consent (of whichever party) calculate that they will suffer little adverse consequence for their gamesmanship if their favorites win. There was nothing terribly special about Florida other than the sudden burst of sunshine on the process. A joint study by the California Institute for Technology and Massachusetts Institute of Technology determined that, out of a hundred million votes cast in the 2000 presidential contest, between four and six million were simply never counted.[15] This is the reserve army of the disenfranchised that reappears in every election to help the official managers of our politics maintain local equilibrium. And so it goes where the "citizen has no federal constitutional right to vote."

The Missing Right to Vote in House and Senate Elections: Disenfranchisement in the District

The shaky foundations of political democracy are not just a threat to the people's participation in presidential elections. The "individual citizen" of the United States also has no federal constitutional right to vote for senators and representatives.[16] Just a few months before *Bush v. Gore*, a majority on the Supreme Court made this point by affirming a two-to-one decision by the United States District Court for the District of Columbia that rejected a claim that American citizens have a right to vote in congressional elections.[17] Although not nearly as famous as *Bush v. Gore*, this case even more directly presented the question of whether American citizens have a democratic right to vote under the Constitution. The answer is no.

The case, *Alexander v. Mineta,* was brought by then–District of Columbia Corporation Counsel John Ferren, a former D.C. Court of Appeals judge and passionate advocate of the rights of Washingtonians.[18] Ferren sued the Secretary of Commerce on behalf of 570,000 American citizens living in the District of Columbia who are denied the right to vote for U.S. Senators and House members (and must rely solely on a single non-voting delegate in the House, a post occupied today by the extraordinary Eleanor Holmes Norton).[19] The 56 named plaintiffs were a rainbow spectrum of American life from all the District's vibrant eight wards, including teachers, firefighters, doctors, veterans, professional athletes, university presidents, writers, artists and the lead plaintiff Clifford Alexander, a former secretary of the army under President Jimmy Carter who had run for mayor in 1976.[20]

Ferren asked the court to order the Secretary of Commerce to include Washingtonians in the decennial reapportionment letter that he would be sending to the Speaker of the House of Representatives in 2000 to report where Americans live for the purposes of congressional redistricting.[21] The plaintiffs also sought declaratory and injunctive relief compelling Congress to provide for their representation in both houses of Congress, either directly, by seating the District's own representatives, or by some indirect mechanism, such as participation in the election of members of Congress from Maryland or another state.[22]

The plaintiffs maintained that their disenfranchisement from congressional elections violates Equal Protection and the privileges and immunities of national citizenship.[23] Brick by brick, they rebuilt a wall of precedent invalidating grandfather clauses, exclusionary white primaries, state poll taxes, restrictions on voting by soldiers away from home, unnecessarily long residency requirements, disenfranchisement of citizens living in federal enclaves, prohibitively high candidate filing fees, and malapportioned legislative districts.[24]

This line of authority, they argued, creates a constitutional imperative of universal suffrage.[25] Indeed, the malapportionment cases specifically established the foundational "one person, one vote" principle. The plaintiffs cited Justice Black's powerful statement in *Wesberry v. Sanders*[26] (1964), a decision that struck down congressional districts with widely disparate populations:

> No right is more precious in a free country than that of having a voice in the election of those who make the laws under which, as good citizens, we must live. Other rights, even the most basic, are illusory if the right to vote is undermined. Our Constitution leaves no room for classification of people in a way that unnecessarily abridges this right.[27]

In the same year, in *Reynolds v. Sims*, Chief Justice Warren wrote:

> [T]he weight of a citizen's vote cannot be made to depend on where he lives. . . . This is the clear and strong command of our Constitution's Equal Protection Clause. . . . This is at the heart of Lincoln's vision of "government of the people, by the people, (and) for the people." The Equal Protection Clause demands no less than substantially equal state legislative representation for all citizens, of all places as well as all races.[28]

The D.C. plaintiffs argued that Equal Protection must extend universal suffrage to people living in the federal city, who share all the essential characteristics of citizens of the states: they pay federal taxes, indeed more per capita than any state but Connecticut; they fight and die in foreign wars and are conscripted into the military whenever there is a draft; they vote for president and vice president under the Twenty-Third Amendment; and they are governed by federal laws and enjoy all other constitutional rights, such as the freedoms of speech, press and assembly. The plaintiffs showed that the selective denial of federal representation to the citizens of Washington is doubly unjust. Congress is not only their national legislature but their local legislative sovereign. It has power to make laws for the District and to veto those passed locally by the Council of the District of Columbia.[29]

In *Alexander v. Mineta*, the plaintiffs pointed out that the Supreme Court determined in 1970 that Maryland could not disenfranchise citizens living at the National Institutes of Health (NIH) federal campus in Rockville.[30] In *Evans v. Cornman*, the Court rejected Maryland's argument that these people were the direct subjects of Congress under Article I, Section 8, Clause 17 of the Constitution, and therefore had no right to vote in Maryland's federal and state elections.[31] By the same token, the plaintiffs argued, Congress, which exercises the same "exclusive Legislation"[32] over District residents as it does over the residents of the NIH campus, could not disregard its obligation to give District citizens the right to vote and be represented in Congress.

The often-heard claim that the District is "too federal" for its citizens to vote in congressional elections was proven illogical. Neither federal employees nor their family members or neighbors are disenfranchised anywhere else in the country, and there are jurisdictions with higher percentages of federal employees than Washington, D.C.[33] So it is hard to see the compelling reason for disenfranchising Washingtonians, only a small percentage of whom work for the federal government. Just as Congress could not segregate public schools in the District of Columbia (any more than states could segregate their own),[34] just as Congress could not shut down the *Washington Post* or establish a church (any more than a state could violate the First Amendment), so Congress cannot deny the basic political rights of voting and representation. That was the plaintiffs' argument.

But all of the Warren Court's old-fashioned rhetoric about the fundamental importance of voting went for naught. The District Court found that there were no basic political rights that applied to all Americans. The majority stated: "The Equal Protection Clause does not protect the right of all citizens to vote, but rather the right of all *qualified* citizens to vote."[35]

To be qualified, you must belong to a "state" within the meaning of Article I[36] and the Seventeenth Amendment[37] and must be granted the right to vote by the state.[38] The court was not moved by the fact that the District of Columbia is treated like a state for more than five hundred statutory purposes, from highway and education funds to Selective Service and Internal Revenue provisions, as well as for every other major constitutional purpose, including the Full Faith and Credit Clause and the Diversity Jurisdiction Clause. Thus, two judges in *Alexander v. Mineta* overruled the senior judge on the panel, Louis Oberdorfer, to find that, however "inequit(able)" condition of residents of the nation's capital may be, simply being United States citizens subject to federal taxation and military conscription does not confer on Washingtonians a right to vote or to be represented in the Senate and House.[39]

We could hardly have it clearer: there is no affirmative, universal, *constitutional* right to vote. This is no longer an eccentric conservative gloss on the document. It is black-letter law based on a haunting textual silence: if you go searching for an explicit popular right to vote in the Constitution, you come up empty-handed. The hard-won language in the Fifteenth, Nineteenth, and Twenty-Fourth Amendments forbidding discrimination in voting establishes no mandatory universal right to vote. Those amendments were *ad hoc* efforts to prevent discrimination against specific populations. They worked pretty well. Thus, the Florida legislature cannot selectively disenfranchise African Americans in its selection of presidential electors today (well, theoretically at least), but it can disenfranchise *everyone*, as the Rehnquist Court kindly reminded us. Similarly, while the Nineteenth Amendment means that Congress cannot selectively disenfranchise women in the District of Columbia, it can disenfranchise all women *and* men living in Washington by denying them a place in Congress. Antidiscrimination amendments simply do not help when government may legitimately disenfranchise everyone in a textually unprotected class.

Territorial Subjects: The People of Puerto Rico, American Samoa, Virgin Islands, and Guam

The people of Washington, D.C. who face taxation without voting representation in Congress, have at least been able to participate in presidential elections since 1964 because of the enactment of the Twenty-Third Amendment three years prior.[40] But there are millions of American citizens living in the American territories[41]—Puerto Rico, American Samoa, Virgin Islands and Guam—who cannot even vote for the president who is their national leader and commander-in-chief in times of war.[42] The American flag waves but there is no voting for president on Election Day.

To be sure, the residents of most of the territories are exempt from federal individual income taxes.[43] But otherwise they possess all of the rights and responsibilities of American citizenship, including military conscription and service,[44] the duty to obey federal laws and policies,[45] local legislative and budgetary autonomy[46] and so on. The lack of federal personal income taxation may roughly excuse the need for territorial voting representation in the Congress that raises and spends tax dollars, but disenfranchisement in presidential elections is a purely gratuitous insult that makes the relationship between the United States and the people of these territories a gratingly neocolonial and obsolescent one. The people of the territories overwhelmingly desire the right to vote for their president. By what logic do we deny it to them? "Despite being a territory of the world's largest exporter of democratic rhetoric," writes Angel Ricardo Oquendo, "Puerto Rico is the only place in all of Latin America where not even a pretense of democracy exists: Puerto Ricans have absolutely no electoral say with respect to the institutions that enact and execute the supreme laws of the land."[47]

According to the U.S. Court of Appeals for the Second Circuit, the "exclusion of U.S. citizens residing in the territories from participating in the vote for the President of the United States is the cause of immense resentment in those territories—resentment that has been especially vocal in Puerto Rico."[48] There are 3.8 million residents of Puerto Rico and another 2.7 million Puerto Ricans living on the mainland.[49] According to Judge Leval, the political exclusion of Puerto Ricans "fuels annual attacks on the United States in hearings in the United Nations, at which the United States is described as hypocritically preaching democracy to the world while practicing nineteenth-century colonialism at home."[50]

"These problems of fairness, resentment, and impaired reputation are serious ones,"[51] Judge Leval wrote in the second of two cases that recently reached the U.S. Court of Appeals for the Second Circuit in New York which essentially challenged the disenfranchisement of citizens living in Puerto Rico. In a world where one person, one vote is the gold standard for democratic society, the current regime is untenable. Each of the territories has a unique history of interaction with the United States in which the dynamics of colonialism, exploitation, dependence and interdependence have all played a part. But in the new century, wherever U.S. citizens live under the U.S. flag, everyone minimally should have the right to vote for president. If the territories leave the American Union, their residents will no longer be U.S. citizens, and if they become states, their residents will have equal rights. But as long as they are with us, and we have every reason to believe this will be a long time, their residents should have a right to cast a vote in national elections for president.

Former Felons

Consider another important example of a suffrage-vulnerable population. Today, eight states permanently disenfranchise all persons who have committed felonies even after they have finished their criminal sentences, and another four states disenfranchise some such ex-offenders based on the offense.[52] A handful of ex-felons in these states win their suffrage back through gubernatorial pardons or legislative action, but this is extremely rare.[53]

Although most states restore voting rights to people who have done good time, the disenfranchised ex-felon population in the others is substantial. All told, more than 1.4 million Americans who did good time and repaid their debt to society are disenfranchised today, and most of them will remain voteless for life.

Disenfranchised ex-offender communities are made up disproportionately of racial minorities. This pattern follows from well documented racial dynamics in our ceaseless War on Drugs. The American inmate population is approximately 70 percent African American and Latino today. In 1999, "close to 800,000 black men were in custody in federal penitentiaries, state prisons, and county jails. . . ."[54] According to the Sentencing Project, in two of the states that deny the vote to ex-offenders, "one in three black men is disenfranchised," and in eight others, "one in four black men is disenfranchised. If current trends in criminal arrest, prosecution and conviction continue, the rate of disenfranchisement for black men could reach 40 percent in the states that disenfranchise ex-offenders."[55]

The practice of stripping people of the franchise for life based on felony convictions has dramatic political consequences. In Florida's 2000 election, where George W. Bush captured the state's 25 electoral college votes on the basis of fewer than five hundred votes, there were more than two hundred thousand ex-felons disenfranchised.[56] Thus, for every single voter in George Bush's margin of victory, there were four hundred American citizens in Florida disenfranchised in the election and for life based on a policy the vast majority of states have rejected.

The 1.4 million voteless ex-offenders nationwide are part of a population of 3.9 million Americans who have lost their voting rights because of a felony conviction.[57] Of this number, 2.5 million are still in prison, on probation or on parole.[58] Although incarcerated felons can vote in many countries, they are denied the right to vote in 48 states and the District of Columbia and retain the right to vote only in Maine and Vermont.[59]

The broader policy of felon disenfranchisement has remarkable effects of its own. Today's prisoners are usually shipped from heavily minority and pro-Democratic urban areas to overwhelmingly white and conservative rural areas where prison construction increasingly has taken place.[60] The prisoners count for census and reapportionment purposes in these rural areas, since these areas are where they live, but they cannot vote there. They thus swell the power of conservative white politicians committed generally to punitive justice policies. Jonathan Tilove writes that the inmates at the famous Attica prison in western New York state "are represented in Albany by state Sen. Dale Volker, a conservative Republican who says it's a good thing his captive constituents can't vote, because if they could, 'They would never vote for me.'"[61] Tilove notes that this phenomenon "raises fundamental questions of fairness: Is it right that America's prison population, now mostly black and brown, should be counted in a manner that augments the power of communities with which they have no real connection or common interests?"[62] His question is all the more trenchant and urgent given the way in which the War on Drugs has targeted the power of the criminal justice system on minority communities.

Of course, most Americans see the logic of disenfranchising people actually serving time for felonies. Losing the vote is part of a general loss of civil liberty arising out of conviction for a serious criminal offense. It might make more sense to have such a deprivation of liberty determined at sentencing by a judge who weighs the nature and gravity of the offense. Nonetheless, it seems reasonable enough that people denied the rights of free movement, intimate association and free speech should also suffer loss of voting rights during the course of their punishment.

The question is whether the loss of voting rights during the course of a criminal sentence should become a permanent mark and brand of second-class citizenship after the sentence is served. The Supreme Court has found that felon disenfranchisement laws do not violate the Fourteenth Amendment Equal Protection Clause because Section 2 of the Amendment authorizes states to strip citizens of their voting rights "for participation in rebellion, or other crime" without fear of losing population basis for representation in the House of Representatives.[63] In its 1974 decision in *Richardson v. Ramirez*, Justice Rehnquist found for the Court that "the exclusion of felons from the vote has an affirmative sanction in section 2 of the Fourteenth Amendment...."[64] Ironically, this provision, which was designed to empower states to disenfranchise ex-Confederate rebels,[65] has come to further erode and undermine the political power of African Americans. The right to vote is not only an emblem of social standing, as Judith Shklar argued, but is also quite clearly a unit of instrumental collective power.[66] When large portions of communities are peeled away from the electorate, the groups to which they belong lose political clout. Prisoners are at the bottom of society and have almost no way to express their needs.

Disenfranchising people who have already served all their time, including probation and parole, serves no criminal-justice purpose. It has no deterrent value. It punishes only in the most gratuitous and silently sadistic way. It does not rehabilitate. On the contrary, it becomes a statement of permanent political estrangement and civic incorrigibility. The criminal sentence becomes a scarlet-letter tattoo, the kind of indelible "Corruption of Blood" that is condemned in Article III, Section 3 of the Constitution relating to treason.[67]

This lifetime branding cuts against everything we believe about citizens having the power to overcome the errors of the past. To the extent that slaves were denied the right to vote (among even more basic liberties), and to the extent that prisoners today have fallen to a level just a cut or two above that of slaves, the official lifetime denial of voting rights to former felons acts as a kind of "badge and incident" of slavery.[68] It is time to get rid of this humiliation and restore a sense of belonging and membership to our fellow citizens returning from prison.

From Visionary to Laggard: America's Missing Right to Vote in International Context

The worldwide movement toward democracy owes more to the United States than to any other nation. In the eighteenth century, the American Declaration of Independence and our Bill of Rights (along with the French Declaration of the Rights of Man and of the Citizen) spread revolutionary notions of popular consent and equality around the globe.[69]

In the last several decades, democratic nations have embraced the concept of "one person, one vote" that infused the struggle of the modern

American Civil Rights movement. As Bob Moses and Charles Cobb tell us in their important book, *Radical Equations*, the movement's door-to-door organizing slogan of "one person, one vote" gave "Mississippi sharecroppers and their allies" in early 1960s a principle of "common conceptual cohesion."[70] The irreducible clarity and mathematical symmetry of the concept created nationwide solidarities of belief among disenfranchised tenant farmers, northern college students, civil rights organizers and opponents of political terror. The doctrine of "one person, one vote" gave birth to a new national and political consciousness. It was soon picked up by the Justice Department as a constitutional argument and then articulated by the Warren Court as Equal Protection doctrine in the redistricting cases.[71]

In *Reynolds v. Sims*, which struck down badly malapportioned state legislative districts in Alabama, Chief Justice Warren peered through the lens of the "one person, one vote" doctrine to reconceive our constitutional and political history as the struggle for the people's sovereignty:

> The concept of "we the people" under the Constitution visualizes no preferred class of voters, but equality among those who meet the basic qualifications. . . . The conception of political equality from the Declaration of Independence, to Lincoln's Gettysburg Address, to the Fifteenth, Seventeenth and Nineteenth Amendments can mean only one thing—one person, one vote.[72]

The aspirational one person, one vote concept, which has since traveled the world from Poland to South Africa to Chile, could have led our current Supreme Court to spell out a robust doctrine of universal suffrage and participatory equality under Equal Protection.

But it was not to be. When the Court took a hard right turn in the 1990s, voting and political participation were treated, once again, a lot more like state-issued privileges than fundamental national rights. As we shall see in the next chapter, the Rehnquist Court repeatedly dismantled majority- African-American and Hispanic congressional districts brought into being under the Voting Rights Act, inscribing into law a presumption that whites shall be in the majority. In *Burdick v. Takushi* (1992), the court allowed states to deny voters the right to "write in" the candidates of their choice, a fundamental democratic liberty where the ballot really belongs to the people.[73] In 1997 in *Timmons v. Twin Cities–Area New Party*, the Court upheld state laws that ban the practice of electoral "fusion" and thus suppress the capacity of new political parties to grow by "cross-nominating" candidates of their choice and creating multiparty political coalitions.[74] And in 2000, the Court not only openly declared that there is no individual right to vote for president but also blithely upheld in a single sentence the disenfranchisement of hundreds of thousands of Americans living in the nation's capital.[75]

In the twenty-first century, America's tolerance for disenfranchisement of large communities in the population is indefensible. "One person, one vote" is now the fundamental expression of political democracy on earth. The constitutions of at least 125 nations, from Angola and Argentina to Yugoslavia, Zambia and Zimbabwe, explicitly guarantee all citizens the right to vote and to be represented at all levels of government.[76] Canada and Mexico guarantee it.[77] Every new Constitution adopted over the last decade makes the right to vote the very foundation of government.

The new Republic of South Africa, for example, defines itself as a "sovereign democratic state" that has "universal adult suffrage" and a "multiparty system of democratic government."[78] Its Constitution provides: "Every adult citizen has the right to vote in elections for any legislative body established in terms of the Constitution."[79] These words do not appear in our Constitution and they are not true as a statement about our political life. While most of us get to vote and feel strongly that it *is* a right, the constitutional underpinnings are feeble.

Our constitutional silence on voting leaves us in backward global company. By my count, fifteen countries have refused in their constitutions to commit to universal suffrage for their people and thus have left voting to the whims of government officials. These are: Azerbaijan, the Bahamas, Barbados, Chechnya, Dominica, Indonesia, Iran, Iraq, Jordan, Libya, Pakistan, Palestine, Russia, Saudi Arabia, and Singapore. Ironically, we have appointed ourselves the task of lecturing to the rest of the world on the construction of democracy by way of the National Democratic Institute. This entity channels tens of millions of dollars a year to the Democratic and Republican Parties to spread the gospel of a political process that officially lacks the right to vote.

This sin of constitutional omission is an affront to international law. Article 21 of the Universal Declaration of Human Rights (1948),[80] inspired by triumph over totalitarianism in World War II, provides that: "Everyone has the right to take part in the government of his country, directly or through freely chosen representatives." Article 25(b) of the International Covenant on Civil and Political Rights (1976) proclaims the right "[t]o vote and to be elected at genuine periodic elections which shall be by universal and equal suffrage and shall be held by secret ballot, guaranteeing the free expression of the will of the electors."[81] The American Declaration on the Rights and Duties of Man, adopted in 1948 and the authoritative interpretation of the Organization of American States (OAS) charter, to which the United States is a signatory, also secures the right to participate in free elections.[82]

In the United States, the principle of universal suffrage now lies in tatters. It's time to catch up with new democratic constitutions abroad, where the citizenries have been more faithful to the spirit of our civilizing movements than we have been ourselves. We need the National Democratic Institute to spend some of the public's money campaigning for the right to vote right here in America.

A Right-to-Vote Amendment

To bring in all of the disenfranchised, to assure that runaway state legislatures and courts do not bypass the presidential votes of the people and the will of the majority, and to prevent a repeat of the dramatic departures from democratic norms we experienced in 2000, we need to amend the Constitution. Try on for size the following proposed Twenty-Eighth Amendment, the Right-to-Vote Amendment:

Section 1. Citizens of the United States of at least eighteen years of age have the right to cast an effective vote in primary and general elections for President and Vice President, for electors for President and Vice President, for their State or District Representatives and Senators, and for executive and legislative officers of their state and local legislatures. Such right shall not be denied or abridged by the United States or by any State.

Section 2. The right of the citizens to vote, participate and run for office on an equal basis shall not be denied or abridged by the United States or by any State on account of political party affiliation, wealth or prior condition of incarceration.

Section 3. The District constituting the Seat of Government of the United States shall elect Senators and Representatives in such number and such manner as to which it would be entitled if it were a State.

Section 4. The Congress shall have power to enforce this article by appropriate legislation. Nothing in this Article shall be construed to deny the power of States to expand further the electorate.

The campaign for this amendment will galvanize Americans for the basic right we wrongly assume is protected already and give national coherence to the scattered, lonely and woefully incomplete efforts that sprang up across the country after 2000 to reform anachronistic and manipulable electoral structures in literally thousands of self-regulating jurisdictions. The movement behind this amendment could quickly sweep away partisan and sectional opposition to the following democratic reforms:

- The push to abolish punch cards and upgrade and equalize voting technology and machinery across county and municipal lines.
- The effort to require equal and adequate funding of voting systems across county and municipal lines.
- The movement to end the scandalous disenfranchisement of nearly six hundred thousand taxpaying, draftable Americans living in Washington, D.C., who presently have no voting representation in Congress.
- The call to give millions of territorial residents the right to vote for president and vice president.
- The movement to restore the vote to disenfranchised ex-felons, hundreds of thousands of citizens who have done their time and are attempting to reintegrate into society.
- Unsung efforts by third parties and independents to end discriminatory practices against candidates and voters based on party identification.

Instead of viewing these seemingly disparate causes as a patchwork of local grievances, the Voting Rights Amendment will lift the agenda of electoral reform to a matter of national self-definition and fundamental constitutional values. The reason why *Bush v. Gore*, that unthinkably radical statement about the urgent need for absolute equality of voting procedures and standards across county lines, simply won't work in these other cases is because of the charmingly candid disclaimer appended to the end of the opinion: "Our consideration is limited to the present circumstances, for the problem of Equal Protection in election processes generally presents many complexities."[83] Like Cinderella's dress, the Court's gallant defense of voting rights in 2000 turned to rags at midnight on December 12, 2000.

So it is left to *the people* to bring the American Constitution in line with the fundamental creed of American political thought that cohered in the aftermath of the modern Civil Rights movement. It is time to amend the Constitution to provide for what was missing when it was first drafted and the "revolution's most democratic leaders"[84] (Thomas Jefferson, Tom Paine, Samuel Adams, and Patrick Henry) were absent from the floor of the constitutional convention: the right of the people to vote and to govern.

The Majority's Missing Right to Rule

The case for a right-to-vote amendment is so irresistible that it is tempting to end the voting rights analysis here. But when it comes to our democracy deficit, a second step needs to be taken. The problem is that even if we give millions of disenfranchised people the right to vote and upgrade state voting systems to count every ballot fairly, we face another structural problem made plain by the 2000 election. Because presidential elections are controlled by the electoral college, the majority does not rule. Al Gore won better than 500,000 votes more than George W. Bush in the national popular election but was defeated in the electoral college by six votes. The popular vote winner lost; the popular-vote loser won.[85] This kind of inversion of democracy has occurred three times before—in 1824, 1876 and 1888[86]—but in the twenty-first century, when people around the world have rejected every form of tyranny, these numbers do not add up to democratic legitimacy.

Therefore, after we inscribe the right of each person to vote, we should amend the Constitution to abolish the electoral college. This change is necessary for one overriding reason: the electoral college directly contradicts the sovereignty of the people. Indeed, what good is it to achieve one vote per person if each person's vote does not ultimately count equally? It is sometimes hard for us to see this point because we instinctively identify what is democratic with whatever happens to be in our Constitution. But an institution that works quite naturally to defeat the will of the national majority is sharply at odds with democracy. The job of small-d democrats is not to pretend that our Constitution is perfectly democratic but to make it more so.

The electoral college has the magical power to frustrate majorities at the national level and roll over minorities at the state level, giving us the worst of all worlds. The winner-take-all "unit voting" character of the electoral college in 48 states depresses and deters participation. In lopsided Democratic presidential states like Massachusetts or New York, Republicans have no incentive to compete and get out the vote; in clear Republican states such as Texas or Georgia, the Democrats similarly give up the ghost long before Election Day.[87] Acting in a perfectly rational way, Governor Bush never challenged Vice President Gore's presumptive victory in Democratic heartland states in the Northeast such as New York, Connecticut, Massachusetts, Maryland and Rhode Island or other slam dunks such as Hawaii. Similarly, Vice President Gore, also acting within his best interests, spent little time or money competing for votes in Republican heartland states in the Deep South and the Great Plains, such as Mississippi, Alabama, Georgia, Virginia, Texas, South Carolina, North Dakota, Montana, Utah and Republican bedrock Alaska.[88] These dynamics in the 2000 presidential election would actually have been much worse had Ralph Nader's surprisingly vibrant candidacy not thrown up for grabs several ordinarily safe Democratic states such as Wisconsin, New Mexico and West Virginia.

The white flag of surrender hoisted by this or that major party in a majority of states not only thwarts turnout among that party's faithful but, in turn, drags down participation by the dominant party's supporters, who correctly see no need to rally the troops to counter a threat. In 2000, the voting rate in Florida soared to 70.1 percent because the state was a fiercely contested battleground.[89] The candidates and their running mates practically bought condos in Miami. But most states were consigned to the safe Democratic or Republican column long before Election Day and therefore saw no campaign—no ads, no mobilization, no competition. Despite surges in voting in swing states, the overall turnout sat at the dismal 47 percent level, which put the United States behind every major democracy on earth.[90] Thus, the electoral college system helps produce elections in which half of Americans do not vote. In 2000, *less than half* of the half that *did* vote— or less than a quarter of the nation—determined the victor.

The major-party candidates have no incentive to spend their scarce time or massive campaign money getting out the vote nationwide because the vast majority of voters—all those in safe states—are structurally rendered superfluous to victory. Campaign resources go instead to persuade "swing voters" in "swing states," which means that the politics of the major-party candidates blur as they compete for voters in the middle, leaving the public without a clear choice between different political programs. When a third–party presidential candidate emerges with some energy, as Ralph Nader did in 2000, all of the pressure in the system is to drive him out of the race as a "spoiler." Or, as Christopher Hitchens parodied the *New*

York Times editorial position on the Nader campaign: "I agree with everything you say, but I will oppose your right to say it."[91]

It is hard to see why the votes of Democrats in Texas or Republicans in Massachusetts should be worthless in presidential elections. It is also hard to see why so many "surplus" Republican votes in Texas or Democratic votes in Massachusetts also should have no electoral salience. If we want people to participate in presidential elections, we should get rid of the state-based electoral college and conduct an honest-to-goodness national presidential election for the first time. If we are going to keep the electoral college, we should at least drop the pretense that the nation's leaders are troubled by lack of participation, stop spending money on all of the expensive national conferences on why people don't vote, and give up the high-minded sermons by our leaders about the importance of showing up at the polls.

The Temporary "Vote Trading" Solution to the Problem of the Electoral College

The sheer irrationality of the winner-take-all arrangement and the mounting frustrations of lesser-evil politics gave rise in 2000 to presidential "vote-swapping" Web sites on the Internet, where citizens created high-tech interparty political coalitions across state and political party lines.[92] This is a phenomenon I am familiar with since I introduced the idea of vote-trading, which I actually first called "vote-pairing," to America in the online magazine *Slate* on October 25, 2000, several weeks before election day.[93]

The idea had its roots in the internal conflict that millions of progressives, including me, were experiencing during the 2000 presidential election.[94] As a lifelong Democrat, I had no doubt in my mind that Al Gore was both a capable public servant and a far more progressive leader than George W. Bush. But Ralph Nader was running a spirited outsider campaign for president on the Green Party ticket. Nader was not only reviving youthful activism across the country but promoting a politics of civic democracy and freedom from excessive corporate power.

Furthermore, Nader had an important process point to make. He had been treated in scandalous fashion by the unctuous and bipartisan Commission on Presidential Debates (CPD), which showed no respect either for him or for basic democratic principles (see chapter 5). I helped him draft his challenge to the CPD's hostile takeover of America's presidential debates. But as the campaign drew to a close, the prospect of a George W. Bush presidency began to concentrate the mind. If I could have my cake and eat it too, I wished that Gore would reach 270 in the electoral college and Nader would reach five percent in the popular vote. This was the unofficial goal of Nader's campaign advisers since it would qualify the Green Party for millions of dollars in federal financing in the next presidential election.

On a sleepless night on October 23, my wife exiled me to the attic. When I came down several hours later, I had with me the article, "How to Save Al Gore's Bacon: Gore and Nader Can Both Win," which would run in *Slate* magazine two days later. I knew the editor, Jack Shafer, a youthful and curmudgeonly libertarian who jumped at the piece (although I suspect he was supporting neither Gore nor Nader).

In the article, I started out by stating the obvious: the election was so close that "a strong showing by Ralph Nader in ten swing states could help give George W. Bush the 270 electoral college votes he needs to win." The closeness of the race "leaves hundreds of thousands of progressive Nader supporters in swing states" with a serious "dilemma," I wrote. "Should they vote their hearts for Ralph Nader and make sure he gets the five percent of the popular vote needed to qualify the 2004 Green Party presidential candidate for federal funding? Or should they vote strategically for Al Gore to stop George W. Bush?"

"Meanwhile," I pointed out, "hundreds of thousands of frustrated Gore voters trapped in the Republican-controlled states of Texas, Louisiana, Virginia, Utah, and Alaska face a quandary of their own. Bush holds such a commanding lead . . . that even if Gore supporters cast their ballot for their man, he won't win any of those states. These are truly wasted votes."

I then suggested putting the two groups together: "There is a way for Gore voters trapped in Republican states to liberate Nader supporters in the toss-up states to vote for Gore without actually abandoning their support for Nader and a strong Green Party in the future." I advocated a "variation on a voting device used in the Senate called 'pairing,' whereby senators on opposite sides of issues match up their votes if they are going to be away from Washington." I suggested a "Gore/Nader vote-swapping" movement on a "Web site to pair individual Gore Democrats in Republican states with individual Nader supporters in swing states."

The article did not advocate a binding contractual arrangement but rather a brief text, under which Gore supporters would append their names, stating that "they have concluded that their best hope for contributing to a Gore victory is to vote for Nader in the explicit hope that Nader voters in swing states will correspondingly cast their ballots for Gore." Those in Nader backer states would add their names under text stating that "as Nader supporters in a toss-up state, they have decided to vote for Gore but do so in the explicit hope that Gore voters in Republican states will correspondingly cast their ballots for Nader." People would add their names to each list and watch the bipartisan coalition grow across state lines. "If just 100,000 Gore supporters and 100,000 Nader supporters in the key states registered and kept their words, both a Gore victory and federal funding for the Greens could be accomplished." This was an accurate prediction about the razor-thin closeness of the election, but, in several key states, prosecution-threatening Republican state attorney generals moved at lightning speed to destroy the vote-trading movement just as it was about to crescendo.

Given the hot emotions between the Gore and Nader camps and the controversy surrounding almost any novel use of the Internet, I had expected explosive controversy to greet this idea. I thus tried to deal with certain anticipated moral and legal objections up front in the article. I acknowledged that I could not convince people who "regard voting as primarily moral and expressive" conduct to join in the coalition. The plan was for "people who regard voting as essentially strategic behavior that requires us to focus on real-world political outcomes and meanings." And indeed the whole system of party primaries suggested that strategic voting is a well-accepted practice in American politics. If it "is immoral to vote strategically," I wrote, "the campaigns should stop trying to convince people—Nader voters, most prominently—to change their votes."

But I vigorously defended the ethics and lawfulness of persuading people to change their vote and of the new cross-party coalition politics brewing on the Internet. It is, I argued, "the highest form of democratic politics to consult your fellow citizens about electoral choices." This was the core political speech: "We are obviously not talking about any kind of binding enforceable contract." Moreover, although "state laws prohibit the selling of votes, this would surely not count as vote-selling," since no money or thing of material value is ever exchanged. Furthermore, I wrote:

> Since no one is bound by their statements, it would not even amount to vote-trading, which is itself a perfectly permissible and ordinary activity. Indeed, vote-trading is the essence of logrolling in Washington: You vote yes on my highway bill and I will vote yes on your tax bill. We compromise to arrive at mutually workable solutions.

If the most explicit vote-trading were to be considered illegal as some kind of trumped-up vote-buying or -selling, then every member of Congress would presumably be guilty of numerous counts of the offense. I urged Gore and Nader supporters to lay down the hatchet and "join forces through the Internet and become professors of the Electoral College rather than dropouts from it."

What happened next demonstrated the awesome political power of the Internet. Cross-partisan voter-to-voter contacts surged all over America. Brad Worley writes in the *North Carolina Journal of Law and Technology*:

> In the immediate wake of Raskin's column, a slew of vote-swapping sites appeared online. At least three sites launched during the following week credited the Raskin column as the impetus. Two of these sites (Voteswap 2000.com and Winchell's NaderTrader), as well as at least four additional sites (PresidentGore.com, Tradevotes.com, votetrader.org, and VotExchange2000.com), featured some variation on the automatic user-matching system proposed by Raskin. With the proliferation of sites available for vote swapping began a rush of media attention and an explosion in user interest.... In its first day of operation (October 26), Voteswap2000. com recorded 500 trades; by the time it closed operations four days later, more than 5000 voters had been matched. During the same time period, VotExchange2000.com reported having registered "a few thousand people," while Steve Yoder's Voteexchange.org, now diverting a good deal of traffic to the larger Voteswap2000.com, had a cumulative total of 230 matches....[95]

Indeed, before the Republican attorney generals struck back a few days later, our best estimate is that at least 35,000 people nationally had explicitly declared online their intention to vote in this bipartisan coalition, with the possibility that, in a ripple effect, tens of thousands of others did the same either over the phone, in person or just independently. Jeff Cardille's flourishing NaderTrader.org experienced more than 650,000 visits in a two-week period.

The legal backlash against the vote-trading movement began with an October 30, 2000, threat letter that ambitious California Republican Attorney General Bill Jones sent to Jim Cody and Ted Johnson, the Generation X creators of www.voteswap.com, which was seeing traffic of thousands of hits. "This letter is to formally notify you that 'Voteswap2000' is engaged in criminal activity in the State of California," Attorney General Jones wrote.[96] The letter suggested that Cody and Johnson were brokering the sale and purchase of votes, each count of which was a felony carrying "a maximum penalty of three years in state prison in California for each violation."[97] With thousands of voters entering into the cross-party political coalition on their site, Cody and Johnson were facing literally thousands of years in jail.

The letter was all bluster, since the legal basis for the threat was flimsy. Attorney General Jones referred to sections 18521 and 18522 of the California Elections Code which criminalize vote-selling and vote-buying. The former provision bans the receipt by any person of "any money, gift, loan, or other valuable consideration, office, place, or employment" in return for having "voted, agreed to vote, refrained from voting, or agreed to refrain from voting for any particular person or measure."[98] The latter provision makes it a crime to "pay, lend, or contribute . . . any money or other valuable consideration to or for any voter" to "vote or refrain from voting at an election for any particular person. . . ."[99]

On their terms, these provisions ban the exchange of money and other material things for votes. The whole point of such laws is to prevent people from creating a financial market in votes, converting financial currency into units of political power. But this is not what the vote-trading movement does. No money (or anything else) changes hands; no one makes a penny on it. The entire motivation for the discussion and agreement is a political one, not financial. How can a vote constitute "valuable consideration" within the meaning of a vote-buying and vote-selling statute when the whole purpose of the statute is to prevent votes from being treated like objects of commercial transaction?

This plain-meaning statutory analysis is constitutionally compelled. For if vote-buying and -selling are read to criminalize vote-trading, then much of what we thought was First Amendment–protected electoral and legislative politics becomes criminal. Vote-trading is the *lingua franca* of real-world local politics, where groups, clubs, factions, and coalitions sit down and form slates with an exchange of promises: you get your constituents to support my guys for council member and state legislature and we'll deliver you our votes for mayor and Congress. Are these slate-making coalitions illegally "brokering" votes? Are political coalitions based on political compromise criminal conspiracies?

Similarly, legislative logrolling is the standard mode of business in Congress and the states. Can it really be the case that two senators who agree to trade votes on two pet projects have both just committed felonies under federal bribery statutes? The theory staggers the mind. Arguably it could be made a crime for two voters in different states to mail one another their yet-to-be-completed absentee ballots: this would be a ballot trade between two people who are nonvoters in the elections they are about to vote in. But for two voters to influence each other's decision about how to vote is First Amendment heartland. If we can't do that, it is hard to see why voters in one state should have a constitutional right to spend money purchasing television ads in another state telling voters there how to vote. The idea that someone could be sent to prison for changing his or her mind about voting based on how someone else is planning to vote is simply astonishing.

But the California threat letter achieved its desired political effect: the creators of Voteswap2000.com shut the site down immediately. Within 24 hours the chilling effect spread: Voteexchange.org and VotExchange 2000.com also terminated operation. Meantime, other officials acted to squelch the threat of vote-trading (suggesting perhaps some coordination among the state officials across state lines). On October 31, 2000, Mary Kiffmeyer, Minnesota secretary of state, issued a similar threat letter to the Web sites, describing vote-swapping as "the ultimate in voter fraud."[100] She elaborated this bit of extravagant silliness with even more remarkable assertions:

> It proposes to change the outcome of the election through an underhanded scheme that induces voters to cast their vote for a candidate they would not normally support. The results, if successful, would discourage and demoralize voters who follow the rules, only to see their candidates defeated.[101]

But how does Secretary of State Kiffmeyer know whom voters would "normally support"? Does this mean that the Gore campaign is engaged in voter fraud whenever it tries to convince Nader supporters to vote for Gore to stop Bush and thereby is inducing voters to "cast their vote for a candidate they would not normally support"? The partisan subtext of her letter is rather shocking: the Republican candidates who would "normally" win may not win, which will "demoralize" their voters, who apparently have some kind of statutory entitlement to win. Kiffmeyer closed her letter: "Vote swapping cannot be permitted and will not be allowed in the State of Minnesota."

Several other states quickly went the way of California. In Oregon, Secretary of State Bill Bradbury, absurdly citing an "undue influence" statute, sent out criminal threat letters. The New York State Board of Elections sent a letter to nadergore.com warning that vote-buying and -selling "is illegal in New York State" and directing its operators "to immediately cease and desist engaging in such activity and to immediately deactivate the web site and access to the activity therein."[102] Arizona followed suit.

As certain Web sites shut down in fear of state prosecution, others came online with more carefully tailored messages and lawyerlike disclaimers. But in large parts of the country, especially the West, the message went out that vote-trading was illegal. California Attorney General Jones, soon to be a candidate for governor of the state, took to the airwaves to denounce vote-trading. I twice debated him on the radio and asked whether he planned to prosecute members of the state legislature for trading votes or George W. Bush for promising public policy benefits—"things of value"— to the voters of California if they voted for him and he were elected. I do not recall him answering.

Jones was primarily interested, I believe, in chilling the Internet coalition, and his campaign had that effect: many people dropped the whole thing in the face of so many reports of official threats. Nonetheless, there were an extraordinary *2.8 million* hits on the various sites, showing that the cat is well out of the bag. The developer of VotExchange2000.com, Alan Porter, has already updated and reregistered his domain name for the 2004 presidential election: Votexchange2004.com.

While the Republican attorney generals shrewdly got the point about the political danger facing the Republican Party from progressive Internet political organizing across state and party lines, neither Gore nor Nader took to the idea nor did anything to bolster it. The Gore campaign kept a huge distance from vote-trading, not realizing that the slightest bit of rhetorical or organizational help would have made his address 1600 Pennsylvania Avenue. For his part, Nader seemed to associate vote-trading with one-way efforts by liberal Democrats to get his backers to vote for Gore. He did not realize that vote-trading actually countered the effect of this well-organized project by making certain that as many progressive Democrats nationally crossed over to vote for Nader as Nader supporters crossed over for Gore.

The irony is that polls show Nader may have lost half of his electoral support in the final 48 hours of the campaign, as the predictable cries of "don't waste your vote" became deafening and the progressive Democrats went home. Had vote-pairing been condoned or at least not frowned upon by the Nader campaign, perhaps hundreds of thousands more Nader votes would have been effectively locked in on a national basis. This was the point missed, I think, by Sam Smith, the editor of the *Progressive Review*, who adopted an absolutist position on voting for Nader in the 2000 campaign and denounced me as a "Washington Democratic operative ... who apparently wanted to get his resume in to Gore early."[103] Not only did Smith call vote-trading a "dirty trick reminiscent of those used by Richard Nixon"[104] but actually, both on the radio and in print, endorsed the idea that Internet vote-trading by progressive Democrats and Nader supporters was a criminally prosecutable activity, which seems a fairly outrageous posture for a long-time champion of political free expression and dialogue.

I understand that, in the heat of battle, it was hard for either the Gore or Nader camps to think clearly about this new idea. It is unsettling for a candidate to condone any political message other than "everybody vote for me." But Nader's standard reply to questions about vote-trading—that people should "vote their conscience" instead—did not fully address either the instrumental character of elections or the pragmatic character of political psychology. Many people's "conscience" told them to do two things at once: build up the political standing of Nader and the Green Party and also promote the election of Gore over Bush. (Similarly, on the right, many conservatives wanted to cast a symbolic vote for Patrick Buchanan while still effectively pushing Bush over Gore; the same drama of vote-trading was acted out on a smaller scale among the Republicans, given Buchanan's declining fortunes in the 2000 race.) Participating in electoral politics in a serious way is not like painting a picture or writing a poem, where all that is called for is sincere expression of one's innermost feelings. Voting is actually a collective exercise practiced individually, or perhaps an individual exercise practiced collectively; in any event, it makes the most sense for people to think of the dynamics of the whole election when they vote.

If we maintain the Electoral College, cross-party and interstate vote-trading will become a hallmark of the Internet age because it liberates people from the tyranny of having their votes mean nothing in states where the result is a foregone conclusion. Vote-trading puts the people, not the consultants, pundits and big contributors, in the driver's seat. Consider some of the comments sent in to NaderTrader.org by participants:

Regarding the Nader Trader idea—I was blown away by the implications of this. I think this sort of mass strategic voting ... is destined to reappear in various contexts in the future.... I think the most important and positive aspect of this concept is that it boosts morale of would-be apathetic voters. I was planning not to vote at all in this election, but was so intrigued by the Nader Trader idea that I changed my mind. For once, it seemed that my individual vote could truly make a difference; whether this was purely psychological or not, it was a strong motivator to get out to the polls.

—New Hampshire voter[105]

I knew the internet would change this election, I just wasn't sure how until now. I told a good friend of mine in Portland that I wanted to vote for Nader, she sent me an e-mail back that said, "if you must vote for Nader, consider this," and she sent me the Nader Trader website. I loved it immediately. Power to the people   now we are not puppets of the electoral college but as voters have found a way get what we want. That is what it is supposed to be about, the will of the people....I traded my vote the first day and within one half hour had e-mailed to 20 friends. Then as the pathetic, "please Mr. Nader step down," e-mails started coming, cc-ed to me and many others, I cc back the Nader Trader site to all of them....I feel great about this, and tomorrow I will proudly go to the polls and vote for Al Gore here in my "swing" state and know that a young woman in Rhode Island will be voting for Nader as her state is Democratic. One really amazing part is the power of the internet—we can connect with each other, without the media—this was a 2 week creation, think what can be accomplished by 2004! I am more excited and hopeful than I have been in the last 7 presidential elections that I have been old enough to vote in. I feel like there are a lot of people like me out there and now we can connect up! It's awesome.

—Wisconsin voter[106]

My family exported/imported four Gore/Nader votes. All were Gore votes leaving Houston, Texas (what could be more beautiful) and we all cast a Nader vote here. Our votes all went to different states: Oregon, Washington and Minnesota. My son in Ohio traded with an old college roommate. They made an election eve trade. My son didn't give up easily on Ohio. Imagine what could have happened with more time.

—Texas voter[107]

There is no way of going back to a presidential politics without vote-trading in the Internet age. Indeed, if there are serious third-party candidates in the future, the organization and technology will be vastly improved over the improvisational efforts of 2000. Still, the legal controversy remains. Much rides on a California lawsuit, *Alan Porter v. Bill Jones*, brought on behalf of Alan Porter, the designer of Votexchange2000.com, by a superb young lawyer at the ACLU of Southern California named Peter Eliasberg and Gregory Luke of the National Voting Rights Institute. (I have been of counsel in this suit along with Harvard Law Professor Laurence Tribe, who dropped out during the *Bush v. Gore* litigation but was replaced by his colleague Alan Dershowitz.) The suit seeks a declaratory statement that the First Amendment protects the creation of voting coalitions on the Internet and an injunction against any further threats of prosecution by Attorney General Bill Jones, who probably changed the outcome of the 2000 election with his transparently partisan threats of prosecution against citizens engaged in free political speech, compromise, and coalition.

The ACLU will almost certainly win this case. Even if it does not, there will always be a way for people to use the Internet to communicate their political desires, even if they must be camouflaged. The only way now to prevent strategic political action on the Internet in presidential elections is to abolish the Electoral College, which makes vote-trading both necessary and logical.

If we move to direct popular election of the president on a national basis, people will vote for the candidate they want to win. A vote will mean the same thing in New York, Texas, Alabama, Oregon and Alaska. Of course, some people will be tempted to vote for their second-choice candidate if they think their first-choice candidate has no chance. But this "lesser evil" problem can be dealt with nicely through institution of an "instant run-off" procedure, as discussed below.

The Electoral College and Political White Supremacy

Because the argument for the electoral college hinges on the presumptive weight we should attach to history, it is important to see how the history of the electoral college is intertwined with the institutions and movements of political white supremacy. The Southern slave states championed the electoral college because it had several clearly advantageous features for them when compared with a majority national vote for president.[108] Awarding a number of state electors "equal to the whole Number of Senators and

Representatives to which the State may be entitled in the Congress" reproduced a number of significant pro–slave state biases already sewn into the constitutional fabric.[109]

The trick was that, by counting slaves as part of the census for the purpose of reapportioning U.S. House seats, the Constitution would vastly inflate Southern white representation in the House. Thus, the slaves, who obviously could not vote, would swell the congressional delegation of the slave masters. The slave states brazenly argued that slaves should be counted as full persons in the census while the Northern states argued they should not be counted at all. The two sides settled on the infamous "Three-Fifths" provision—a clear victory for the slave power (though a historical irony, since most people do not realize that had the slave states had their way, slaves would have been counted as full persons).[110]

Article II then reproduced this effect in presidential elections by awarding states presidential electors in a number "equal to the whole Number of Senators and Representatives to which the State may be entitled in the Congress."[111] The two "add on" electors for each state's senators gave further disproportionate power to the less populous states, especially those with fewer eligible voters—that is, the slave states.[112]

The proslavery, pro-small state tilt reappeared in the provision for a so-called "contingent election" in the House of Representatives upon the failure of any presidential candidate to collect a majority in the electoral college. In such case, "the House of Representatives shall immediately choose by Ballot the President," but "the votes shall be taken by states, the representation from each state having one vote...."[113] In such an event, the smaller slave states, such as South Carolina or Alabama would receive a major boost up to a level of parity with more populous Northern states such as New York, Massachusetts, or New Jersey. Everywhere you looked in the intricate electoral college provisions, the South had dug in its heels.

The subsequent history of the Electoral College illuminates its racial character, as the slave power proved adept at winning and manipulating presidential elections. Four of the first five U.S. presidents were slave masters who brought their slaves with them into the presidency and the White House: George Washington, Thomas Jefferson, James Madison, and James Monroe (with only the second president, Massachusetts's John Adams, interrupting the reign of slave masters). The failure of the proslavery forces to defeat Abraham Lincoln in the election of 1860 immediately precipitated Southern secession and the Civil War.[114] The 1876 election was thrown into turmoil because of the failure of any candidate to assemble an electoral college majority, and then Southern forces, operating in a chaotic post-election environment not unlike that of 2000, traded the presidency for a commitment from Republican Rutherford B. Hayes to withdraw federal troops from the Reconstruction South.

In the second half of the twentieth century when the modern Civil Rights movement became a critical political force, "white Southern politicians ... repeatedly and deliberately attempted to manipulate the machinery of the electoral college to influence national policy on race and civil rights."[115] In the 1948 presidential campaign, J. Strom Thurmond, the then-Democratic governor of South Carolina, ran for president on a fiercely segregationist "states' rights" platform. Following through on a brilliant electoral college strategy suggested by racist theorist Charles Wallace Collins, an Alabama lawyer and public servant who had served as law librarian of Congress and librarian of the Supreme Court, Thurmond convinced four state Democratic parties, those of Alabama, Louisiana, Mississippi and South Carolina, to nominate slates of electors pledged to vote for him.[116] The national Democratic nominee, Harry Truman, found a way onto the ballot to compete against Thurmond in three of those four states, but Thurmond still won in all four states and captured 39 electoral college votes. Truman carried the national election by the skin of his teeth, but the Democratic Party received Thurmond's message loud and clear.

In 1960, ardent foes of the Civil Rights movement played the electoral college card again when Alabama and Mississippi selected fourteen unpledged "free electors" in the presidential contest. These electors ended up voting for Virginia Senator Harry F. Byrd, an architect of "massive resistance" to *Brown v. Board of Education*, and declared their overriding opposition to attempts to "integrate our schools, do away with literacy tests as a qualification for voting [and] otherwise undermining everything we hold dear in the South."[117]

In 1968, Alabama Governor George C. Wallace, who had famously declared "segregation now, segregation tomorrow, segregation forever," perfected and nationalized the strategy of appealing to race prejudice to move the whole political spectrum rightward.[118] Wallace's racially charged blue-collar campaign helped move large numbers of white southerners out of their traditional home in the Democratic Party and created fertile terrain for the new Republican "Southern strategy." Wallace won in Alabama, Arkansas, Georgia, Louisiana and Mississippi, and Richard Nixon, campaigning on a similar socially authoritarian platform, took Florida, Kentucky, North Carolina, South Carolina, Tennessee and Virginia. Racist southerners had successfully used race as a lever to move presidential electors out of the Democratic column.

In 1980, Ronald Reagan launched his presidential campaign in the Mississippi town where civil rights activists Schwerner, Chaney and Goodman had been murdered in 1965. Reagan turned the solid Democratic South into the solid Republican South. Although Arkansas's Bill Clinton cut into this Republican hold on the South, these underlying dynamics remain powerful. In the 2000 election, George W. Bush launched his southern campaign at the fundamentalist Bob Jones University, which banned interracial dating. Bush swept the South: Alabama, Arkansas, Florida, Georgia, Kentucky, Louisiana, Mississippi, North Carolina, Oklahoma, South Carolina, Texas, Tennessee and Virginia. These thirteen southern states control 163 electoral votes, which is more than half of the 270 needed to win the election. The Deep South remains the beating heart of the Republican presidential electoral college coalition.

Because of the nation's racial demography and geography, the winner-take-all electoral college in the states means that most of the votes cast by African Americans in presidential elections will count literally for nothing. In 2000, more than 90 percent of African Americans voted for Democratic nominee Al Gore for president, something as close to a unanimous endorsement from a community as one might find.[119] Yet 58 percent of voting African Americans, or 20,202,137 people, live in states that gave 100 percent of their electoral college votes to the Republican nominee, George W. Bush. Thus, most African Americans voted in states where their votes ended up having no effect on the ultimate outcome of the election. [See graphic.] African Americans voted overwhelmingly for the popular vote-winner but it made no difference. The one Southern state where the African-American vote clearly might have made a difference was Florida. This fact makes the strategies deployed to cancel out African-American voting power in Florida all the more appalling and the Supreme Court's tying of a little bow on the whole process all the more cynical.

Florida aside, the structural cancellation of African-American votes in presidential elections in the South reflects the general operation of the winner-take-all Electoral College system. This is the basic reason to get rid of the Electoral College today: each person's vote should count equally in a presidential election, regardless of geography, and the winner should

The Racial Dynamics of the
Republican Presidential Electoral
College Coalition

- 90% of African Americans voted for Al Gore.

- 58% of voting age African-Americans live in states where 100 percent of the electoral college votes went to George W. Bush

- 20,202,137 African Americans live in states whose electors went to George W. Bush

- The 13 Southern States (AL, AR, FL, GA, KY, LA, MS, NC, OK, SC, TX, TN, VA) control 163 electoral votes, or more than half of the electoral votes needed to win the election (270).

actually *win*. But the electoral college has grown up with America's sordid racial history, and it continues in its underground fashion to embolden the minority voice of white racial conservatism in the multi-cultural America of the new century.

The "Faithless Elector"

A common argument against the Electoral College which I do *not* make refers to the danger that a presidential elector, having been elected pledged to this or that candidate, may later betray that candidate by voting for someone else. This is silly, because the Framers designed the Electoral College as a deliberative political institution. It cuts against this purpose to try to hem the elector in. For example, since we have this institution, what would be wrong with an elector who had originally pledged to Bush saying, "since the Supreme Court decision is flawed, the Florida result is in grave doubt, and Gore won a robust popular majority, I plan to cast my vote for Gore"? This didn't happen, but wouldn't it have reflected the kind of political wisdom and deliberative judgment the Framers desired and we expect from our elected leaders?

Moving from a hypothetical example to a real one, didn't we see a profile in courage in Barbara Lett-Simmons, a Democratic elector from the District of Columbia who cast a blank ballot to protest the Democratic nominee's seeming indifference to disenfranchisement in the District of Columbia? Why should we have an Electoral College if the electors are not supposed to use their minds between Election Day and the day they cast their ballots?

The Obsolete and Empty Arguments for the Electoral College

History

Arguments in defense of the Electoral College inevitably turn to history: this was the way the Framers *intended* to have us elect presidents, we are told, so this is the way we should do it.[120] But the Electoral College was a kind of awkward compromise between advocates of direct popular election and advocates of congressional election within a context suffused with political arguments favoring the slave power. If we summon up the imagination to discard this obsolete and undemocratic plan for electing presidents—that is, if we become constitutional framers ourselves—we will be doing nothing uncharacteristic in American history. We have often replaced the handiwork of the Framers when it has thwarted popular control over government. The Thirteenth, Fourteenth and Fifteenth Amendments after the Civil War wiped out the original exclusionary assumptions of white supremacy in politics and government.[121] In 1913, we replaced the indirect method of electing U.S. senators by state legislatures with direct election "by the people" as provided for in the Seventeenth Amendment.[122] The Nineteenth Amendment rejected the sexism of our Framers by writing women into the body politic.[123] And we have repeatedly modified the Electoral College itself to bring it closer in line to our values.

Changing the mode of presidential election would honor the democratic values of the Framers far more than adhering unthinking to the electoral college. Many Founders voiced hopes that future generations would not become mindless slaves to antiquated and mystified constitutional traditions. Judith Shklar has reminded us that in his time Thomas Jefferson "detested the 'sanctimonious reverence' with which some men looked at the Constitution. Ancestor worship was an irrationality no democracy could afford; on the contrary, we should, he wrote, 'avail ourselves of our reason and experience to correct the crude essays of our first and inexperienced councils.'"[124] Following Thomas Paine, Jefferson insisted that: "The earth belongs in usufruct to the living. The dead have no rights, the earth belongs to the living."[125]

Federalism

The energy for the pro–Electoral College argument now comes from small states, which have in recent years fallen hook, line and sinker for the claim that they benefit politically from the two-elector "add-on" for senators. The myth is that presidential candidates spend more time in smaller states than they otherwise would because these states' electors are more of a prize in the current regime than their people-votes would be in a popular election. Ask any smallish-state senator and you get the same answer: take away the electoral college and you take away the extra leverage we have to get candidates to pay attention to our interests.

This claim, however, is factually wrong. Presidential candidates go disproportionately to *swing* states, not *small* states, and even within the swing states, they go disproportionately to the larger ones, not the smaller, because of the winner-take-all effect. In 2000, the candidates bypassed and took for granted small states that were safely in one column or the other, for example Republican-controlled North Dakota and Idaho or Democratic-controlled Rhode Island and the District of Columbia. To the extent that a jurisdiction's political interests are deemed to be taken seriously when candidates visit them (a dubious assumption in any event), none of these places picked up any influence by virtue of being small. The states that profited from the electoral college were large swing states such as Florida, Pennsylvania, Michigan, Missouri and Ohio, and then, and only to a much lesser extent, small swing states such as New Mexico, West Virginia and New Hampshire.

The mathematical rationale for the intuitively predictable candidate behavior of favoring large swing states against small ones was explained in a superb law review article in 1968 by John F. Banzhaf III, who proved that, under the electoral college system, individual voters in large states enjoy much greater voting power than those in small states.[126] Through a meticulous examination of the chance that voters have to "affect the outcome in a given situation,"[127] Banzhaf found that a voter in New York in 1968 had more than three times the "voting power" of a voter in Washington, D.C.[128] Many scholars have since corroborated and elaborated the Banzhaf thesis that, all other things being equal, it makes more sense in the Electoral College regime for candidates to invest resources in larger states than in smaller ones.[129]

It is important to see why there is so much confusion over this point. The Framers undoubtedly intended the smaller states to have a disproportionate share of the power in selecting a president, and indeed it worked like this when electors were chosen by state legislatures and acted deliberatively, on an individual basis, to decide who should be president. In that system, the two-elector add-on could really help this or that small-state elector-politico to broker a deal that would somehow benefit his state.

But when states moved from this process of appointing freewheeling electors to the winner-take-all unit system of pledged electors, all that mattered in political terms was moving majorities of voters in the largest swing states to vote for the right slate of electors. In other words, the Banzhaf factor took over.[130] Senators from smaller states swear by the electoral college today because they know in their bones that the Framers' compromise was designed to help them and that the Electoral College is structurally linked to the composition of the Senate. But today the joke's on them, because in reality the Electoral College no longer works in their favor.

The shrewder small states recognized this fact long ago. In 1966, in the aptly named *Delaware v. New York*, Delaware and a group of other small states tried unsuccessfully to sue New York and other large states on Equal Protection grounds for awarding their electors in the unit bloc fashion.[131] The Court refused to entertain the filing of an original jurisdiction action, but the political logic of the new regime was clarified.[132] The smaller states saw that the traditional pro-small state bias in the electoral college had been defeated and completely reversed by the big states' winner-take-all method of distributing electors.[133]

Even if it were true that the Electoral College regime differentially helps jurisdictions such as Delaware, North Dakota and the District of Columbia (and it is demonstrably false), such a disproportion would be indefensible as a matter of democratic principle (as opposed to raw political assertion). The president is presumably the leader of the nation and not of the patchwork of electoral majorities in particular states that gave him all their electors. But the Electoral College can only encourage presidents to think of the country in the red-and-blue terms of a CNN election-night map: friendly regions, where the base needs constant watering and replenishment, and unfriendly regions that should be generally avoided and gently disregarded. If we move to a direct popular vote where every vote counts, presidents will have effective voting constituents everywhere, even in the most "hostile" areas, and will be motivated to represent the full breadth of the nation. Presidents elected by the people will govern mindful of the whole nation, not just 270 electors. The irony of today's deadlock over the Electoral College is that the small states are saving an undemocratic institution that benefits the large states.

The Popular Election of the President Amendment

Consider the following amendment to adopt direct popular election of the president which includes a built-in "instant run-off" provision to guarantee that the winner actually has majority support of the voters:

> The President and Vice President shall be elected by direct popular vote of all U.S. citizens eighteen years of age and older, but no person shall be elected President who has not attained at least 50 percent support among the votes cast. Whenever there are three or more candidates listed on the ballot, the ballot shall ask voters to rank their choices in order of preference. If no candidate receives at least 50 percent of the first-place votes cast, the last-place candidate's ballots shall be redistributed to the second-choice candidates

of these voters. This instant runoff method shall continue until a candidate has achieved a majority of all votes cast.

Of the several important changes embodied in this Popular Election of the President Amendment, the enactment of majority rule is only the most obvious. The development of direct election by the people means that all Americans will, for the first time in history, participate together as citizens in a single and truly national election. Our first direct election of the president will mark an important political emancipation for American civil society, which has been artificially segmented and divided into 51 separate voting jurisdictions with different rules, procedures and ballots. State lines are meaningful and defensible in congressional elections but puzzlingly irrational and out of place when choosing a president, a unitary executive who acts for the entire nation. Americans should vote as one nation with *a single presidential ballot* that looks the same in Maine and Hawaii, California and Florida. Furthermore, by granting all citizens the right to vote for president, the amendment would for the first time allow millions of American citizens living in the territories of Guam, American Samoa, Puerto Rico and the Virgin Islands to vote for president. Since they do not belong to states and do not pay federal taxes, territorial residents would continue to have only nonvoting representation in Congress, but their existing place in the American regime would be properly recognized by giving them a role in presidential elections.

The shift to popular election of the president would also redistribute political power. A similar transformation took place in 1913 when the Seventeenth Amendment shifted the mode of election of U.S. senators from state legislative selection to direct election by the people.[134] The new method ended the practice of out-of-state businesses purchasing the friendship of so-called "corporation senators" through well-placed bribes and covert campaign contributions in state legislatures. A progressive reform pushed by the Populists, direct election of senators removed multiple levels of political filtering that blocked real democratic accountability and responsiveness. Today, when presidential elections are influenced by hundreds of millions of dollars in corporate soft money, closed corporate-sponsored debates, the taking for granted of most of the population, and fine-tuned pollster-driven manipulation of the rest, a changeover to popular election would break the current top-down dynamics of the system.

The Popular Election of the President Amendment replaces the bizarre

Rube Goldberg–type contraptions of the electoral college—the two-vote add-on, the lengthy delays between popular voting and the casting of the electoral-college votes, the contingent House election based on state-by-state voting, the recurring possibilities of popular-vote losers winning the election—with clean and simple majority rule. A majority is guaranteed by virtue of the "instant runoff" mechanism, which assures that the winner will achieve a popular mandate without requiring that an expensive second (or third) runoff election be held. This method of voting not only guarantees that candidates will take office with majority support but also dampens partisan invective and rancor during the campaign. Candidates have no interest in polarizing things because they want to become a group of voters' second favored choice even if they cannot be their first. This instant runoff mechanism is gaining increasing support around the country. On March 5, 2002, the people of San Francisco voted by 56 percent to 44 percent to adopt instant runoff voting for election of local officials. Rob Richie and Steven Hill of the Center for Voting and Democracy in Takoma Park, Maryland, who organized the drive, have made a signal contribution to public discourse by putting the instant runoff on America's democracy agenda.

Popular election of the president advances the one person, one vote principle. The Banzhaf analysis, which measures the chances of a vote affecting the outcome of the presidential election, tells us that individual votes in large states are worth much more than individual votes in small states.[135] If we disregard that dynamic analysis and just consider abstractly what percentage of a single electoral college vote each voter controls, then the effect reverses and voters in small states have a clear advantage. Each voter in Vermont or Idaho thus has more say in the electoral college than each voter in New York or California. Moreover, the vagaries of voter turnout also create distortions in the Electoral College: other things being equal, a single vote in a high turnout state is worth less than a single vote in a low turnout state. In sum, if we really want each citizen's vote to count equally in presidential elections, we need to move to direct popular election of the president.

Amazingly, the government of the United States conducts and provides no official count of the vote for president. So, we never know in any reliable sense who actually won the most votes. This is a dramatic problem. In 2000, the people were completely dependent upon private media to report vote totals from thousands of jurisdictions around the country, based on some hazy combination of precinct returns, polling and exit interviews.

The public was utterly helpless before the ever-changing projections and declarations of victory issued by broadcast entities. It now looks as though that process may have been contaminated by strategic partisan manipulation.[135] There is no reason for it not to happen again.

The vagaries of vote counting put the icing on the cake that is baked behind the scenes by state secretaries of state, electors, party bosses, television news anchormen and women, state legislatures and Supreme Court Justices—almost everybody but the people. We need to establish a constitutional right to vote and then replace the Electoral College with direct national majority rule in presidential elections. We need a national ballot for president based on a national election with a national system of reporting the tally. It is time for the people to claim America's presidential elections as our own and fulfill our lost promise of becoming a democratic nation.

CHAPTER FOUR

Unequal Protection
The Supreme Court's Racial Double Standard
in Redistricting

Clarence Thomas: The Only Black Vote That Counts
—Sign carried by protester at the Supreme Court
after the Court's decision in *Bush v. Gore*

The Voting Rights Act of 1965

In his book *Radical Equations*, Bob Moses recalls an epiphany he had in 1960 when he got to know Amzie Moore, president of the Cleveland, Mississippi branch of the NAACP. A 26-year-old teacher from the Horace Mann school in the Bronx, Moses had traveled to the Deep South to join the Civil Rights movement. He quickly fastened onto Moore, a ubiquitous force in the black community who reminded Moses of his own father. This natural-born politician in the destitute Mississippi Delta became a mentor to the young Civil Rights organizer from the North.

Moore was "not interested in sit-ins to desegregate Mississippi's public accommodations,"[1] nor was he focused on the legal battles for school desegregation. What Moore wanted to do was to get African Americans the vote back after a near-century of disenfranchisement following Reconstruction. Moore opened Moses's eyes to what political participation could mean in an area where a system of violent intimidation and oppression had left 98 percent of African Americans off the voter rolls and too petrified even to try to register. Moore, writes Moses:

> had concluded that at the heart of Mississippi's race problem was denial of the right to vote. Amzie wanted a grassroots movement to get it, and in his view getting that right was the key to unlocking Mississippi and gaining some power to initiate real change. I had not given that idea any thought at all; *I didn't know before I began talking to Amzie that the Mississippi Delta where he lived was a congressional district that was two thirds Black.* I had been

sitting up hearing about oppression behind the *iron* curtain and the meaning of the vote for freedom all through my college years and graduate years
*without knowing about the Delta and its congressional district with a Black
majority.* I had not made the connection to the denial of the right to vote
behind the *cotton* curtain.[2]

The Civil Rights movement mobilized around the right to vote and tore
down the cotton curtain. The blood sacrifice of the people who transformed Mississippi and the South created a dynamic of action that led to
President Lyndon Johnson's signing of the Voting Right Act on August 6,
1965.

The Voting Rights Act and the movement that brought it into being
changed the character of American politics. The Act destroyed the literacy test, the character exam, the polling-place constitutional law quiz and
other "first-generation"[3] suffrage obstacles. The result was that the African-
American population in the South, which had a voter-registration rate
averaging less than 25 percent in 1956, reached 62 percent registration by
1968, just three years after the act was signed into law.[4]

The nascent black-majority congressional district that political vision-
aries Amzie Moore and Bob Moses could perceive through the darkness
of Mississippi apartheid was suddenly coming into focus across the South.

But in politics, as in physics, every action creates an equal and opposite
reaction. The first reaction against the prospect of serious black political
power came from conservatives in the states. The second one, as we shall
see shortly, came from conservatives on the Supreme Court.

It was not long after the Voting Rights Act passed that Southern whites
developed subtle structural techniques to thwart the dread prospect of
African-American representation and multiracial democracy. They realized
that black voting would mean little if whites could still control the outcome of elections. So they imposed a "second generation"[5] of seemingly
neutral discriminatory mechanisms: majority "runoff" requirements that
guaranteed that a divided white field would not produce a black winner;
at-large elections that prevented black majorities from forming in single-
member territorial districts; and carefully gerrymandered boundary lines
in single-member district plans to break up potential African-American
majorities and bury them safely in different districts.

The Justice Department used the Voting Rights Act to counter these
ploys, and courts found that their clear effect was to dilute the black
vote. But, in 1980, a conservative plurality on the Supreme Court upheld

Mobile, Alabama's at-large election plan in *Mobile v. Bolden* and found that structural vote dilution was neither unconstitutional nor illegal under Section 2 of the Voting Rights Act unless the plaintiffs could demonstrate a racially discriminatory purpose behind the adoption of allegedly diluting mechanisms.[6]

This "purpose test" marked a major step backwards. While it was easy to show that runoff provisions or the submerging of a black population undermined black political power, it was much harder to prove that such political disempowerment was the deliberate purpose of white politicians. By now even the most primitive white officials had scrubbed their public rhetoric clean of racial animus in deference to the Civil Rights laws. Nothing short of a lie detector test or a heart X ray could show the deliberate malice of these schemes to the satisfaction of a conservative Supreme Court majority weary of the race problem.

In Congress, the Civil Rights forces, mobilized by Congressman John Conyers and the Leadership Conference for Civil Rights, responded by pressing for enactment of the 1982 amendments to the Voting Rights Act. These amendments restored the "results" test by rendering unlawful any voting procedure or standard that *resulted* in racial minorities having "less opportunity than other members of the electorate to participate in the political process and to elect representatives of their choice." The amendments provided that: "the extent to which members of a protected class have been elected to office in the State or political subdivision is one circumstance which may be considered: *Provided,* That nothing in this section establishes a right to have members of a protected class elected in numbers equal to their proportion in the population."[7] Thus, African Americans won no right to numerical proportional representation in legislative delegations ("quotas"), but Congress made clear it would not tolerate the effective dilution and submergence of the black vote in states with a history of discrimination and polarized racial voting.

In the wake of these amendments, several appeals courts found that at-large voting systems violated the Act where there had been "racially polarized voting."[8] In 1986, the Supreme Court in *Thornburg v. Gingles* found that North Carolina violated the Act by redrawing single-member districts for state House and Senate seats in such a way as to systematically dilute black citizens' votes. The decision was not based on an evidentiary showing of subjective intent to discriminate but on a set of structural factors reflecting unlawful vote dilution. Justice Brennan held that, to successfully challenge a legislative redistricting as a violation of the Act, there must be racially polarized voting, the potential and political will for a minority community to elect a candidate of its choice (not necessarily a candidate of its *race*), and the consistent obstruction of such a possibility by a white majority drawn into the district.[9] Under this test, "the degree of racial bloc voting is the key element of a vote dilution claim."[10]

The 1990 decennial reapportionment was the first in which states redrew congressional and state legislative district lines under the new "results" test, and it had exciting consequences for minority political power. For the first time at least since Reconstruction, white-controlled state legislatures that had carefully drawn lines in the last redistricting to prevent the emergence of black voting majorities now redrew district lines to permit such districts to come into being. Because of the pervasive residential segregation in the South, this task was not generally tough to accomplish; the tricky part was how to create such districts and at the same time protect as many white incumbents as possible, especially the Democrats who had long counted on black votes for a margin of victory. This political imperative, combined with dramatic improvements in computer redistricting technology, produced the fancy new cartography.

In historical terms the new districts were a triumph. Just as the 1965 Act brought down man-made barriers to black voter registration, the 1982 amendments brought down man-made barriers to blacks constituting electoral majorities and holding public office.

The 1990 census and subsequent redistricting produced "historic increases in the number of majority-black and majority-Hispanic congressional and legislative districts and accompanying advances in the numbers of black and Hispanic members of Congress and state legislators."[11] The nation saw a doubling of "majority-minority" House districts from 26 to 52, resulting in a 50 percent jump (from 26 to 39) in the number of African-American members of the U.S. House and a 38 percent increase (from 13 to 18) in Hispanic representation in the House.[12] There were corresponding stunning increases in the number of majority-minority legislative districts and minority representatives in the states.[13] Although racial minorities still remain statistically "very much under-represented"[14] in Congress and state legislatures in relation to population, the 1982 amendments substantially integrated Congress and the state legislatures.

With a real racial integration of American politics in place, the stage was now set for Supreme Court backlash in the name of—you guessed it—Equal Protection itself.

Shaw v. Reno and Miller v. Johnson

Shaw v. Reno (1993) came from North Carolina, where the state legislature had drawn two majority-African-American congressional districts out of the twelve to which the state was newly entitled.[15] Although this configuration still left white citizens, who were 76 percent of the state's population, as a voting majority in 83 percent of the districts (ten out of twelve), the two new districts with slender African-American majorities in 1992 elected the first African-American members of Congress from North Carolina since Reconstruction. They were Mel Watt and Eva Clayton, who became the first African-American women ever to reach Congress from North Carolina, a watershed event in the home state of Senator Jesse Helms.

As Bob Moses's and Amzie Moore's political vision was coming to fruition, conservatives across America perceived a dangerous shift in political power taking place. The *Wall Street Journal* and neoconservative critic Abigail Thernstrom angrily denounced the new majority-black districts as electoral quotas and a form of political segregationism.[16] Conservatives began to delight in ridiculing majority-minority districts and the politicians they elected.

In North Carolina, a group of white plaintiffs, led by a constitutional law professor at Duke University named Robinson O. Everett, brought an Equal Protection lawsuit to have the new districts thrown out. They alleged not that white voters had been disenfranchised, nor that their votes had been diluted, nor that they had been subjected to poll taxes or literacy tests, but that "the deliberate segregation of voters into separate districts on the basis of race violated their constitutional right to participate in a 'color-blind' electoral process,"[17] as Justice O'Connor recaptured it for the *Shaw* majority. What irked Professor Everett and the other plaintiffs was the oddness of the lines on the map: "What appellants object to is redistricting legislation that is so extremely irregular on its face that it rationally can be viewed only as an effort to segregate the races for purposes of voting, without regard for traditional districting principles...."[18]

This grievance seemed a most wobbly legal claim, since the Court had never before required districts to be of any special shape, compactness or aesthetic. The invocation of segregation was baffling, since the congressional districts at issue were the most closely *integrated* districts in North Carolina history: the first district was 53.4 percent African American and

45.5 percent white, and the twelfth was 53.3 percent African American and 45.2 percent white. How could these districts, responsible for integrating the state's century-old, lily-white congressional delegation, be compared to segregated schools, for example, where 100 percent of whites went to one public school and 100 percent of African Americans to another? The emphasis on "traditional districting principles" was equally puzzling, since the controlling constitutional standard of "one person, one vote" was honored in North Carolina's plan. Beyond that, of course, the most time-honored "districting principle" in the South was that African Americans would never constitute the electoral majority. The white plaintiffs were actually contending that they had a right under Equal Protection not to live in a majority-African-American district, a claim that was logically absurd even if fairly reflective of the way many white voters felt.

In a display of stupefying judicial activism, Justice O'Connor, with Justices Scalia, Thomas, Kennedy and Chief Justice Rehnquist (yes, the *Bush v. Gore* five), found that the *Shaw* plaintiffs stated an actionable claim by alleging that "the legislation, though race-neutral on its face, rationally cannot be understood as anything other than an effort to separate voters into different districts on the basis of race...."[19] Although she was perfectly conscious of, and untroubled by, the fact that "the legislature always is aware of race when it draws district lines," Justice O'Connor nonetheless found that a majority-minority district like the one in question "bears an uncomfortable resemblance to political apartheid."[20] A law creating such a district "reinforces racial stereotypes and threatens to undermine our system of representative democracy by signaling to elected officials that they represent a particular racial group rather than their constituency as a whole...."[21]

The *Shaw* decision produced a flood of lawsuits throughout the 1990s that washed away many majority-minority districts. The original quasi-aesthetic principle targeted majority African-American and -Hispanic legislative districts whose perimeters appear to the Court to be "bizarre,"[22] "extremely irregular,"[23] "twisted,"[24] "snakelike,"[25] "iguana-like,"[26] like a "Rorschach ink-blot test,"[27] or "a 'bug splattered on a windshield.'"[28] But the notion soon expanded outward in *Miller v. Johnson.*[29] In this 1995 decision, Justice Kennedy wrote for the Court majority that a bizarre shape is only *evidence* of the constitutional wrong, not the *essence* of it.

A legislature actually violates Equal Protection, according to Justice Kennedy, whenever it can be shown that its redistricting map has "subordinated traditional race-neutral districting principles, including but not limited to compactness, contiguity, respect for political subdivisions or communities defined by actual shared interests, to racial considerations...."[30] Thus, the real sin of the new districts lies not in their strange perimeters but rather in what sympathetic law professor Richard Pildes called the "excessive use of race."[31] Not racism, not racial subordination, not segregation but the "excessive use of race." Hmm.

A profound mystery presents itself immediately. According to the Court, states have a right to draw districts in any shape they please. According to the Court, states also have a right to use race and ethnicity in drawing up districts so long as there is no disenfranchisement or vote dilution taking place. But suddenly, when the Voting Rights Act finally works to give African Americans real political voice, these two constitutional rights are magically transformed into one constitutional wrong.[32]

Racial Double Standards

The conservative Justices' line of cases toppling majority-minority districts has transplanted astounding racial double standards to the heart of Equal Protection law. According to the new doctrine, strict scrutiny attaches whenever state legislatures consciously create African-American or Hispanic majorities in local, state or federal legislative districts, especially where the perimeters of such districts are "bizarrely" drawn. But when legislatures consciously assemble white majorities in legislative districts, it is taken as a simple matter of course, a kind of natural background condition, and no such scrutiny applies no matter how bizarre the district looks. Under this asymmetrical doctrine, whites have gained a presumptive constitutional right to be in the majority in territorial districts at every level of government unless minorities can form majorities by being concentrated in enclosed geographic areas.

Imagine that Congress had passed this double standard as a statute, declaring that "any districts with nonwhite majorities must not have a bizarre perimeter." Leaving aside the comical vagueness of this command, its racial discrimination is a classic violation of Equal Protection. The basic idea of Equal Protection, as the Court emphasized in *Romer v. Evans*,[33] is "the principle that government and each of its parts remain open on impartial terms to all who seek its assistance."[34] Thus, "[a] law declaring that in general it shall be more difficult for one group of citizens than for all others to seek aid from the government is itself a denial of equal protection of the laws in the most literal sense."[35] Racial classifications are the most suspect of all.

We know that the rule discriminates, because African Americans, Hispanics, Asian-Americans and others have no corresponding Equal Protection right not to be part of majority-white districts that have a bizarre shape. For centuries, legislatures have drawn white-majority districts that look extremely irregular, twisted, snakelike, iguana-like, like a Rorschach ink-blot test, or a bug splattered on a windshield.[36] The word "gerrymander" goes back to the early nineteenth century to describe the cartographic handiwork of crafty Massachusetts Governor Eldridge Gerry. And yet distorted-looking iguana-like majority-white districts escape strict scrutiny and are upheld by the Court, the assumption being that, by definition, they reflect "traditional districting principles."[37] On this point, a picture is worth more than a thousand words: Consider the following maps of four districts from *Bush v. Vera*, comparing two bizarrely shaped majority-minority districts struck down by the Supreme Court as racial gerrymanders and two bizarrely shaped majority-white districts upheld *in the very same case*.[38] These maps give the game away.

The white-supremacist character of the *Shaw* doctrine now becomes clear. When legislatures deliberately create majority-minority districts in order to empower minority populations whose votes have been historically diluted by racial gerrymandering, they violate Equal Protection. But when they purposefully create majority white districts to entrench white incumbents who have benefited from racial gerrymandering, they do not.

In many states with large minority populations, histories of racially polarized voting and records of consistent defeat of minority-preferred candidates, state legislatures have tried to comply with the Voting Rights Act by fashioning majority-minority districts.[39] In all of these cases, there is an explicit motivation to create a majority-minority district to remedy past violations.[40] Why this should be described as a *racial* motivation rather than an *antiracist* one is intriguing. In any event, there will be a plain documentary record of what the Court considers to be illicit "racial" motivation. There will often be a set of hearings about vote dilution and race discrimination, and elaborate discussion of how districts can be structured to empower minority voters.[41] There may be an active correspondence between the legislature and the Justice Department and relevant speeches on the floor of the legislature.[42]

Thus, it is easy to show legislative design to create majority-minority districts. Indeed, there is little chance that majority-minority districts will be created without such design. Nothing happens by accident in legislative

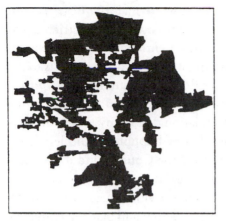
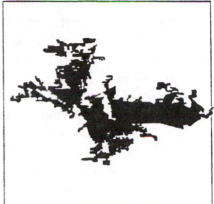

DISTRICT 18 | DISTRICT 29

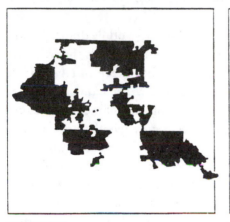

DISTRICT 6 | DISTRICT 3

Figure 4.1 A three-judge federal district court panel in *Bush v. Vera* struck as unconstitutional District 18 (50.9 percent African American and 15.3 percent Latino) and District 29 (60.6 percent Latino and 10.2 percent African American), while upholding districts 6 and 3, which are 90 percent white and 89 percent white respectively.

redistricting, certainly nothing to benefit racial minorities. After all, majority-white legislatures tend to create majority-white districts wherever they can, not for reasons of explicit racism necessarily, but simply because state legislators want to go to Congress or help their (white) friends and family get there. The baseline assumption is to maximize the number of majority-white districts. So most white legislators do not have to express themselves as did the plainspoken Joe Mack Wilson, former Chairman of the Georgia House Reapportionment Committee, who stated with epigrammatic cogency: "I don't want to draw nigger districts."[43]

The Court's presumptive hostility to nonwhite majority districts contrasts dramatically with its enthusiastic endorsement of redistricting for purposes of incumbent reelection or partisan entrenchment. In *Burns v. Richardson*,[44] the Court rejected the argument that tailoring districts to the electoral interests of incumbents violates Equal Protection.[45] In *Gaffney v. Cummings*,[46] the Court upheld against Equal Protection attack a redistricting plan that caused substantial population deviations among districts in order to create "a proportionate number of Republican and legislative Democratic seats."[47] In *Abrams v. Johnson*,[48] the Court found it permissible to redistrict with the intent of protecting "incumbents from contests with each other."[49] In fact, in all of the congressional reapportionments leading to *Shaw* challenges, incumbency protection and partisan entrenchment have been dominant factors controlling the shape of congressional districts.

In *Bush v. Vera*,[50] the Court struck down three new, oddly drawn, majority-minority congressional districts in Texas on the grounds that race was the predominant factor in their configuration.[51] But the record was replete with evidence of pervasive manipulation of the redistricting process by incumbents and by a group the Court deferentially calls "functional incumbents," the "sitting members of the Texas legislature who had declared an intention to run for open congressional seats."[52] These actual and functional incumbents drew zigzag doodles all over the map in order to produce the right combinations of voters to satisfy their career goals.[53] As Justice Stevens argued, the intricately drawn Texas plan was far more the result of political gerrymandering by the Democratic-controlled legislature than anything else.[54] In 1992, under the new map, more than two-thirds of the districts—including each of the new ones—elected Democrats, even though Texas voters are arguably more likely to vote Republican than Democrat. Incumbents of both parties were just as successful: 26 of the 27 incumbents were reelected, while each of the three new districts elected a state legislator who had acted with the privileges of an incumbent in the districting process, giving "incumbents" a 97 percent success rate.[55]

Deploying new technologies and "informational advances that allowed the state to adjust lines on the scale of city blocks,"[56] legislators "were able to further fine-tune district lines to include likely supporters and exclude those who would probably support their opponents."[57] Legislators even drew complicated squiggly lines all over the map in order to exclude the home residences of "potential primary challengers" or to "contain particularly active supporters."[58] The Court even noted that plans for "a relatively compact 44 percent African-American district" respectful of county lines were overthrown by white incumbents in favor of a less compact and more heavily African-American district simply to protect their own bases.[59] As then–state senator Eddie Bernice Johnson put it, "the incumbents 'have practically drawn their own districts. Not practically, they have.'"[60]

The Court is nonchalant about accepting incumbent and partisan self-entrenchment as valid state interests for creating extravagantly bizarre districts. (Consider the maps again.) The Court proceeded in *Bush v. Vera* on the assumption that perpetuating incumbency is a "legitimate districting consideration."[61] And yet it is a far greater affront to democratic principles to build a congressional district around the political career of a single person than it is to shape a district to enable hundreds of thousands of citizens belonging to a long-gerrymandered-out racial group to take a turn at being in an electoral majority.[62] "[T]he government's abuse of the power of incumbency for the purposes of perpetuating its own power is one of the worst possible offenses against the polity."[63] Here we find something close to what the Court warned against in *West Virginia v. Barnette*:[64] incumbent public officials prescribing what shall be orthodox in politics—namely themselves.

Moreover, allowing incumbent self-entrenchment through creative line drawing has an unavoidable racial meaning.[65] Incumbents are "still disproportionately white."[66] And yet the Court's conservative majority cannot see that the system of incumbent self-promotion it blesses has a subordinating racial meaning. It does not consider oddly drawn majority-white districts favoring white incumbents to be racial gerrymanders at all. All the burdens of racial association fall on minorities. Whiteness is not seen as racial but as natural.[67] To be white is to rise above race.

Paradox and Contradiction

With this essential double standard in place, the constitutional law of redistricting is now riddled with paradox and contradiction. Minority plaintiffs challenging racially gerrymandered districts under Equal Protection must show that the district lines were motivated by a racially discriminatory purpose. But white plaintiffs challenging government creation of majority-minority districts under Equal Protection do not have to show either a racially discriminatory purpose *or* effect to get them struck down.

Since the Supreme Court's 1976 decision in *Washington v. Davis*,[68] the Court has required every minority plaintiff who challenges government action as a violation of Equal Protection to prove that there was a racially discriminatory purpose motivating the action.[69] In *Davis*, the Court rejected an Equal Protection challenge by disappointed African-American applicants to the personnel-testing procedures used by the District of Columbia Metropolitan Police Department.[70] Although the Police Department test clearly had a racially discriminatory impact in that disproportionate numbers of African Americans failed, the Court found that the discriminatory impact standard for employment cases under Title VII was not the standard for proving Equal Protection violations.[71] Rather, the Court reaffirmed what it described as "the basic equal protection principle that the invidious quality of a law claimed to be racially discriminatory must ultimately be traced to a racially discriminatory purpose."[72]

In every succeeding decision in which minority plaintiffs invoked Equal Protection to challenge government action, the Court has reaffirmed the *Davis* standard. Most dramatically, in *Mobile v. Bolden*,[73] as we have seen, the Court in 1980 upheld the use of at-large city commissioner elections that constantly frustrated the political aspirations of the city's African-American population because, as the Court emphasized, "only if there is *purposeful* discrimination can there be a violation of the Equal Protection Clause."[74]

Indeed, it is so difficult for minority plaintiffs to prove Equal Protection violations under this exacting standard that, astonishingly, Justices Scalia and Thomas have *never* found as Supreme Court Justices that a minority plaintiff's Equal Protection rights were violated. The only exception to this pattern that I could find was in *Bush v. Vera* itself, where the conservatives voted to uphold a conservative Hispanic's Equal Protection challenge to majority-African American and -Hispanic congressional districts in Texas. (But, as we shall see, no showing of purpose was required in that case.) Other than that, I have not been able to locate a case where the Court's ultraconservatives found that the government violated the Equal Protection rights of minority Civil Rights plaintiffs. This is a fact so dumbfounding that I would be only too happy to stand corrected.

In any event, the stifling "purpose" requirement for proving Equal Protection violations has never been applied in the *Shaw* cases, where the conservatives have repeatedly granted Equal Protection relief to white plaintiffs. The Court simply never asks whether the government's creation of bizarre-looking majority-minority districts is motivated by the *purpose* of discriminating against whites or diluting their votes. In none of the cases do any of the plaintiffs even *allege* a discriminatory purpose. Nor, amazingly, has the Court found, or any plaintiff alleged, that there was even a discriminatory *effect* caused by the districts. Nor could any plaintiff from *Shaw* or the other cases have made such a showing. Every white voter in North Carolina enjoyed the right to vote, to speak, to run for office and to contribute money—all of the same rights enjoyed by African-American voters in majority-white districts in the state. No one has a constitutional right to be in the racial majority in a district (or at least so we thought), and no one has the right to be represented by someone of his own racial group (or at least so we thought).

Given that there is neither discriminatory intent nor effect in the creation of a majority-minority district, it is equally hard to see why *Shaw* plaintiffs have any standing to sue at all. Where is the injury? Justice O'Connor suggested that a law creating a bizarre district "reinforces racial stereotypes and threatens to undermine our system of representative democracy by signaling to elected officials that they represent a particular racial group rather than their constituency as a whole...."[75] Of course, there is no empirical proof offered anywhere for this proposition, and it contradicts just about everything we know about how politicians work. The idea that an African-American representative from a 52 percent African-American district would disregard his nonblack constituents is not only wrong as a statement about reality but borderline deranged. Politicians are eager to please as many voters as possible.

In any event, the alleged symbolic harms that give rise to white plaintiff standing to challenge majority-African-American and -Hispanic districts are not valid in any other type of Equal Protection case. For example, Justice O'Connor, author of the majority opinion in *Shaw v. Reno*, wrote an opinion denying standing to African-American parents who challenged an IRS policy of granting tax exemptions to private schools that discriminate on the basis of race.[76] She found that these parents had no standing to challenge the government's allegedly unlawful actions because their claim depended on an "abstract stigmatic injury" that could theoretically "extend nationwide to all members of the particular racial groups against which the Government was alleged to be discriminating."[77] Unless the parents had actually applied to the schools for their children and had been rejected, then the only harm was "a claim of stigmatic injury, or denigration,"[78] something not legally actionable or cognizable.

Yet this is the exact kind of diffuse and ethereal injury recognized in *Shaw* cases: the putative injury of being stigmatized by the perceptions allegedly caused when a white person lives in an oddly drawn majority-

African-American or -Hispanic district.[79] In the *Shaw* sequence of cases, "denigration" or "stigmatic injury" not only confers standing, but doubles as the very basis of the cause of action. It is putatively by showing that the government has forced you to live in a majority-minority district, where, apparently, everyone is presumed to think alike, that you have proven an Equal Protection violation.

In no other voting context do people have Equal Protection standing to challenge a law or policy that makes them feel bad. Many minorities undoubtedly feel stigmatized by being forced to live in legislative districts drawn to create a white majority. Many people feel offended by virtue of being forced to live in a legislative district drawn with the purpose of facilitating the reelection of an incumbent. Many people feel stigmatized by the operation of the private campaign finance system, which benefits the wealthy, who are disproportionately white and male. Many independents and members of third parties feel marginalized, excluded and stigmatized by the imbalanced public funding of the two "major parties" under the Federal Election Campaign Act.[80]

Yet in none of these cases have we ever recognized—or is it imaginable that we would recognize—standing by those with hurt feelings to challenge policies on that basis, no matter how powerful the underlying claim.[81]

Ironically, the Court's double standard is undertaken in the name of fairness. The offending Justices actually believe that they are holding up the banner of Civil Rights. They repeatedly liken majority-black and -Hispanic districts to racial segregation and apartheid.[82] In *Shaw*, Justice O'Connor suggested that the districts in question "segregate the races for purposes of voting." In *Holder v. Hall*,[83] Justice Thomas described the creation of majority-minority districts as "an enterprise of segregating the races into political homelands that amounts, in truth, to nothing short of a system of political apartheid."[84]

But "segregation" in the hands of Justices abolishing majority-minority districts does not mean "segregation" as anyone else ever understood it. Indeed, it is quite the opposite of segregation as the Warren Court grasped the concept. The segregated schools ruled invalid in *Brown v. Board of Education*[85] were 100 percent white or 100 percent black, and parents had no right to transfer their children from one to the other.[86] By contrast, in *Shaw*, the congressional districts targeted for destruction were the most closely *integrated* in the history of the state. They led to interracial political coalitions and the first interracial North Carolina House delegation since Reconstruction. Families of every race enjoyed a perfect right to move into the geographical confines of this district and to vote there or to move outside the district and vote elsewhere. Moreover, far from being apartheid-like Bantustans, the two well-integrated districts were home to a *minority* of the state's African-American residents, 57 percent of whom actually lived in majority-white districts.[87] If North Carolina had created 100 percent white districts and walled them off from 100 percent African-American districts, then all of the promiscuous and morally self-flattering talk of "apartheid" might be warranted. But here the Court is describing integrated districts and House delegations as a form of political segregation. Labeling integrated districts "apartheid" and "segregation" corrupts our moral language and insults the memory of people who lost their lives resisting racial apartheid, both in its South African and American guises.[88]

Remarkably, the term "apartheid" has never been used by the Court's majority to describe disenfranchisement of African Americans, poll taxes, literacy tests, grandfather clauses, or Jim Crow. The concept of "apartheid" has not been used to refer to a majority-white state's criminal-justice system in which murderers of whites are 400 percent more likely to receive the death penalty than murderers of African Americans;[89] to the erection by a majority-white city council of a physical traffic barrier between majority-white and majority-black parts of town;[90] to the pervasive use of race by police in traffic stops, stop-and-frisk situations or criminal profiles;[91] or to the existence of *de facto* segregated public school systems.[92] Thus, the lingering social and legal features of apartheid as they exist in the real world are not constitutionally suspect; only the threat of minority political power is.

Of course, not all majority-African-American and -Hispanic legislative districts violate Equal Protection under *Shaw*. They pass muster when their inhabitants are clustered together. For example, the Fifth Congressional District in Georgia "is sufficiently compact and, being an urban minority population, has a sufficiently strong community of interest to warrant being a majority-minority district."[93] Therefore, majority-minority districts based on *actual* geographic and residential segregation are not "segregated" for Equal Protection purposes.[94] As long as ghettoized minority communities are not linked to communities in other areas, they will be allowed to have majority-minority status in legislative districts. Again in the name of integration, this doctrine reinforces racial distance, class separation and the political interests that certain incumbents may have in maintaining patterns of residential segregation.

Although *Shaw* is allegedly based on the need to combat negative stereotypes about the political behavior of racial minorities, the doctrine actively promotes them. Because the *Shaw* cases have never specified any injury actually suffered by any person, Justice O'Connor's original statements about the problem remain authoritative. The problem, she thought, is that designing such districts "reinforces the perception that members of the same racial group—regardless of their age, education, economic status, or the community in which they live—think alike, share the same political interests, and will prefer the same candidates at the polls."[95] In such districts, "elected officials are more likely to believe that their primary obligation is to represent only the members of that group, rather than their constituency as a whole."[96]

But all of these assertions are quite nearly the obverse of reality. The majority of African Americans and Hispanics still live in majority-white districts, but allowing minorities sometimes to be in the majority has not only integrated state legislatures and Congress but also forced white voters and white legislators to deal with minority legislators as individuals, not group stereotypes. Moreover, the growth in minority legislative presence has, by definition, forced the creation of many more interracial legislative and political coalitions, which have the effect of knocking down stereotypes and directly acquainting people with one another. Giving white voters the opportunity to have African Americans and Hispanics as representatives and leaders (just as minority voters have long had the opportunity to have whites as representatives and leaders) has a generally liberating effect in a society where whites have been conditioned to see minorities in subordinate positions.

Furthermore, it is false that, in an oddly drawn majority-minority district, elected officials are "more likely to believe that their primary obligation is to represent only the members"[97] of their group "rather than their constituency as a whole."[98] If you think of the original district struck down in North Carolina,[99] it would have been political suicide for an elected member of Congress of whatever race to decide to serve only or primarily the 53 percent of the population that was African American and ignore the other 47 percent of the population. There is no evidence whatsoever for this proposition.

In fact, it is the *Shaw* cases themselves that stigmatize minorities by insinuating that they cannot be trusted to participate as equal actors in the redistricting process and by declaring them unfit to form an electoral majority unless they are geographically ghettoized. The subtextual consequence is to cast a cloud of suspicion and illegitimacy over members of Congress and state legislators elected from oddly drawn majority-minority districts. The deep semiotics of *Shaw* are to suggest that white officials are elected legitimately while others are now coming to office in an illegitimate way. White privilege here becomes not only "invisible" and "weightless,"[100] in Peggy McIntosh's terms, but omnipresent, authoritative, natural, neutral and all-encompassing.[101] Everything that does not qualify as white-defined from start to finish becomes suspect and deviant. The *Shaw* doctrine has the quality of a racial slur, and its authors—with their compulsive projections about "legislative quotas," "race-based gerrymandering to protect black candidates from white competition," "a Jim Crow system of elections,"[102] and quota districts[103]—prove themselves not only historically disoriented but morally dyslexic.

Political White Supremacy in the Age of "Color Blindness"

The Court's sudden new focus on "traditional districting principles"[104] and enshrines a history of racial domination in which "southern white officials have long known the dilutionary effects" of particular "laws when used in a racially polarized setting."[105] Indeed, the Court's method of turning customary practices in the states into constitutional law revives the 1896 reasoning in *Plessy v. Ferguson*, where the Court upheld Louisiana's segregation of whites and blacks on train cars. Rejecting Homer Plessy's Equal Protection attack on Jim Crow, Justice Brown found that *de jure* segregation in public places was a "reasonable ... exercise of the police power"[106] because the state "is at liberty to act with reference to the established usages, customs, and traditions of the people...."[107] The *Plessy* Court thus defined the content of Equal Protection by reference to racist practices that the Equal Protection Clause was designed to overthrow.[108] Similarly, in legislative reapportionment today, no districting principles are more "traditional" than states ensuring that African Americans will never form an electoral majority and allowing white incumbents representing white majorities to map out their own districts.[109]

The animating spirit of the cases is what we might think of as "color-blind white supremacy."[110] Justice O'Connor spoke of the *Shaw* plaintiffs' "constitutional right to participate in a 'color-blind' electoral process" and likened the most integrated district in North Carolina's history to "political apartheid." Justice Thomas stated in *Holder v. Hall*[111] that the "enterprise of segregating the races into political homelands," which is an appalling Orwellian description of integrated districts where whites are not in the majority, is "repugnant to any nation that strives for the ideal of a color-blind Constitution."[112]

What does color blindness in the electoral process mean to the Court's majority? It certainly does not mean that legislators may not take race into account in the redistricting process. As Justice O'Connor put it in *Shaw*: "the legislature always is aware of race when it draws district lines." Here, Justice O'Connor speaks from experience. She was the Republican majority leader of the Arizona State Senate in 1972 and knows how politics works. Indeed, anyone who believes that state legislators draw district lines without knowing the precise racial and partisan demographics of the resulting districts is too innocent to be let out of the house by himself. Political color blindness also does not mean that voters cannot make voting choices according to race since the Court is perfectly aware of racially polarized voting and assumes it is not directly addressable by law.

What political color blindness means is that states cannot act intentionally to promote the political empowerment of African Americans and Hispanics. A bizarrely drawn district that is 55 percent white will be upheld; a bizarrely drawn district that is 55 percent African American will be struck down.

In this sense, the use of "color blindness" in the electoral context mirrors its overall function in the parlance of modern backlash conservatism. By the time *Shaw* reached the Court in 1993, the Rehnquist Court's racial reaction was already swinging. The conservatives gathered excitedly around the mantra of "color blindness," a magical turn of phrase that justified not only the dismantling of affirmative action programs at both the local[113] and national[114] levels but judicial disengagement from the project of active school desegregation.[115]

The use of "color blindness" by conservatives is profoundly ironic, and not just because American conservatism has trafficked in racism and been anything but color-blind for most of its history. For self-proclaimed "originalists," "textualists" and "strict constructionists," the totally invented notion of "color blindness" should carry no intellectual appeal at all. The words "color blindness" appear neither in the Constitution nor anywhere in the legislative history of the Fourteenth Amendment. Indeed, the Radical Republicans in Congress who voted to add the words "equal protection" to the Constitution were themselves also anything but "color-blind." Unlike the conservatives on today's Court, however, they were progressives who wanted to challenge in color-conscious ways the vicious reign of white supremacy.

The framers of the Fourteenth Amendment designed Reconstruction in a radically race-conscious way to uplift the recently freed black population and to prevent the political, economic and social restoration of the slave masters. The Radical Republicans created the Bureau of Refugees, Freedmen and Abandoned Lands, the so-called Freedmen's Bureau, which was set up to distribute free food, clothing and other supplies directly to African Americans.[116] It was also authorized to take abandoned and confiscated lands to divide into forty-acre lots for rental and eventual sale to the black population.[117] Other important aspects of Reconstruction included the establishment of schools for black children and the development of economic independence for some number of blacks.

In other words, the Congress that made Equal Protection part of the Constitution and gave itself the power to enforce its purposes clearly regarded affirmative race-conscious legislation as within the spirit and contemplation of the Fourteenth Amendment.

The originator of the color blindness metaphor was Justice John Marshall Harlan, who employed it to great effect in his famous dissenting opinion in *Plessy v. Ferguson*.[118] Harlan wrote: "[o]ur Constitution is color-blind, and neither knows nor tolerates classes among citizens. In respect of civil rights, all citizens are equal before the law."[119] Significantly, in filing this opinion against forced race segregation on railway trains, Justice Harlan never cast doubt on the validity of public policies designed to *benefit*, as opposed to harm, the black population. It is thus weird and unfair for today's conservatives to enlist him posthumously to this reactionary cause, especially given his statement that the purpose of the Reconstruction constitutional amendments was "to secure 'to a race recently emancipated, a race that through many generations have been held in slavery, all the civil rights that the superior race enjoy.'"[120] Moreover, he repeatedly invoked the authority of the Thirteenth Amendment ban on slavery and involuntary servitude to explain what was wrong with public segregation: "[t]he arbitrary separation of citizens, on the basis of race, while they are on a public highway, is a badge of servitude wholly inconsistent with the civil freedom and the equality before the law established by the Constitution."[121] Can the same be said of affirmative action and majority-minority districts?

It is a logical and moral error to uproot the original idea of "color blindness" from its place in the rhetorical struggle against the segregationist period of white supremacy.[122] It is doubtful that Justice Harlan would have deployed the color blindness metaphor to strike down efforts to assist—

as opposed to oppress—the emancipated black population. But even if we want to project modern-day conservative understandings of color blindness onto Justice Harlan, one need look no further than his own dissenting opinion to see that this kind of fetishized color blindness can act as a thin legal veneer for white supremacy. Consider the chilling (and almost always redacted) sentences that precede Justice Harlan's famous passage about color blindness:

> The white race deems itself to be the dominant race in this country. And so it is, in prestige, in achievements, in education, in wealth and in power. So I doubt not, it will continue to be for all time, if it remains true to its great heritage and holds fast to the principles of constitutional liberty. But in view of the Constitution, in the eye of the law, there is in this country no superior, dominant, ruling class of citizens. There is no caste here. Our Constitution is color blind. . . .[123]

Thus even if we (quite unreasonably) assume that Justice Harlan's vision of color blindness was intended to stop positive efforts such as affirmative action, such a vision becomes entirely suspect because it seeks to reconcile the pretense of legal neutrality with the injustice of perpetual white supremacy. One might forgive Justice Harlan, a former slave owner and Know-Nothing crusader struggling to articulate a racial liberalism, for the limitations of such a vision. As for his modern-day enthusiasts on the Court—that is, the racial conservatives of our time—their conversion to color blindness seems too little, too late, and all too convenient and transparent.

Like color blindness itself, the doctrine targeting oddly drawn majority-minority districts has no basis in the history of the Equal Protection Clause. This explains why the self-proclaimed "originalist" Justices who have signed on to it have not once mentioned the original intent or understanding of the framers of the Fourteenth Amendment in this context. As Jeffrey Rosen has observed, "during the heyday of the Warren era, the conservative judicial revolution was founded on the principle that the Fourteenth Amendment has nothing to say about apportionment."[124] He quotes Justice Harlan's statement in dissent in *Reynolds v. Sims* that: "The history of the adoption of the Fourteenth Amendment provides conclusive evidence that neither those who proposed nor those who ratified the Amendment believed that the Equal Protection Clause limited the power of the States to apportion their legislatures as they saw fit."[125]

Yet now, several declared originalists on the Court believe not only that Equal Protection controls apportionment, but that it forbids bizarrely drawn districts if they create the wrong racial majority.[126] If anything, the Radical Republicans who framed the Fourteenth Amendment and promoted black suffrage in the South wanted to see African Americans replace their slave masters as representatives in Congress. Surely they would be turning over in their graves to learn that the Fourteenth Amendment was being used to dismantle long-suppressed districts with black political majorities in them.

The Court's preclusion of certain districting choices that would create majority-minority districts subverts democratic sovereignty.[127] The U.S. House Representatives is the people's House and was created to represent of all of the people in their splendid variety.[128] The Senate membership is composed of representatives of the fifty states, all of which except Hawaii are dominated by whites. Thus the only real possibility for minorities to be in a numerical majority in a legislative jurisdiction is in the House context. By removing possibilities for creating such districts and badly chilling others, the Supreme Court has tilted constitutional structure in order to skew the design of democratic institutions along preferred racial lines. Injecting a one-sided racial filter into the districting process, the Court undermines the principle of popular democratic sovereignty by which the citizenry controls the government rather than vice versa.[129]

The fact that the Supreme Court itself invented this double standard in the name of Equal Protection,[130] without any basis in the text, history or doctrine of the Constitution, reflects a historically resilient and protean racial ideology on the Court. This ideology appeared first in the form of original-intent analysis in *Dred Scott v. Sanford*,[131] later in the guise of deference to social custom and judicial restraint in *Plessy v. Ferguson*,[132] and now in the judicial activism associated with free-floating "color blindness" rhetoric in *Shaw*[133] and its progeny.[134] The legal doctrines change shape, form, and justification, but the reality of political white supremacy endures.[135]

Turning the Fourteenth Amendment Inside Out

Like *Plessy v. Ferguson* before it, and *Bush v. Gore* after it, the *Shaw* line of authority represents a racially inflected judicial assault on democracy. *Shaw* laid the track for *Bush v. Gore* by abandoning legal precedent and logical analysis in order to redeem and privilege the political will of white majorities. Just as *Shaw* "took back" many congressional and state legislative districts from African-American and Hispanic majorities and handed them off to white majorities, *Bush v. Gore* "took back" the presidency from a candidate supported not only by a popular majority in the nation but by commanding majorities of African Americans and Hispanics and handed it off to the candidate favored by the majority of white voters.

States that still want to live up to the meaning of the Voting Rights Act can focus on the Court's statement that it will tolerate districts based on nonracial "communities of interest."[136] Although this idea is itself obscure, states can concentrate on developing records in apportionment plans "that will give voice to genuine interests in the community and withstand constitutional challenge."[137] Indeed, it now appears that Justice O'Connor, shifting in the wake of *Bush v. Gore* from an ideological commitment to "color blindness" to a more partisan commitment to maximizing the fortunes of the Republican Party, may be turning more tolerant of majority-minority districting.[138] Many Republican strategists believe majority-minority districts can benefit Republicans by packing black votes and draining loyal Democrats away from swing suburban districts. These partisan considerations should ideally have nothing to do with constitutional analysis.

However the Rehnquist Court rules on particular districts in the future, it has placed federal judges in command of our congressional and state legislative elections. It has lost the thread of self-government, progressive democratic inclusion and the true meaning of Equal Protection. It has turned the Fourteenth Amendment inside out.

Ultimately, the way for the people to escape from the box that the Court has built for us is to leave single-member districts behind and move to the at-large proportional-representation electoral systems used by democracies around the world. Just as the Voting Rights Act gave us a way to move beyond the literacy test, proportional representation may give us a way to transcend the Court's deeply unprincipled but resilient brand of color-blind white supremacy, the key transparency now laid down over all legislative district maps.

CHAPTER FIVE

America's Signature Exclusion

How Democracy Is Made Safe for the Two-Party System

I give the sign of democracy / By God! I will accept nothing which all cannot have their counterpart of on the same terms.
—Walt Whitman, *Song of Myself*

Long before elections are stolen at the ballot box, in the redistricting back-room, or in late-night five-to-four decisions of the Supreme Court, they are stolen in your mind. This is because our political expectations are structured by the ballot choices offered and suppressed by the mysterious operation known as the "two-party system." Even if everyone had a right to vote, even if this right were not racially double-crossed, even if majorities had a right to prevail, the electoral process would not be democratic unless all parties were allowed to compete on a free and equal basis.

This principle is self-evident and foundational in democracy. Even with ubiquitous confusion about a "two-party system," Americans endorse the principle of free and pluralistic elections and not only in the abstract. A strong majority of Americans consistently backs the idea of a new major political party coming into being to keep the Democrats and Republicans honest and to confront their complacencies. A CNN/Gallup/ *USA Today* poll in July 1999, for example, found that 67 percent of adult Americans supported "having a third political party that would run candidates for President, Congress, and state offices against the Republican and Demo-cratic candidates."[1]

But to establish a truly open political process today would require a sweeping overhaul of the Supreme Court's elections jurisprudence, which is deeply under the spell of the self-entrenching and extraconstitutional "two-party system." Indeed, it was the Court's unprincipled endorsement of a two-party system that set the stage for America's dramatic collapse into a one-party system in *Bush v. Gore*. After all, if they do not conform electoral process to principles of strict neutrality, what will keep the justices from aligning their judicial analyses with their partisan sympathies? If the Court can uphold the suppression of all political parties but two, why not all but one?

We will see that the Court upholds laws that discriminate against third parties by keeping their candidates off the ballot, out of debates and off the public's radar screen. The Court has even authorized states to ban "write-in" ballots, thus emphatically defining the ballot as the government's property, not the people's. The Court has recently upheld anti-"fusion" laws enacted in the late nineteenth century to destroy progressive multiparty coalitions. Its famous decisions about money in politics have constitutionalized plutocratic arrangements, turning the central part of the election process into what I call a "wealth primary" that is heavily slanted towards the perpetuation of incumbent parties.[2]

The Court cannot seem to find democratic principles in the Constitution protecting the right of the people freely to form our political will and make unmanipulated choices in elections. But this should not be so hard. The First Amendment's free speech clause creates a political anti-establishment principle that corresponds to the ban on state endorsement of religion in the Establishment Clause. This was the point Justice Jackson was getting at in *West Virginia v. Barnette*,[3] the challenge by Jehovah's Witnesses to a compulsory Pledge of Allegiance in public schools. Justice Jackson shifted the grounds of discussion from religious free exercise to freedom of political thought and conscience. "Authority here is to be controlled by public opinion, not public opinion by authority,"[4] Justice Jackson wrote. "If there is any fixed star in our constitutional constellation, it is that no official, high or petty, can prescribe what shall be orthodox in politics, nationalism, religion, or other matters of opinion...."[5]

The right not to be forced into the state's approved political orthodoxies is complemented by the affirmative right to launch a political party of your own and to be treated equally by the government in the process. This right is the political free speech equivalent of the religious free exercise principle: you can say or think whatever you want in politics and the government may not discriminate against you because of it. As Justice Brennan put it in that other great flag case, *Texas v. Johnson*: "If there is a bedrock principle underlying the First Amendment, it is that the Government may not prohibit the expression of an idea simply because society finds the idea itself offensive or disagreeable."[6]

The current Supreme Court has often had a surprisingly difficult time applying this principle to electoral politics. But it is easily translated: the government must remain neutral and stand aside when the people are forming their political will.[7] To respect the political sovereignty of the people, the government must never endorse a political party (or even two of them) against its competitors. The campaign period, the kind of process Habermas calls "political will-formation,"[8] must feature formally equal opportunities for all candidates to be heard. Indeed, we can define democracy as the system in which the government is not permitted to manipulate the sovereignty of the people over the continuing reconstitution of their political leadership.

States Adding Unconstitutional Qualifications to Federal Officeholding: *U.S. Term Limits v. Thornton* and *Cook v. Gralike*

The Supreme Court has rightly defended this principle of government neutrality in the context of state efforts to drive incumbents off the ballot. In the 1995 case *U.S. Term Limits v. Thornton*,[9] the Court held that Arkansas violated the Qualifications Clause of Article I of the Constitution when it tried to deny incumbents a printed line on the ballot if they had already served three terms in the House of Representatives or two in the Senate.[10] Incumbents could run, but only as write-in candidates.[11] Justice Stevens found for the majority that designing a special rule to disadvantage incumbents in elections essentially added an impermissible fourth candidacy qualification. The three requirements of Article I are exhaustive: that House Members be at least 25 years old and Senators 30, that they be residents of the United States for at least seven years or nine years respectively, and that they be inhabitants of the states they represent.[12] These requirements cannot be altered by the states.[13]

It is important to see why the Court strongly rejected Arkansas's effort to impose term limits through ballot manipulation. The Constitution was created not by the states but by the American people, and it established Congress as the sovereign legislature of the people. Because the organic sovereignty of the populace over election of their representatives is complete, the qualifications for running for office are exclusively those set forth in the Constitution itself. Any state-imposed effort to change these qualifications, Justice Stevens found, "is contrary to the 'fundamental principle of our representative democracy,' embodied in the Constitution, that 'the people should choose whom they please to govern them.'"[14] This is an old principle. As Chief Justice John Marshall stated in *McCulloch v. Mary-*

land, "The government of the Union ... is emphatically, and truly, a government of the people. In form and in substance it emanates from them. Its powers are granted by them, and are to be exercised directly on them, and for their benefit."[15]

This governing principle is so foundational that Congress itself lacks the power to add to the constitutional qualifications for congressional service, as the Court found in *Powell v. McCormack*.[16] There, the Court overthrew an effort by Congress in 1969 to deny a House seat to Congressman Adam Clayton Powell, who clearly met the age, residency and citizenship qualifications but had allegedly engaged in serious misconduct in the prior Congress.[17] The Court found overwhelming historical, textual and theoretical support for the proposition that the Framers intended the Qualifications Clause to be "fixed and exclusive,"[18] leaving no room for any body to add new qualifications short of constitutional amendment. Alexander Hamilton, in *The Federalist* No. 60, stated that candidate qualifications for Congress are "defined and fixed in the Constitution, and are unalterable by the legislature."[19] James Madison warned at the constitutional convention that: "If the Legislature could regulate [the qualification of electors or elected], it can by degrees subvert the Constitution. A Republic may be converted into an aristocracy or oligarchy as well by limiting the number capable of being elected, as the number authorized to elect."[20]

In *Thornton,* the Court emphasized that Arkansas's attempt to drive certain citizens off the ballot—incumbent officeholders—contradicted the essential "principles of our democratic system."[21] One such principle is "the egalitarian concept that the opportunity to be elected" must remain "open to all."[22] Here the Court essentially merged the concerns of the Qualifications Clause with Equal Protection, which calls for equal treatment of equally situated persons, and the First Amendment, which insists upon government neutrality in the treatment of different political views. A second "critical postulate" was that "sovereignty confers on the people the right to choose freely their representatives to the National Government."[23] The Court quoted Hamilton's powerful statement before the New York Convention: "This great source of free government, popular election, should be perfectly pure, and the most unbounded liberty allowed."[24] The Court agreed with the sentiment that "the right of the electors to be represented by men of their choice, was so essential for the preservation of all their other rights, that it ought to be considered as one of the most sacred parts of our constitution."[25] Finally, the Court found that "the right to choose representatives belongs not to the States, but to the people."[26] Thus Arkansas could not "make it significantly more difficult"[27] for incumbents to win by forcing them to run as write-in candidates. The Court would not allow Arkansas to "evade the Qualifications Clauses by 'dress[ing] eligibility to stand for Congress in ballot access clothing,'" as this "trivializes the basic principles of our democracy...."[28]

Even more recently, in *Cook v. Gralike*,[29] the Court rejected an effort to manipulate public consensus by placing slanted information on the ballot next to candidates' names characterizing their voting records and positions on a term limits constitutional amendment.[30] The Missouri law in question required that "DISREGARDED VOTERS' INSTRUCTION ON TERM LIMITS" and "DECLINED TO PLEDGE TO SUPPORT TERM LIMITS" be added next to the names of candidates guilty of the various sins being combatted.[31] Again the Court rallied to the principle that the Constitution does not allow government to thwart the will of the people by using the ballot to engineer a public consensus tilting in one direction. These ballot rules had the impermissible "intended effect" of "handicap[ping]" certain candidates.[32] At the moment voters cast their ballot, the moment of public choice, the state must be completely neutral, as it must also be all along the way in composing and designing the ballot. It seems well accepted in state courts, for example, that public officials may not have a policy of automatically placing incumbents first on the ballot.[33]

America's Self-Appointed Political Establishment: The "Two-Party System"

It is a commonplace in both public rhetoric and the law of American politics that we have a "two-party system." This is a kind of civic religion that we feel pious and mystical about, but no one really bothers to define the term.[34] The phrase appears in our discourse in three different ways: 1) as an empirical observation or political science hypothesis that, in a majority-rule electoral regime based on single-member districts, voters will sort themselves into two main partisan tendencies at any given time in history; 2) as a claim that the Constitution requires political arrangements in which all participation is channeled into two major parties; and 3) as a description of the collusive agreement by the Democratic and Republican parties over time to make the perpetuation of their political dominance a public policy and the defining feature of election law.

In order to assess the fairness of our electoral process, we need to know the extent to which America has a two-party system in each of these senses.

The "Two-Party System" as an Empirical Political-Science Finding and Hypothesis

Some political scientists have observed that in a single-member-district rep-resentative democracy with winner-take-all elections, the electorate will over time group and regroup into two main political camps. Based on such data, they have predicted that this two-party arrangement is relatively durable over time even if a third party periodically emerges to challenge or replace one of the two main parties. This is known as "Duverger's Law," after Maurice Duverger, who remarked upon the phenomenon.[35]

There are several things to note here. First of all, the factual premise of this empirical claim—the existence of *single-member* congressional and state legislative districts—does not reflect any constitutional requirement. For part of our history, it was common for members of the House of Repre-sentatives to be elected on a statewide basis, not in territorial districts. Single-member districts were not made a federal requirement until the 1960s. And other methods have also been used for electing legislators, such as Illinois's use of cumulative voting, a method of proportional-represen-tation vote-allocating that is commonly used by corporations. Thus the prediction of a permanent two-party system rests on a purely contingent and permissive feature of contemporary American politics.

More important, even political scientists who see the two-party system as structurally determined in this way do not claim that any two specific parties must emerge over time, just that two will ultimately win out until the next "realigning" event or issue causes a strong third party to emerge to supplant one of the two incumbent parties. This is the way the current Republican Party began just before the Civil War. Thus even if this empir-ical claim is accurate, it tells us nothing about which two parties must be in power at any point in time nor does it recommend the insulation or propping up of any specific two parties at a moment in time. On the con-trary, the fact that a healthy and supple two-party system is open to outsider parties toppling the incumbents argues against institutionalizing incum-bent parties and for maintaining maximum ease of entry by new parties.

The hypothesis of even a fluid two-party system being a necessary by-product of single-member districts is a political-science prediction that may or may not be accurate. There are contrary indications in our own history suggesting that single-member districts do not foreclose the emergence of competitive multiparty arrangements. Under election laws in the nine-teenth century that permitted the "fusion" of two or more parties behind particular candidacies, progressive and populist parties in the Midwest thrived alongside the Democrats and Republicans despite the existence of single-member districts. (It was this history that the New Party hoped to revive in challenging Minnesota's law banning cross–party endorsement fusion candidacies in *Timmons v. Twin Cities Area New Party*. The majority in *Timmons* even noted the success of third parties without fusion.[36] This period of multiple competitive parties producing state legislators and House members from outsider parties simply makes the point that nothing even in single-member districting obliges us to have a closed or static "two-party system."

We recently have seen numerous independent or minor-party candidates beat the odds to defeat standard-bearers of the two major parties. In 1998, Minnesota Reform Party nominee Jesse Ventura trounced his Democratic and Republican rivals to become governor of Minnesota. Independent Congressman Bernie Sanders has repeatedly vanquished Democratic and Republican opposition for Vermont's lone U.S. House seat.[37]

Whatever its historical validity, the empirical claim that we are historically prone to a two-party system must be sharply separated from the normative constitutional claim we examine now: that the two leading parties today should be able to confer upon themselves public advantages to entrench their rule over others. By analogy, it is one thing to observe empirically that the United States is a majority-Christian nation and quite another to conclude that the government may therefore establish Christianity as the official religion of the nation. We have to monitor carefully this tendency to slide over from alleged facts to constitutional norms.

The "Two-Party System" as a Constitutional Claim

It is sometimes directly asserted and very often assumed that the Constitution creates, or authorizes creation of, a two-party system. This claim is wrong.

In a constitutional sense, America has no two-party system. The Constitution does not mention political parties, much less a two-party system, much less still two specific parties. We no more have a constitutional two-party system than a three-party system or nine-party system. As to the elements of the intermediate political organization of society, the Constitution gives us only principles of citizen political freedom and governmental nondiscrimination. The First Amendment protects the rights of citizens to speak, associate and participate in politics without regard to ideology or party. Equal Protection forbids interference with the right to vote once granted and bans discrimination against minority political groups.

The Framers despised the spirit of partisan faction, and Richard Hofstadter did not exaggerate when he described our original covenant as a "Constitution against parties."[38] Thomas Jefferson said that, "if I could not go to Heaven but with a political party, I would not go there at all."[39] And when he was president, Jefferson uttered the immortal words: "We are all Republicans—we are all Federalists." In his farewell address, President George Washington urged his countrymen to "discourage and restrain" the "common and continual mischiefs of the spirit of party."[40]

Of course the Framers understood, as Madison argued famously in *The Federalist* No. 10, that faction is, in some sense, an inescapable part of politics and the human condition. They wanted to plan a constitutional structure that would manage the dangers of faction by offsetting political ambitions and designs. All of the Framers themselves, when acting not as authors of the Constitution but as politicians and statesmen, engaged in healthy amounts of partisan conspiracy and intrigue. Such is the real world of politics and such is human nature. But while the first generation of Americans living under the Constitution undoubtedly fought their battles as Federalists and Republicans, with shifting alliances both from within and without, none ever remotely thought that the Constitution legislated the existence of two specific political parties.

The "Two-Party System" as a Collusive Effort by the Democratic and Republican Parties to Make Their Dominance a Public Policy Objective and Defining Feature of Election Law

Here, the "two-party system" is neither a historical trend nor a constitutionally driven public institution but a kind of vast political antitrust conspiracy.[41] Although they are otherwise cutthroat competitors for public office, the two major parties at any given time will band together in government to design laws to guard their overwhelming market shares in votes and to drive out any effective competition from other parties.

This kind of "two-party system" is a vibrant historical and powerful political reality. Although it lacks any constitutional foundation, it has successfully reshaped the essential features of our electoral institutions, from ballot-access laws to the antifusion laws to debate-access laws to presidential campaign public financing laws. This "two-party system" exists indeed, and with a vengeance.

The Unconstitutionality of Election Rules Favoring the "Two-Party System"

From the three possible senses of the phrase "two-party system," we can arrive at some conclusions that permit us to judge the validity of current electoral arrangements. To the extent that it is just an empirical generalization and prediction, a "two-party system" political-science thesis may be more or less true at different points in time. This thesis does not claim to notice the inevitability of any two specific parties taking power and makes no normative claims at all. Thus, the empirical existence or nonexistence of a political two-party system is no more relevant to defining the requirements of free speech and Equal Protection than is the empirical existence or nonexistence of a sociological "two-church system" or "three-church system" for understanding the Religion Clauses.

If the "two-party system" is a claim about what the Constitution requires, it is plainly wrong from both the text and the history of the Constitution. No one had any such thing in mind. The whole idea conflicts with the values of "robust, uninhibited, and wide-open"[42] political debate, factional pluralism and the antidiscrimination norms of Equal Protection. To the extent that our jurisprudence translates empirical observations about the two-party system into a normative assumption that parties in government may validly act to endorse it, this assumption is illegitimate, just as illegitimate as translating empirical observations about the "Judeo-Christian tradition" into a normative assumption that parties in government may act to endorse Judeo-Christianity. Everything in our Constitution calls out for neutrality as to contending political sects as well as religious sects.

Thus the real "two-party system," collusion by the Democratic and Republican parties to make their joint dominance public policy and the central goal of election law, actually describes not a constitutional mandate but unconstitutional state action. This self-installing "two-party system" is unlawful. Let us see what this means in terms of specific electoral practices, beginning with the key issue of who gets to appear on the ballot and run for office.

No Place on the Ballot: How Alternative Parties Are Suppressed

Imagine that you were launching a new democratic society based on periodic popular elections. How would you set up the ballot? From its beginnings in the eighteenth century through around 1890, American election authorities furnished no official printed ballot. The earliest elections were conducted by voice vote and then replaced by a homespun paper ballot. As the Supreme Court records: "Individual voters made their own handwritten ballots, marked them in the privacy of their homes, and then brought them to the polls for counting."[43] Soon political parties "began to produce their own ballots" which they handed to voters on their way to the ballot box, "often printed with flamboyant colors, distinctive designs, and emblems so they could be recognized at a distance."[44] In this bring-your-own-ballot regime, all people were situated relatively equally to cast a vote. To be sure, paper costs something and the wealthy have more of it than the poor, but there were always parties ready and willing to provide voters with preprinted ballots with their nominees' names on them. In this low-tech environment, the parties outside the polls heavily pressured voters on Election Day, but parties in government had no ability to manipulate voter choice through the inclusion, exclusion or placement of names on an official ballot.

This system lasted until the introduction of the so-called "Australian ballot" in 1888 in Massachusetts, where the government prepared official ballots with the names of candidates already printed on them. The success of this new system "set off a rapid and widespread adoption of the Australian system in the United States," and by 1896 the greater part of the country had embraced it.[45] The impetus for the change in most places was the public's hope that a neutral government-issued ballot would liberate popular choice in the electoral process from domination by two ruling parties that aggressively hustled party-printed ballots outside the polls.[46] In other words, the development of the government-prepared ballot actually started as an effort to undermine the two-party arrangement, not entrench it.

At the beginning it worked this way. Many states simply allowed all parties automatic space on the ballot for their candidates.[47] Others set up relatively modest signature requirements. According to Richard Winger, America's leading authority on ballot-access issues, the most common state-law petition requirement in the early years of the official government-issue ballot was five hundred voter signatures, and the second most common was a thousand, all due thirty days before the general election.[48]

Such rules made it relatively easy at the beginning of the twentieth century for all active political parties to get their candidates' names printed on official state ballots. In Maryland, for example, in the ten state elections that took place between 1903 and 1938, the general election ballot featured candidates of the Democratic Party, the Republican Party, the Socialist Party, the Labor Party, the Prohibition Party, and the Communist Party. During this time frame, there were never fewer than three candidates for statewide offices such as governor, comptroller, attorney general and clerk of the Court of Appeals.[49] In all of the statewide elections but that of 1926, there were at least four party-nominated candidates for governor on the ballot and in four elections there were five. The state essentially permitted any organized party to secure its candidates ballot access by payment of a fee.

In a determined effort by the major parties to eliminate left-wing opposition, many state legislatures began in the 1940s to severely restrict the ability of parties other than the Democrats and Republicans to get on the ballot.[50] Before granting parties a line on the ballot, they demanded that outsider parties show either that their candidates had received a certain percentage of votes in the prior election or that they had collected petition signatures from a certain percentage of registered voters or a certain percentage of those who cast votes in the last election. Major parties had no problem qualifying under the prior electoral performance-standard, but minor parties faced an increasingly complex and demanding state-by-state regime of mandatory signature-gathering. In Illinois, for example, the state legislature, hostile to the Communist Party, "increased the petition signature requirement from 1,000 to 25,000 signatures, and added a requirement that 200 signatures be collected from each of fifty counties."[51] This move succeeded in wiping the Communist Party off the ballot for the next four elections.[52]

In Maryland, tough signature requirements targeting new parties have meant that since 1940, not a single nominee of a political party outside the "two-party system" has succeeded in meeting the signature requirements for getting on the ballot for statewide office.[53] This is a remarkable fact given the rich history of third-party candidates running for statewide office in Maryland in the first four decades of the twentieth century. As in most states, Maryland's elections grew far less democratic and pluralistic over the course of the twentieth century.

Today in Maryland, structural political exclusion persists in government-imposed requirements that force minor parties—and their candidates separately—to collect tens of thousands of signatures to join a process that Democrats and Republicans participate in automatically. A new political party must first obtain and submit the signatures of at least ten thousand Marylanders supporting its formation, but this is just the beginning. Each candidate nominated by a qualified alternative party must conform to the same rules that apply to an independent, which means that, even though a party is recognized and enjoys ballot status, its candidates must still submit a nominating petition signed by at least one percent of citizens eligible to vote in the election for a particular office in order to run for it.

In 2002, this meant that approximately thirty thousand signatures had to be collected for each new party candidate for statewide office. A party that seeks to nominate candidates for governor, comptroller and attorney general must find another ninety thousand signatures, an additional 120,000 signatures statewide for a full complement of state legislators, and another thirty thousand signatures to run candidates in each U.S. House district.[54] This gauntlet of hurdles means that a new party—the kind with the least resources, no patronage jobs or sweetheart contracts to offer, and few or no elected officials to help build support—must collect 240,000 signatures to field a full slate of candidates. Meanwhile, all Democratic and Republican nominees have their names placed on the ballot automatically without having to collect a single signature (other than their own statement of candidacy) because they qualify simply based on their parties' past electoral performance. Laws like this—and they are everywhere— are ruinous to the fortunes of third parties and constitute a major impediment to broad public participation in elections.

America's Signature Fetish: *Jenness v. Fortson*

When two parties in government collude to block other parties from competing against them, this should be the paradigm case for judicial intervention in the "political thicket"[55] to restore a free market in political competition. The First Amendment forbids political-viewpoint discrimination and rejects any government interference with the rights of political association not justified by some compelling rationale. The Equal Protection Clause forbids any state action that burdens the right to vote or discriminates against minorities in the political process. Most important, the Qualifications Clause prevents states from adding qualifications to the three explicit Article I requirements for running for office. All of these values make signature-gathering requirements totally obnoxious to constitutional democracy.

But a 1971 Supreme Court case called *Jenness v. Fortson* continues to haunt the jurisprudence of ballot access law.[56] We need to confront the fallacies of this case in light of *U.S. Term Limits v. Thornton* and of modern free-speech law in order to get beyond the nation's political signature hang-up.

In *Jenness*, the Socialist Workers Party (SWP) of Georgia and its candidates for governor and two U.S. House seats brought an action against Georgia's draconian ballot-access regime. Under this system, candidates nominated by parties that had received 20 percent or more in the most recent gubernatorial or presidential election (read Democrats and Republicans) won an automatic place on the general-election ballot. Candidates whose parties did not qualify this way were forced to collect signatures equal to at least 5 percent of the electors who were eligible to vote in the last appropriate election. Thus Linda Jenness, who was the SWP's candidate for governor, had to collect an eye-popping 88,175 signatures, and the SWP's two House candidates had to collect separately more than 10,000 signatures apiece. It is well known that candidates must collect far more signatures than the actual statutory target, since huge numbers of signers are disqualified because they do not actually know their right district, have moved from a prior address and failed to reregister, have made a mistake in filling out the form, or have illegible handwriting. It is often estimated that third-party candidates need to collect at least 25 percent more signatures than the statutory minimum to have their petitions clear the validation process. Linda Jenness would have been crazy to submit anything less than a hundred thousand signatures.

For anyone who has tried to get the autograph of a celebrity, a document notarized by a notary public, or members of a family living in different places to sign a birthday card, you will recognize what an astounding thing it is to require a third-party candidate for Governor to collect from one hundred thousand citizens, mostly belonging to other political parties, their signatures, including printed names, addresses and zip codes. It is doubly amazing when juxtaposed with the fact that Jenness's major-party opponents sailed onto the general-election ballot based on their parties' prior electoral performances without having to gather so much as a John Hancock from their mothers and fathers.

But the Court in *Jenness* upheld Georgia's system, contrasting it with the Ohio plan the Court had condemned in *Williams v. Rhodes* in 1968. That Ohio plan, which totally abolished write-in ballots and independent candidacies, favored "two particular parties—the Republicans and the Democrats—and in effect tend[ed] to give them a complete monopoly," making it "virtually impossible" for outsider parties to be placed on the

1968 presidential election ballot.[57] It required a new party to get petitions signed by a number of voters equal to at least 15 percent of the number of voters who cast ballots in the last gubernatorial election. The state added numerous other disabling administrative obstacles and deadlines.

The *Jenness* Court called Ohio's law "vastly different"[58] from Georgia's. The Ohio law required 15 percent of those who voted in the last election to sign the petitions, while Georgia's law required the signatures of only 5 percent of all registered voters. Georgia freely allowed write-ins and recognized independent candidacies. It did not impose unreasonably early filing deadlines or require the creation of "elaborate primary election machinery."[59] There were no "suffocating restrictions" placed upon "the free circulation of nominating petitions," since a voter could sign multiple petitions, remained free to vote in major-party primaries, was not required to pledge to vote for the petitioning candidate, and did not need to have his signature notarized—all provisos found in other states.[60] Moreover, the Court found in *Jenness,* there was no invidious discrimination against minor-party candidates because collecting tens of thousands of signatures to get on the ballot is not "inherently more burdensome" than trying "to win the votes of a majority in a party primary."[61] In sum, the Court said, "Georgia's election laws, unlike Ohio's, do not operate to freeze the political status quo,"[62] and Georgia has "an important state interest in requiring some preliminary showing of a significant modicum of support before printing the name of a political organization's candidate on the ballot—the interest, if no other, in avoiding confusion, deception, and even frustration of the democratic process at the general election."[63]

With these words the Court constitutionalized an outrageous double standard that has since afflicted third parties, who are essentially forced to leap tall buildings just to put their candidates' names on the ballot. Nothing about the *Jenness* opinion makes sense, and yet it continues to defoliate our barren political terrain. Richard Winger has counted 126 lower-court cases in which minor-party and independent candidates lose constitutional claims about unequal treatment where the deciding court invokes the canonical authority of *Jenness v. Fortson.*[64]

Cleansing and Gerrymandering the Ballot: The Court's Disoriented Treatment of Ballot-Access Restrictions

The arguments and interests invoked by the Court in *Jenness* on behalf of massive signature requirements are absurdly trumped up. To the extent they have any empirical validity at all, they could be much better served through far less drastic means.

First of all, it is hard to see the relevance of the fact that Georgia permitted write-in ballots. The SWP candidates did not want to run as write-ins but rather as full-fledged, balloted, partisan candidates. In the *Thornton* case, the Court rejected Arkansas's argument that incumbents were not actually being kept off the ballot because they retained an option to run as write-in candidates. Everyone knows that being forced to run on a write-in basis will, as the *Thornton* Court put it, "make it significantly more difficult"[65] to win.

Although the SWP candidates clearly did experience state laws as politically "suffocating," the Court disagreed, because it found that a Georgia voter could sign multiple petitions, was not required to pledge to vote for the petitioning candidate, remained free to vote in major party primaries, and did not need to have his or her signature notarized.[66] But these statements about how free other Georgians were to sign the minor-party petitions beg the central question. Why should the SWP candidates be forced to collect *anyone's* signature to qualify for what is already their constitutional right to run for office? In the federal context, the right to run is rooted in the people's sovereignty over their own government. The test for candidate eligibility for federal office is embodied exclusively in the Qualifications Clauses. Why should a citizen's right to run for public office depend on the decision of other citizens to sign their names to a paper?

The Court disingenuously maintained that forcing minor-party candidates to collect tens of thousands of signatures to get on the ballot is not "inherently more burdensome" than trying "to win the votes of a majority in a party primary."[67]

But this is comparing apples and oranges. Jenness and the SWP claimed that it violated Equal Protection to treat the Socialist Workers Party *as a party* differently from the Democrats or Republicans. The proper comparison is thus not between how hard it is for *any* SWP candidate to get on the ballot (very hard) and how hard it is for a *specific* Democrat or Republican to emerge from a competitive primary battle (very hard). The proper comparison is between the chances that *any* Democratic or Republican nominee will be placed on the general election ballot (100 percent) and the chances that *any* SWP candidate will be placed there (minuscule under Georgia's laws). When the Court states that Georgia's election laws "do not operate to freeze the political status quo,"[68] this is either bad research or disinformation. The whole point of the SWP's litigation was that these laws were making it impossible for them to get on the ballot to challenge the two larger parties. Today in Georgia, there have been no minor-party U.S. House candidates for Congress in the last sixty years. This is not for lack of trying. The status quo seems awfully frozen, indeed.

The Court in *Jenness* nodded to the fact that Georgia's 5-percent rule was "somewhat higher than the percentage of support required to be shown in many States."[69] But the Court suggested that Ohio's law was actually worse because it required signatures from 15 percent of the number of voters in the last election. Yet 5 percent of registered voters is often going to be more in hard numbers than 15 percent of those who actually voted. What should matter is the hard-number totals actually being imposed, since they define the arduousness of the task. For most of the relevant history, it would have been easier to get signatures to qualify for the ballot under Ohio's invalidated law than under Georgia's upheld law.[70]

Most important, the *Jenness* Court found that Georgia has "an important state interest in requiring some preliminary showing of a modicum of support before printing the name of a political organization's candidate on the ballot—the interest, if no other, in avoiding confusion, deception, and even frustration of the democratic process in the general election." The Court has been cruising on this conclusory statement ever since, blithely assuming that a state that requires third parties to collect tens of thousands of signatures is, by definition, pursuing important valid interests rather than camouflaging a bipartisan political attack on outsider parties. These alleged interests, and the means adopted to promote them, need to be carefully dissected to determine whether this whole line of authority reflects anything but a cynical power grab.

Alleged State Interests in Cleansing the Ballot

Avoiding Confusion

The *Jenness* claim of a state interest in "avoiding confusion" has become the dominant argument for upholding severe restrictions on third-party access to the ballot. It is sometimes reformulated as "voter confusion" or ballot "overcrowding."[71]

Is there actually an important valid interest in avoiding voter confusion on the ballot? Do signature-gathering requirements advance such an interest?

The state interest in preventing "voter confusion" and "ballot over-crowding" seems potent at this high level of generality. But neither the state legislatures involved nor the Supreme Court have told us precisely how many candidates they believe voters can handle seeing on the ballot before growing "confused." Is it Fifteen? Ten? Seven? Five? Three? Or just two? This slipperiness as to the confusion tipping point means that the state never has to offer hard empirical evidence of voter confusion or specific documentation of the point at which voters lose their ability to understand a ballot.

Nor do the states even give us anecdotal examples of voters being confused by too many candidates. Astonishingly, the *Jenness* Court invoked its interest in preventing confusion against the background of a Georgia general election ballot that offered only one candidate for governor and one candidate for the vast majority of U.S. House and state legislative races from 1944 to 1962.[72] This was the upshot of the restrictive statutory change of 1943. Before that time, Georgia had generously allowed third parties a place on the ballot without any signature or fee requirements at all. In this open period, there was no confusion and no confusion alleged: there were never more than six candidates on a statewide general-election ballot.[73]

In the secret code of the two-party system, "avoiding confusion" simply means avoiding choice. There is nothing less confusing than a one-party state. Say what you will about closed political systems, but they are easy to understand and never tax the intellectual capacities of the citizenry.

I am perfectly willing to believe that voters can be confused by the design of a ballot, such as the infamous butterfly ballot in Palm Beach in the 2000 presidential election. But that is because the ballot design was confusing. Other presidential ballots in other parts of Florida and in other states had the same number of candidates but confused no one because they were designed effectively. I am also perfectly willing to believe that a ballot with 25 candidates on it for one office (and I have never heard of remotely this number of candidates) might look strange and might even be time-consuming (it might take three minutes to read all the names). But is it really confusing? Would I really lose track of the fact that in the final analysis I need to choose one? I have more than a hundred channels of cable television at home, and my elementary school-age children are perfectly able to make viewing choices on a daily or even hourly basis. Is it really the case that *adults* cannot handle more than—what?—four candidates on the ballot at a time every two or four years? What about all the counties and cities where citizens vote for four, five, or six commissioners or council people in every election? The government should be forced to document this most dubious claim as a compelling interest before imposing massive "signature" duties on citizens running for office.

The same states that use Kafkaesque signature requirements for minor-party candidates make it easy for Democrats and Republicans to run in their party primaries. Most major-party primary candidates for governor, senator or other high federal or state office simply fill out a form or pay a small filing fee and—presto!—appear on the ballot. Thus, we often see primary elections with upwards of eight or ten candidates running without facing any roadblocks based on the claim that voters will be confounded by too much democracy.

Can a state that authorizes large multicandidate primaries plausibly claim that its voters will be overwhelmed by more than two candidates in a general election? Why does the individual voter's attention span lose so much capacity between the primary and the general election? The real interest in reducing the field reflects not the voters' political attention deficit disorder but the obsessive-compulsive desire of politicians to control electoral outcomes.

But even if we pretend that there is a valid state interest in keeping candidates off the ballot to make the ballot tidy, the means adopted—requiring minor-party candidates to collect tens of thousands of signatures to secure a ballot position—have nothing to do with this interest.

If the state wants to assure that its ballot will be limited to a finite number of candidates—say five—signature requirements will obviously not work. In theory, ten, fifteen or more candidates could go out and collect the requisite number of signatures to qualify. The law is thus radically *underinclusive*. It does not effectively address the identified problem.

Conversely, if there are only five potential candidates (or less), and thus no danger of the field going over the five-candidate attention ceiling, selectively requiring the minor-party candidates to go out and collect thousands of signatures from nonsupporters is simply an unnecessary, unjust and somewhat cruel drain on the candidates' political time and resources. Moreover, the means will often sweep too broadly, since a perfectly comprehensible field of five will be artificially reduced to a field of two because the signature requirements are so onerous and often impossible to meet. The signature laws thus also operate in an *overinclusive* way.

There are far less restrictive means available to vindicate the state's interest in keeping the pool of candidates down to the right number—assuming that the states can commit themselves to what that number is. Say it is five. Why not simply allow the first five party-nominated candidates who sign up to get on the ballot? If there are frustrated candidates left over, a second page of the ballot could be prepared and voters given a warning that says: "Academic studies show that voters grow confused after looking at a list of five candidates. There are two candidates whose names appear on the next page. You are free to read their names and consider them as ballot choices or to disregard them, but consider them at your own risk." We could even create two separate ballots—a tidy ballot with five candidates or less and a messy ballot with more than five names—and then allow voters themselves to select which ballot they want and feel they can handle.

Now, some may object to these solutions on the grounds that they are not fair to the leftover candidates on the second page or those whose names appear only on the larger ballot. But these are forms of relatively minor unfairness compared to the gross injustice of systematically driving minor-party candidates off the ballot because their presence will be assumed to confound the voters. If we bristle at creating a second-class group of citizens by making them appear on the ballot in an inferior way, what of the outrageous injustice of forcing them off the ballot altogether? I am not arguing that this is an ideal solution, just a far superior one to forcing all minor-party candidates to waste their resources on a Sisyphean make-work assignment of collecting tens of thousands of signatures from members of other parties.

If there is truly a scarcity of ballot space (and we have reason to be dubious), a serious solution that would avoid the blatant inequitable treatment of minor parties today would be to require *all* parties to collect signatures in a competitive way and then award the top five signature-gathering parties the available lines on the ballot in the order of the number of signatures they raised. This solution would give the major parties a chance to return to grassroots work and make everyone suffer equally under the petition-gathering regime.

Deception

It is hard to know what Justice Stewart meant by invoking "deception" as a possible state interest for signature requirements, but Richard Winger has looked at the oral arguments in *Jenness* and has concluded that Justice Stewart was referring to the possibility raised by Chief Justice Burger that a major political party might deceive voters and sabotage its main opponent by instigating a phony third-party candidacy by someone with the identical or similar name to the opponent. This would siphon away votes from the major-party candidate. Of course, the answer to such a hypothetical possibility is not to shut down the full breadth of political diversity in society, but for the state to identify the proper party affiliation of each candidate on the ballot. Presumably the honest people involved will expose such a plot in the media with the full expectation that the public would punish such a scheme.

Frustration of the Democratic Process

It is impossible to know what this phrase means and no elaboration was offered by the Court. One would think that curtailing the opportunity for all political viewpoints to be represented on the ballot is the relevant threat to democracy.

Some Preliminary Showing of a Modicum of Support

The *Jenness* Court did not assert that demonstrating a "modicum of support" was a state interest served but the means, of serving other interests. But the various terms of this problem have gotten mixed up, and it is sometimes asserted that the state itself may have a valid interest in requiring third parties to show "a modicum of support." It is important to see why this is false.

If we concede that the state has no separate independent interest in cleansing the ballot to prevent voter confusion, then it is hard to divine what its interest might be in making sure that a party's candidate has a "modicum of support." After all, it is the voters, not the government, who will determine a candidate's level of support on Election Day. It reverses the proper order of things for the government to make predictions about the level of candidates' support and then bar them from the ballot on that basis. Public opinion must control authority, not vice versa. The gatekeeper of the democratic will must be the people themselves.

Even if the state had a valid interest in making candidates show a "modicum of support" before finding a place on the ballot, the petition-gathering requirement does not promote this interest. In every state it is clear that the voter's signature does *not* express political support for the candidate.

In truth, no one really knows what the signature means. It probably expresses the voter's hazy assent to the proposition that the candidate should not be denied a place on the ballot simply because he or she did not collect enough signatures. Thus, if it is a "modicum of support" we are seeking to establish, we should not force the candidates to collect thousands of signatures from pedestrians and strangers willing to grant them a democratic right that is already rightfully theirs. Rather, we should require candidates to provide a signed statement by one hundred or two hundred people that they actually plan to vote for the candidate. Of course, this procedure would underscore the dubiousness of the whole inquiry, because the state has no valid interest in deep-sea fishing in the political waters of civil society before an election. Let the candidates appear on the ballot: this is where they belong.

Avoiding the Presence of "Frivolous Candidacies"[74]

Some later cases, implicitly recognizing that the state advances no defensible interest in preventing ballot overcrowding or voter confusion by imposing huge signature-gathering requirements on third parties, focus on the alleged interest in keeping frivolous candidacies off the ballot. But in the federal context, this interest in making sure all balloted candidates are deemed *serious* by the state obviously imposes an unconstitutional additional qualification for federal office. To run for the House under this theory, you must be thirty years old, a state resident, a citizen for seven years—and must be deemed to be "serious" under state law. This system fails the *Thornton* test.

A seriousness requirement imposed for candidacy for state office would also be unconstitutional under any minimally democratic reading of the Constitution. In a democratic society, seriousness lies in the eye of the beholder. It is ultimately the voters who must judge the seriousness, or frivolity of the candidate and his or her platform. In any event, it is difficult to see how the level of signatures obtained is a mark of seriousness since those signatures, by law and in fact, do not represent people pledged to vote for the candidate. A far less burdensome and repressive means of showing seriousness would be to ask candidates—all of them, including "major party" nominees—to document how much time they have spent campaigning. Or perhaps they could be asked to mobilize a thousand personal and volunteer hours, not for the perfectly useless task of collecting signatures, but for different kinds of useful community service. This approach would more closely link officeholding to meaningful community action. Indeed, if we are going to treat ballot access as a reward rather than a right, the best plan would be to require candidates to register 250 or 500 new voters before receiving a ballot position. Voter registration would help the community and the candidate simultaneously.

The whole signature-gathering obsession should be abolished by the states or, if not, revisited carefully by federal courts asking hard questions about what purposes are actually being served by these petitions. The petition process is a colossal state-ordered waste of time, an invisible but massive structural harassment in the electoral process designed for no purpose other than to frustrate challengers to the two-party system. Our model here should be Great Britain, which "has never required more than 10 signatures for anyone to get on the ballot for members of Commons."[75]

Confusion about Fusion: *Timmons v. Twin Cities Area New Party*[76]

The Supreme Court has authorized states to engage in other kinds of ballot manipulation to cordon off the two-party system. In the nineteenth century, progressive and populist parties thrived through electoral "fusion" coalitions in which the parties of the left would "cross-nominate" each other's candidates. If the Populists placed the Democratic candidate for governor and the Greenback candidate for treasurer on their ticket, they could get reciprocal commitments to have their candidate for lieutenant governor "fused" onto the other parties' tickets. This arrangement allowed for power-sharing, patronage-sharing and the formation of large political coalitions. As Chief Justice Rehnquist noted in *Timmons*:

> Fusion was a regular feature of Gilded Age American politics. Particularly in the West and Midwest, candidates of issue-oriented parties like the Grangers, Independents, Greenbackers, and Populists often succeeded through fusion with the Democrats, and vice versa.[77]

After introduction of the Australian ballot, the Republican Party-controlled legislatures worked hard to defeat this practice at the turn of the twentieth century by making it illegal to have the same candidate appear on different party lines. Most states got rid of electoral fusion. Today, it exists as a remnant in a handful of states, such as New York, where it continues to give life to a healthy third-party sector, including the Conservative Party, the Liberal Party, the Right-to-Life Party, and the impressively creative Working Families Party.

But the trend in the states has been to impose strict controls on the ballot, and often specifically to break up cross-partisan electoral coalitions. The ultimate inversion of the original practice of voters bringing their own personally drawn ballots to the polling place has been states mass-producing ballots and then forbidding voters the opportunity to write in the names of their choices. In *Burdick v. Takushi* (1992), the Supreme

Court, quite shockingly, approved Hawaii's practice of narrowing ballot access and throwing away ballots where voters write in the names of their chosen candidates. The Court stated by way of explanation that it has "repeatedly upheld reasonable, politically neutral regulations that have the effect of channeling expressive activities at the polls."[78] This case was a dreadful omen for the Court's consideration of the ban on fusion.

In 1997, the Twin Cities Area New Party, which was part of a national effort to launch a third party to the left of the Democrats, challenged Minnesota's 1901 antifusion law as a violation of the First Amendment associational rights and Equal Protection rights of its members. The party wanted to cross-nominate a progressive Democratic-Farmer-Labor candidate, State Representative Andy Dawkins, on the New Party line. Dawkins agreed to be the standard-bearer of the New Party but confronted a law that provided: "No individual who seeks nomination for any partisan or nonpartisan office at a primary shall be nominated for the same office by nominating petition...."[79] The Eighth Circuit ruled in the New Party's favor, finding that the fusion ban was a "severe" burden on its "freedom to select" its own "standard bearer" and its right to "broaden the base of public participation in and support for [its] activities."[80]

Voting six-to-three, the Supreme Court reversed and rejected the plaintiffs' claims.[81] Splitting hairs, Chief Justice Rehnquist separated the right of the New Party to nominate its own standard-bearer, which he agreed exists, from its right to place its nominee's name on the ballot, a right that he said is not "absolute."[82] The New Party could still endorse Dawkins and campaign for him, but Minnesota did not severely burden the New Party's political associational freedoms by wiping its chosen nominee's name off the ballot. Chief Justice Rehnquist thus imagined that parties have private rights that do not translate into public rights.

To justify its rule, Minnesota cited all of the familiar airy interests in "protecting the integrity, fairness and efficiency of their ballots and election processes...."[83] What do these terms mean in this context? Chief Justice Rehnquist liked the state's argument that candidates and parties might "exploit fusion as a way of associating his or its name with popular slogans and catch phrases,"[84] a suggestion seemingly refuted by the long history of fusion and its contemporaneous practice in states like New York.

More significantly, Chief Justice Rehnquist stated that:

> voters who might not sign a minor party's nominating petition based on the party's own views and candidates might do so if they view the minor party

as just another way of nominating the same person nominated by one of the major parties. . . . The State surely has a valid interest in making sure that minor and third parties who are granted access to the ballot are bona fide and actually supported, on their own merits, by those who have provided the statutorily required petition or ballot support.[85]

But this argument badly begs the question because the New Party and Representative Dawkins went to Court to establish that he *was* the party's own candidate and that it was only state law that prevented him from being its official ballot nominee. More to the point, Chief Justice Rehnquist gives the game away when he says that the state has an interest in making sure that third parties "granted access to the ballot" are "actually supported by" those who sign their petitions. This assertion contradicts the theory behind petitions, which is *not* that voters who sign their names actually support the candidate or will vote for him but that they approve of granting him ballot status. If signing a candidate's petitions denoted support, it would be literally impossible for the vast majority of third-party candidates, and probably major-party candidates as well, to collect tens of thousands of signatures. Yet Chief Justice Rehnquist is implicitly acknowledging that the state has delegated control over ballot status to the busy guy in the street who can either register his vague approval for the party by signing or express visceral disgust by walking away.

Chief Justice Rehnquist was intellectually honest enough to recognize that his decision in *Timmons* landed hard on the side of constitutionalizing the "two-party system":

States also have a strong interest in the stability of their political systems. This interest does not permit a State to completely insulate the two-party system from minor parties' or independent candidates' competition and influence, nor is it a paternalistic license for States to protect political parties from the consequences of their own political disagreements. That said, the States' interest permits them to enact reasonable election regulations that may, in practice, favor the traditional two-party system, and that temper the destabilizing effects of party-splintering and excessive factionalism. *The Constitution permits the Minnesota legislature to decide that political stability is best served through a healthy two-party system.*[86]

Of course, a "healthy two-party system," speaking now in the political-science sense, is a fluid one open to challenge and change, the kind that gave rise to the Republican Party and Abraham Lincoln prior to the Civil War. But the two-party system Minnesota aimed to entrench is a fortified political establishment built on the violation of other citizens' political rights. This self-entrenching two-party system our progressively democratic Constitution should not tolerate, much less endorse.

Taking John Anderson's Case Seriously

The modern test for election restrictions today is found in the 1983 case of *Anderson v. Celebrezze*,[87] a rare triumph for outsider candidates and open democracy. In this case, the Court struck down Ohio's early presidential-candidate filing deadline for Independents when it was challenged by former Republican Congressman John Anderson, who was seeking the presidency in 1980 as an Independent. A man of old-fashioned political integrity and virtue who does not understand why the machinations of party operatives should thwart the sovereignty of the people, Anderson brought challenges to many electoral restrictions, and his Supreme Court victory, if its meaning is taken seriously by the Court, could topple our absurd signature fetish.

When testing the constitutionality of regulations that burden election rights, *Anderson v. Celebrezze* requires us, first, to assess the magnitude of the injury to the rights, which is obviously very great with hefty signature-gathering requirements; second, to measure the legitimacy and strength of the state's asserted interests, which rapidly disappear with respect to signatures under any kind of serious scrutiny; and, third, to determine whether protecting the state's interests actually requires burdening the injured party in this way. The inescapable conclusion from this means-ends test is that signature requirements, at least in their present form, have nothing to do with any important state interest and simply inflict political hard labor and compelled expression on fledgling and maverick parties.

Furthermore, based on *Thornton* and *Cook v. Gralike*, we can see that a state law requiring a candidate for Congress to collect ten thousand signatures to achieve a place on the ballot has most assuredly imposed an unconstitutional qualification for federal office. Just as a state cannot effectively ban incumbents from the ballot, it cannot effectively ban those who lack the resources or status of incumbents. Yet that is what most of the states are doing. The purpose of the Qualifications Clause was to open up public office to people of merit from every station in life. The petition requirement subverts this goal. Indeed, it confers a kind of title of politi-

cal nobility[88] on those officials and candidates aligning themselves with the
the two-party system.

Through its shameless gerrymandering of the ballot, the two-party system keeps a tight grip on American politics. This is why our burden of
hope as a society falls to the Supreme Court, which should zealously enforce
rules of fair play in elections. But the Court has made itself part of the
assault on democracy rather than its champion. As we have seen, it would
not be hard to discredit the two-party system, its bizarre signature fetish
and all of its phony, arrogant claims about "ballot overcrowding" and "voter
confusion." But we would need principled judicial analysis, something in
desperately short supply right now. It will take a democratic movement
from below, using nimble and creative tactics, to change these dynamics,
because the two-party system has also been swallowing up our national
political debates, the occasions upon which we might otherwise get to
talk about the integrity of the political process, and the very events around
which public political consciousness is formed.

CHAPTER SIX

"Arrogant Orwellian Bureaucrats"

How America's Electoral-Industrial Complex Controls Our Political Debates and Gerrymanders Your Mind

Public sentiment is everything—he who moulds public sentiment is greater than he who makes statutes.

—Abraham Lincoln, in his first debate with Stephen A. Douglas, Ottawa, Illinois, August 21, 1858

No democracy without debate: surely that must be our ethos. President Lincoln, who championed "government of the people, by the people, and for the people,"[1] taught us that debate is democracy's lifeblood. As a candidate for U.S. Senate in Illinois in 1858 from a new third party, he met Democrat Stephen Douglas in eight raucous debates "before huge, ardent audiences" and participated in "twenty-one hours of speeches, rebuttals, and rejoinders—all punctuated by choruses of cheers and jeers."[2] Lincoln's loss to Douglas in the state legislature's selection of a Senator did not render his campaign or these lively exchanges a waste of time. Based on the antislavery politics he spelled out in the heat of argument, Lincoln went on to win the White House two years later.[3]

If debate practices are any measure of democratic vitality, we are in a bad slump. Our presidential debates are content-starved, made-for-TV spectacles staged by the Commission on Presidential Debates (CPD), a money-swollen creation of the two-party system. This inside-the-Beltway private corporation was set up in 1987 by lawyer-lobbyists Frank Fahrenkopf Jr. and Paul Kirk Jr., the former chairmen of the Republican National Committee and Democratic National Committee respectively, with the mission of ousting the League of Women Voters, which had the gall to invite Independent John Anderson to debate in 1980.[4] Cochairmen Fahrenkopf and Kirk designed the CPD on an explicitly "bipartisan" basis to sponsor "nationally televised joint appearances conducted between the presidential and vice-presidential nominees of the two major political parties."[5]

The CPD collects millions of dollars from politically active mega-businesses such as Philip Morris, R.J. Reynolds, Dow Chemical, Sprint, Sara Lee and Anheuser-Busch, the beer giant that ponied up $550,000 in the 2000 election and won the right to sponsor what I cannot resist calling the Anheuser Bush-Gore Debate in St. Louis, Missouri, the company's hometown. In every pundit's revealing metaphor, debates have become the "Super Bowl of American politics," a bipartisan commercial event brought to you by big tobacco, big beer and other corporate sponsors that profit from America's money politics regardless of which team prevails on Election Day. According to the CPD, as I told an audience at Harvard Law School on the evening of the first 2000 presidential debate in Boston, "bipartisan" means that corporations can *buy* a party, and when they buy one, they get the other for free.

The debates are designed not as a focal point in a broad public dialogue among our divergent political forces—Democrat, Republican, Independent, Green, Libertarian—but as a ritual celebration of the two-party system and its incestuous common-law marriage to corporate capital. Although they bill the debates as key moments in the campaign for the whole electorate, our self-appointed debate managers brazenly declare third-party and Independent candidates "not viable" and exclude them—even if they represent the views of millions of Americans, as Perot did in 1996, and Nader did in 2000.

At the first 2000 presidential debate in Boston at the University of Massachusetts, the Green Party's nominee Ralph Nader, who had been given a ticket to watch the debates, was met by a phalanx of Massachusetts state troopers and security guards who threatened to arrest him if he entered the building. But the real offense against democracy was not this personal insult to Nader, a man who has devoted his entire life to public service, but the organized suppression of competing political viewpoints in the debates. When Nader was excluded, it meant that the two pro-NAFTA, pro-GATT, pro-WTO, pro–free trade, pro–death penalty, pro–Taft-Hartley Act and anti–national health insurance candidates could "jointly appear" in peace. In a two-way debate where other significant candidates have been excluded, the major party nominees can maintain an implicit conspiracy of silence on a range of issues where they agree but depart from the views of a large group of other Americans, perhaps even most of the public.

When compared to pluralistic debate practices in almost every other democratic nation, our electoral-industrial complex produces one of the most constricted and vacuous political discourses on earth. These exclusionary practices are embarrassing in light of the policies of our neighbors Canada, where in 2000 five presidential candidates participated in debates,[6] and Mexico, where in 2000 all six presidential candidates debated several times and Vincente Fox then shocked the world by sweeping away decades of PRI rule.[7] The first presidential election in a free South Africa offered a debate with more partisan diversity in a general election than we have ever seen on television in America. By contrast, our debates recurrently establish the collusive two-party system as the nation's official political church. This establishment is untenable, given not only basic Equal Protection and First Amendment norms, but also the Twelfth Amendment's overlooked provision that, in the event no candidate receives a majority in the electoral college, the House of Representatives shall choose a president from the top *three* leading candidates.[8]

Allowing more candidates actually adds tens of millions of viewers. When Ross Perot was permitted to debate Governor Bill Clinton and President George Bush in 1992, there were more than a hundred million more viewers (over the course of the three debates) than there were in 1996, when Perot was excluded from the debates with President Clinton and Senator Robert Dole.

Yet the CPD does not care that tens of millions of Americans have left the Church of the Two Parties by tuning out its "televised joint news appearances." The lifeless sound-bite exchanges between the two major party candidates are a striking political success for the two-party system because they demoralize large segments of the dissenting public and reinforce the two-party dogma for those who do watch. When third-party candidates are allowed to participate, dangerously unexpected—that is to say, democratic—things can happen. In 1998, Reform Party candidate Jesse Ventura participated in all ten gubernatorial debates in Minnesota and proceeded to trounce his major-party opponents.

As Ross Perot's lawyer challenging his exclusion from the presidential debates in 1996, I argued that corporate subsidies to pay for exclusionary two-candidate debates constitute illegal business contributions to the featured candidates. This argument is grounded in the fact that the Federal Election Campaign Act categorically forbids corporations to engage in any spending "in connection with" federal elections. The general counsel of the Federal Election Commission (FEC) ultimately agreed with this analysis but, as we shall see, the Democrats and Republicans who serve on the FEC overruled their chief lawyer and upheld lavish corporate sponsorship of two-party debates as a perfectly neutral and lawful event.

You can hardly blame the three Democratic and three Republican FEC commissioners for their Pavlovian defense of the political duopoly. They were following the lead of the Supreme Court, which actually found *governmental* debate exclusion to be compatible with the First Amendment. In a remarkable 1998 case called *Arkansas Educational Television Commission v. Forbes*,[9] the Court upheld the gerrymandering of congressional candidate debates by the managers of a state-owned public TV network. By a vote of six-to-three, it affirmed the exclusion of Ralph Forbes, a conservative Independent running for Congress in Arkansas, from the state public cable TV channel's 1992 debate between his Democratic and Republican rivals. This was an astonishing decision, not just because the political viewpoint censorship was so blatant but because the government's slanted interference almost certainly changed the outcome of the election. The Court's shocking decision in this case compels special attention because it shows the casual but relentless destruction of democratic principles in the Court's constitutional jurisprudence.

Ralph P. Forbes v. The Arrogant Orwellian Bureaucrats of the AETN; The Crooked Lying Politicians; and The Special Interests[10]

Throughout the 1980s, a maverick Christian conservative in Arkansas named Ralph Forbes irritated the state's Republican establishment with increasingly successful primary campaigns for public office. In 1990, he ran for lieutenant governor and captured 46.8 percent of the vote in a three-way race for the Republican Party nomination, defeating two rivals. Although he lost in the runoff to the candidate backed by the party establishment, it was clear that Forbes, who swept fifteen of the sixteen counties in his home congressional district, had become a force to be reckoned with. When the House seat in the Third District opened up in 1992, he declared for Congress as an Independent. He knocked on doors through the summer, sweating his way across the rural district to collect more than six thousand signatures, earning a ballot position next to Republican Tim Hutchinson and Democrat John Van Winkle.

In the sprawling mountains of the Third District, television plays a key role in elections. So it was significant when the Arkansas Educational Television Network (AETN), the state agency operating five public TV stations, decided to sponsor debates in Arkansas' four U.S. House districts. There were only nine candidates for Congress in the state in 1992: four Democrats, four Republicans and one Independent, Forbes. AETN invited everyone but Forbes to debate. He only found out about the debate by accident from AETN's promotional newspaper ads that featured photographs of his rivals under the headline: "Do you know your candidates?" When Forbes asked to be included, AETN said it was going to "stick with the major candidates" instead. On the evening of the debate, Forbes showed up, but was turned away after being told the station would rather show reruns of *St. Elsewhere* than have a debate with him in it.

Forbes sued *pro se*. He gave his First Amendment case the irresistible caption *Forbes v. The Arrogant Orwellian Bureaucrats of the AETN; The Crooked Lying Politicians; and The Special Interests.* He prevailed in the Eighth Circuit Court of Appeals, where Chief Judge Richard Arnold found that the televised debate was a "limited public forum"—public property opened by the government for specific speech purposes. In such a forum, a speaker may not be excluded unless the government shows a compelling reason.[11] As a balloted candidate, Forbes naturally belonged to the class of speakers invited to the forum, and Arkansas lacked a compelling reason to exclude him. The "government cannot, simply by its own ipse dixit, define a class of speakers so as to exclude a person who would naturally be expected to be a member of the class on no basis other than party affiliation."[12] AETN's putative reason for excluding Forbes—its perception that he was not "viable"—violated the First Amendment because his political viability was a "judgment to be made by the people of the Third Congressional District, not by officials of the government in charge of channels of communication."[13]

AETN appealed, urging the Supreme Court to treat its debate not as a public government forum of any kind but as private journalism. On this theory, AETN did nothing more unlawful than, say, the *New York Times* did by failing to cover Forbes' campaign.

By a vote of six-to-three, the Supreme Court reversed the Eighth Circuit and upheld AETN's closed debate. Writing for the majority, Justice Anthony Kennedy started sensibly by rejecting AETN's extreme claim that the First Amendment protects the government channel against Forbes rather than vice versa. The First Amendment does apply to government-sponsored candidate debates, Justice Kennedy wrote, because such debates are designed as "a forum for political speech by candidates" and "candidate debates are of exceptional significance in the electoral process."[14]

At this point, Forbes' case should have been clinched. The First Amendment forbids government from practicing "viewpoint discrimination" in any type of public forum. To silence political candidates on the grounds that they are not "viable," which simply means that someone thinks they are likely to lose, is plainly to discriminate against them based on their (allegedly) unpopular viewpoints. The First Amendment protects both popular and unpopular speech, winning arguments and losing ones.

But Justice Kennedy retreated from the implications of his understanding that a state-sponsored debate must respect freedom of speech. He rejected the Eighth Circuit's conclusion that the debate was a limited public forum. Squinting hard, he wrote that AETN "did not make its debate generally available to candidates for Arkansas' Third Congressional District seat," but rather—follow this closely, now—"reserved eligibility for participation in the debate to candidates for the Third Congressional District seat (as opposed to some other seat). At that point ... [AETN] made candidate-by-candidate determinations as to which of the eligible candidates would participate in the debate.... Thus, the debate was a nonpublic forum."[15]

In this most oxymoronic concept, a "nonpublic forum" is one the government does not make generally available but opens only to certain people for specific purposes. In a nonpublic forum, a government can make "reasonable" exclusions so long as they are not viewpoint-based. But even if we charitably grant that this was not a real public forum, was the exclusion of Forbes in fact viewpoint-neutral? No invitation policy was ever announced. The network simply invited two of the candidates and rejected the third based on the fact that he was neither Democrat nor Republican. The freewheeling "candidate-by-candidate determination" method that Justice Kennedy invokes as proof that the debate was a nonpublic forum was itself the essential violation of Forbes' First Amendment rights. For there were no viewpoint-neutral standards used in making these selections: not whether the candidates were balloted, not whether they had run for office before nor how well they performed—nothing. (Had there been a standard at least based on past electoral performance—dubious in itself—Forbes would have made the grade, having drawn more than 46 percent of the statewide vote in his run for lieutenant governor in the Republican primaries just two years before. He had received more votes in state elections than either of his two opponents. But it was, of course, critical to the partisan selection process that no actual standards be defined.)

Justice Kennedy dangerously weakened the doctrine of First Amendment viewpoint-neutrality by allowing government officials to predict a candidate's "viability" and then exclude him from a public debate on this basis. He endorsed the trial jury's finding that Forbes' exclusion was not based on "objections or opposition to his views," and quoted approvingly AETN's executive director, who

> testified Forbes' views had "absolutely" no role in the decision to exclude him from the debate. She further testified Forbes was excluded because (1) "the Arkansas voters did not consider him a serious candidate"; (2) "the news organizations also did not consider him a serious candidate"; (3) "the Associated Press and a national election result reporting service did not plan to run his name in results on election night"; (4) Forbes "apparently had little, if any, financial support, failing to report campaign finances to the Secretary of State's office or to the Federal Election Commission"; and (5) "there [was] no 'Forbes for Congress' campaign headquarters other than his house."[16]

Justice Kennedy concluded: "It is, in short, beyond dispute that Forbes was excluded not because of his viewpoint but because he had generated no appreciable public interest."[17]

This argument, framed to make Forbes seem laughable, is a house of cards. First of all, the conclusions about how the voters and the media regarded Forbes were based on no actual empirical research—not even a poll—and therefore were pure speculation. Second, these conclusions are irrelevant. The constitutional rights of candidates (or other speakers) in public fora do not depend on their political popularity, estimated favor with the media or fund-raising prowess. In elections, poverty cannot constitutionally be used to disadvantage citizens, which is why the Court has invalidated practices that slouch toward plutocracy, such as poll taxes and high candidate filing fees.[18]

Of course, AETN did not even pretend to apply any of its arbitrary standards to Democrats and Republicans. The modest sums Forbes raised were more than what was collected by two Republican congressional candidates invited to participate in AETN's televised 1992 debates. As for the fact that Forbes's headquarters were in his house, the same was true not only of the loser Republican candidates in neighboring districts but also of John F. Kennedy, who ran his victorious 1960 presidential campaign from his home in Hyannisport, which served as campaign headquarters. This uppity *Better Homes and Gardens* standard obviously cannot be a lawful screen for debate participation, but it goes to show how much the

Court has absorbed the plutocratic snobbery of the "wealth primary" into election law.

At bottom, Justice Kennedy misapplied the doctrine of viewpoint discrimination. The trial jury's factual finding that Forbes's exclusion was not based on the network's "objections or opposition to his views" does not control the legal question of whether his exclusion was viewpoint-based. The test of First Amendment viewpoint neutrality is an objective test focused on the nature of a governmental classification that treats two classes of speakers differently. It is not a subjective test focused on the motivations of government actors in suppressing someone's speech. Subjective animus may be evidence of objective viewpoint discrimination, but is no necessary element of it.

The objective character of the viewpoint discrimination test was essentially established by Justice Kennedy himself in a fine majority opinion he wrote in *Rosenberger v. Rectors and Visitors of University of Virginia*.[19] In that 1995 case, the Court struck down the University of Virginia's practice of reimbursing the publishing costs of all student-run periodicals except those religiously identified. Although there was no allegation of animosity towards religious students in the case, the Court found that religiously motivated expression provided a distinctive viewpoint that could not be blocked out from public consideration. The university bore no malice towards religion, but when it declined to give the same speech privileges to religious student publications as it did to secular ones, the Court found that it was engaged in unconstitutional viewpoint discrimination.[20]

In the same way, the whole purpose and effect of excluding Forbes's appearance as a candidate was to block out presentation of a political viewpoint deemed unpopular by a candidate deemed unpopular. This is political viewpoint censorship. The fact that AETN would also have excluded unpopular candidates of the left does not rescue the policy. As Justice Kennedy perceptively wrote in *Rosenberger*: "The dissent's declaration that debate is not skewed so long as multiple voices are silenced is simply wrong; the debate is skewed in multiple ways."[21]

I hardly need to point out that I have no sympathy for Ralph Forbes's barbed-wire right-wing politics, but democracy is for everyone, and what one person can be cheated out of, all of us can be cheated out of. If the First Amendment means anything, surely it means that government actors cannot use taxpayer money to set up political debates among certain candidates in a congressional election and then arbitrarily exclude others with untraditional or dissenting politics.

The Electoral-Industrial Complex: How the Commission on Presidential Debates Took Control

In presidential elections, the gatekeeper of our political discourse is not a public bureaucracy but the Commission on Presidential Debates. The CPD is a private corporation in the District of Columbia made up of ten commissioners divided equally between the two major parties. Its cochairs and cofounders, Frank Fahrenkopf Jr. and Paul Kirk Jr., are not only former national Republican and Democratic party chairs but activists in their party networks. The CPD is funded by friendly large corporations that independently pumped millions of dollars directly into the Democratic and Republican national committees in "soft money" contributions until the McCain-Feingold legislation took effect. With the current ban on corporate "soft money" contributions to the national parties, the Commission on Presidential Debates becomes an even more critical conveyor belt to carry political money from rent-seeking corporate America into the cooperating wings of the two party system.

In 1988, when the CPD took over the presidential debates in the George Bush–Michael Dukakis contest, the League of Women Voters decided it wanted nothing more to do with the debates. Its language was unusually sharp. "The League of Women Voters is withdrawing its sponsorship of the presidential debates scheduled for mid-October because the demands of the two campaign organizations would perpetrate a fraud on the American people," League President Nancy M. Newman told the press on October 3, 1988: "It has become clear to us that the candidates' organizations aim to add debate to their list of campaign-trail charades devoid of substance, spontaneity and having to answer tough questions. The League has no intention of becoming an accessory to the hoodwinking of the American Public."[22]

In 1992, the CPD wanted to exclude Ross Perot and his running mate Admiral James Stockdale from the debates between President Bush and Bill Clinton and between their respective running mates, but then "the Bush campaign insisted, and the Clinton campaign agreed, that Mr. Perot and Admiral Stockdale be invited to participate in the debates."[23] Ironically, Perot was thus invited not because the CPD thought it was right—in their reflexive bipartisanship, the commissioners planned to keep him out— but because both candidates ultimately thought it would be to their advantage. (It turned out that Clinton, not Bush, was right about that.) In other words, the CPD will exclude third-party candidates unless the major-party candidates tell them not to.

Having had this chance to debate Bush and Clinton in 1992, Perot won a smashing 19 percent of the popular vote and helped increase turnout by a remarkable 12 million votes. When he ran again in 1996, he not only had much broader name recognition and ballot status in fifty states and the District of Columbia but had been given $30 million in public funding based on his 1996 performance. Everyone assumed that the CPD would permit him to debate again.

But the CPD had a surprising announcement. Clinton and Dole would automatically be invited to participate because they were "the respective nominees of the two major parties." As for Perot, after consulting a mushy eleven-factor test, the CPD unanimously concluded that he was not "electable" and therefore ineligible to debate. The CPD reported that among the factors it considered were: "the professional opinions of the Washington bureau chiefs of major newspapers, news magazines, and broadcast networks"; "the opinions of a comparable group of professional campaign managers and pollsters not then employed by candidates under consideration"; "published views of prominent political commentators"; and "the findings of significant public opinion polls conducted by national polling and news organizations."

Perot went to U.S. District Court in the District of Columbia to stop the closed debates. He complained that the CPD's decision-making process was arbitrary and subjective and violated the FEC's rules requiring debate sponsors to use only "preestablished objective criteria" in determining which candidates to invite and forbidding them to "use nomination by a particular party" as "the sole objective criterion."[24] As one of Perot's lawyers, I argued that if a corporate debate sponsor is not scrupulously neutral, its spending to promote certain candidates runs afoul of the key provision in the Federal Election Campaign Act (FECA) stating that corporations may contribute no money to federal candidates nor spend any money on their behalf.

Judge Thomas Hogan cut off this argument on procedural grounds. Citing FECA's requirement that injured parties first go to the Federal Election Commission to exhaust their administrative remedies, Judge Hogan refused to enjoin the closed debates.[25] He recognized the candidate's "frustration" and even "perhaps unfairness in the process," but opined that "the complaint should be with Congress and the statutory framework established for the FEC to operate...."[26]

The District Court sent Perot to the FEC, the administrative graveyard for claims of illegal campaign practices. In the meantime, a most damning piece of evidence surfaced to show that the CPD probably never even applied its manipulable multifactor test.

The published proceedings of a post-election conference at the Harvard Kennedy School's Institute of Politics contain details of the real story.[27] George Stephanoupolos, who was then Senior Adviser to President Clinton, said in reference to the Dole-Kemp campaign's bargaining position when the two parties negotiated about debates: "[t]hey didn't have leverage going into the negotiations. They were behind, they needed to make sure Perot wasn't in it. As long as we would agree to Perot not being in it we would get everything else we wanted going in. We got our time frame, we got our length, we got our moderator."[28]

Tony Fabrizio, the Dole-Kemp pollster, added: "And the fact of the matter is, you got the number of dates." Later he reiterated: "George made very good observations about the positions we walked into the negotiations [with]."[29]

Stephanopoulos even pointed out that the Democrats themselves had no reason to want Perot in the debate: "we didn't want [people] to pay attention. The debates were a metaphor for the campaign. We wanted the debates to be a nonevent...."[30]

The following exchange between journalist Chris Matthews and Stephanopoulos brings the point home with eye-popping emphasis:

> MATTHEWS: Did they accept that deal to keep Perot out of the debate? Was that part of the deal? In other words, they [Dole] wanted Perot out and you wanted the debates over with, so you basically decided to keep the other guy out?
> STEPHANOPOULOS: Well, we didn't want Perot in either.
> MATTHEWS: You didn't?
> STEPHANOPOULOS: No.
> MATTHEWS: Well, why did you make us think you did?
> STEPHANOPOULOS: Because we wanted Perot's people to vote for us. [Laughter] How's that for candor? [Laughter][31]

It seems the real decision to exclude Perot in 1996—as to include him in 1992—was a strategic political one made secretly by his rivals. In other words, the CPD ignored its own terrible rules; it did not even *cheat* Perot fairly. This was no impartial debate sponsor. The CPD was a "political committee" acting in service of the two parties. The secret agreement entered into between the two parties and ratified by the CPD turned the 1996 debates into an illegal corporate contribution of millions of dollars of television time to the Clinton and Dole campaigns by the CPD's commercial sponsors. These corporate benefactors, major companies such as Philip Morris, Anheuser-Busch, Dun & Bradstreet and Lucent Technologies, had found one more way to funnel money to the two-party system. It is hard to imagine a more vivid and shameful display of "corporate democracy" at work.

The FEC held Perot's complaint through the debates, the election and calendar year 1997. But then, in 1998, something amazing finally happened: someone told the truth. Lawrence Noble, the FEC's general counsel, issued a 37-page report, breathtaking for its factual honesty and analytic lucidity, agreeing with Perot '96 that there was "reason to believe" that millions of dollars in corporate contributions to the CPD were illegal contributions to the Democratic and Republican campaigns and that the CPD itself was acting as an unregistered "political committee" on behalf of the two candidates. He proposed a full-scale investigation and subpoenas to determine exactly what took place when the CPD voted to exclude Perot.

When General Counsel Noble gave his report to the Democratic and Republican commissioners of the FEC, true to form they voted unanimously to override his analysis and recommendations. They found "no reason to believe" that the debate commission had "violated the law by sponsoring the 1996 presidential debates or by failing to register and report as a political committee."[32] Their statement was dishwater regurgitation of the CPD's selection criteria, topped off with nauseating Beltway nonsense such as: "The pool of experts used by CPD consisted of top-level academics and other professionals experienced in evaluating and assessing political candidates. By basing its evaluation of candidates upon the judgment of these experts, CPD took an objective approach in determining candidate viability."[33]

With the kind of analysis you might get from the CPD's own press office, the FEC found that "viability" is an objective criterion for selecting debate participants, that public opinion poll results are valid criteria for deciding who debates,[34] and that the amount of money a candidate has available to him or her "is certainly an objective factor which can be legitimately used by a sponsoring organization."[35] There the matter has rested with the FEC.

However, no truth-telling goes unpunished in Washington, and not long after Noble's very noble report was released, there was a move among Republicans in Congress—also apparently unhappy with Noble's reformist energy in cases involving Newt Gingrich's GOPAC, the Christian Coalition and corporate soft money—to remove him as general counsel by limiting his term. Noble weathered that crisis but left not long after. Today he is the executive director of the Center for Responsive Politics, the key clearing-house on money in politics.

The 2000 Presidential Election and the Anheuser-Bush-Gore Debates

Although the bipartisan CPD was saved at the last minute by the biparti-san FEC, the CPD's managers realized that their manipulable eleven-part test fooled no one. They faced a growing legitimacy crisis. On January 6, 2000, the CPD revealed a new standard requiring that presidential candi-dates who want to debate have "a level of support of at least 15 percent of the national electorate as determined by five selected national public opin-ion polling organizations, using the average of those organizations' most recent publicly reported results at the time of determination."

The new standard was clearer but no less arbitrary or unfair. Polling citizens on who they support before they have seen the candidates debate puts the cart before the horse. How do they know whom they support and why is it relevant at this point anyway? If we are going to use polls, surely the relevant question is: Who would you like to see debate in order to make up your mind on whom to vote for?

Ironically, a majority of the American people, for whom the CPD claims to speak, flatly reject the 15-percent preference rule. Some 51 percent of the people told the NBC News and *Wall Street Journal* poll that they believed third-party candidates should *not* have to meet the CPD's 15 percent requirement, and polled majorities regularly favored the inclusion of both Ross Perot in 1996 and Ralph Nader in 2000.

If the CPD was determined to use preference polling, it could far more defensibly have chosen 5 percent as the level of necessary support, since that is the percentage of the national popular vote a presidential candi-date must achieve in order qualify his party for public financing in the next election. Yet the CPD tripled this federal statutory figure in a way certain to reduce the chances of third parties qualifying for debates. The 15-percent figure raises the bar absurdly high. A candidate who stands at a disquali-fying 10 percent in the polls commands the allegiance of more than 10 million voters, who are apparently to be given the cold shoulder by our self-appointed debate managers.

In 2000, the major third-party candidate was the Green Party nominee, Ralph Nader, who ran a vigorous populist campaign focused, appropriately enough, on the dangers of excessive corporate power. He wanted to debate this problem with his rivals, but the corporations clearly would not have it. Nader attracted tens of thousands of citizens to old-fashioned "super-rallies" across America, but needed to confront Bush and Gore directly in order to penetrate mainstream political consciousness. Yet he hovered between 6 percent and 9 percent in the polls during the summer and early fall and thus fell short of the CPD's newly announced numerical polling cutoff mark.

On the evening of October 3, 2000, the night of the first presidential debate between Vice President Gore and Governor George W. Bush, Nader showed up with a ticket to watch the debate at the University of Massachusetts. The ticket was not actually for the debate hall but for the neighboring Lipke Auditorium, where the debate was being broadcast for an overflow audience on closed-circuit television. But even the symbolism of having Nader seated with the overflow audience in a separate facility was too much for the CPD. Nader was met by a security force that threatened him with arrest if he did not immediately leave the premises. Meantime, thousands of people kept at a distance from the debate hall were outside protesting his exclusion, chanting "Hey, hey corporate state, let Ralph debate!"

In his book about the 2000 presidential election *Crashing the Party*, Nader recounts his anger at the moment he faced arrest at the hands of state trooper Sergeant McPhail and the CPD's security officer, John Vezeris. Here is Nader's telling of the incident:

> The trooper became more impatient to get me back on the shuttle bus, and the sergeant said, "Mr. Nader, is it your intention to be arrested here?" My immediate thought was: What the hell? In the United States of America, I have a ticket to a public function at a public university, and without any cause or disruption, the authorities are throwing me out of the place. A private corporate power is using the state's police for its partisan political ends. Sounds like a corporate state. See you in court, man.[36]

And what an historic turning point it would have been to submit to arrest at that moment, to dramatize to the nation how the corporatized two-party system would use the police power of the state to jail opposition candidates. Had Nader been joined by close advisers such as Randall Robinson, who launched the Free South Africa Movement in the 1980s, best-selling author Michael Moore, Harvard Professor Cornel West, Phil

Donahue and rock artist Patti Smith and submitted to arrest, their civil disobedience would have stolen the thunder of the official debate presentation and radically changed the dynamics of the campaign.

However, Nader left the scene, only to return once again and then walk away from another opportunity to be arrested:

> But as I always prefer to be a plaintiff rather than a defendant, my associate and I instead repaired to the shuttle and returned to a Metro train stop several miles away.... No sooner did we get off the shuttle than we were met again by state troopers. But this time NBC's *Today Show* had a big camera with a bright light right there and did an interview with me.... All the while, Sergeant McPhail was threatening me with arrest "for trespass" if I did not leave within three minutes. Nearby, two Secret Servicemen from the Boston office were observing. They said they had no role regarding this situation, but they wanted to be helpful, escorting us onto the shuttle and riding with us back to the T stop. On the bus I had a good conversation with one of them, Chief Boston Agent John O'Hara, regarding the abuse of authority without cause that we had just experienced. He couldn't have been more understanding....[37]

In a cleverly improvised presidential campaign, Nader's decision not to be arrested was one of only two real mistakes, the other being his failure to embrace the logic of Internet vote-trading (see Chapter Three). Many great lawyer-reformers, like Nader himself, have consented to arrest, that is, to becoming defendants, in order to demonstrate graphically the logic of political repression. Mahatma Gandhi and Nelson Mandela are two famous examples. And what of William Kunstler? Although Nader's campaign shrewdly focused on the closed debates as a metaphor for the hostile corporate takeover of our democracy, the lack of vivid photographic images of democracy under arrest undercut Nader's ability to galvanize public sentiment over the next few weeks as the closed debates took place. Had he spent the night in the Boston jail, his act of conscience would have unleashed civil disobedience to swamp any attention that the banality-packed debate might have received. Nader never recovered politically from the phenomenal setback of being excluded from the debates and left standing out in the cold, his candidacy tagged "not viable" for all America to see.

Legally, however, Nader was finally able to win some rough justice for being unlawfully excluded from the nearby public facility where he wanted to watch the debates. On April 16, 2002, the day before a federal district court in Boston was to hear his claim that the CPD had violated Massachusetts's public accommodations and civil rights laws, the CPD's executive director Janet Brown and its co-chairs, Paul Kirk, Jr. and Frank Fahrenkopf sent Nader a formal letter of apology and made an undisclosed monetary settlement with his lawyers. The CPD's security consultant also apologized and agreed to pick up part of Nader's attorney fees.

In federal court in Boston, Nader also attacked the FEC's rule authorizing private corporations to sponsor debates as outside of its granted authority under the Federal Election Campaign Act. Although the district court found he had standing to sue, the court did not see the debate rule as unlawful. The Supreme Court's decision in *Forbes* and the FEC's rejection of the Perot suit in 1996 had set the table for Nader's loss, and the First Circuit Court of Appeals dined easily on his statutory claims.

What's Wrong with Debate Gerrymandering? The Fallacies of "Viability" and "Cacophony"

Whether it assumes a "public" or "private" character, debate gerrymandering is defended in two related ways. The first defense maintains that only "viable" candidates have a right to debate. The second is that, without a viability screen, we would suffer an impossible "cacophony" of political voices rendering candidate debates all sound and fury. Both of these arguments are specious and deeply at odds with our constitutional values.

The "Viability" Test Reflects Viewpoint Discrimination

Viability means that a candidate is perceived to be popular and a good prospect to win.[38] But the First Amendment protects equally the political speech of *popular* citizens with mainstream views and *unpopular* citizens with minority views. The Court emphasized this axiom of free speech in *Texas v. Johnson*, which upheld the right of political dissenters to burn the American flag: "If there is a bedrock principle underlying the First Amendment, it is that the government may not prohibit the expression of an idea simply because society finds the idea itself offensive or disagreeable."[39] Surely this principle must have "its fullest and most urgent application precisely to the conduct of campaigns for political office."[40] Otherwise we are saying that dissenters have a right to make jerks out of themselves by burning flags but have no right to be part of the political dialogue that takes place among citizens at election time.

A state-controlled "viability" screen in congressional elections—the *Forbes* case—offends the Qualifications Clause, the First Amendment and Equal Protection. In our democracy, state government has no rightful power to predict winners or losers in an election, especially a federal one, much less publicize its predictions to voters and selectively favor chosen candidates with free television time.[41] If the government cannot add the words "abandoned term limits pledge" or "(not viable)" or "(likely winner)" next to candidates' names on the ballot, it should not be able to send such messages during the campaign.[42]

The citizenry must decide which candidates are "electable" by electing them. The government's role is to guarantee fair process and secure counting of the ballots. If the people, through their government, decide that a publicly sponsored debate is necessary for enlightenment of the electorate, then the government must find an equal place for *all* ballot-qualified candidates.[43] By picking and choosing "viable" candidates, the government usurps the role of the people.

This is not a metaphor. In *Forbes*, it is likely that, had Forbes been invited to debate by AETN, his participation would have changed the outcome of the race. The Republican victor, Tim Hutchinson, received 125,295 votes, or 50.2 percent of the total, compared to Democrat John Van Winkle, who received 117,775, or 47.2 percent.[44] Meanwhile, Forbes captured 6,329 votes or 2.5 percent.[45] If Forbes, a strong conservative with proven vote-getting power, had been allowed to debate and had converted just one out of every fifteen eventual Hutchinson voters, the election would have gone to Democrat Van Winkle. You might love the result or you might hate it, but the government's decision to sponsor and close this debate probably elected Congressman Hutchinson.

Why Don't Democrats and Republicans Have to Be "Viable"?

In the real world, the "viability" screen operates as a pretext for excluding third-party and independent candidates. We know this because debate sponsors never ask whether Democratic and Republican candidates are "viable." The other congressional debates that AETN sponsored in Arkansas in 1992 provide a dramatic example of this double standard at work. In every case, Republican challengers credited with no chance to win were nonetheless invited to debate.

Arkansas's First Congressional District is one of the most Democratic in the country and has not sent a Republican to Congress since 1868.[46]

In the eight elections prior to 1992, the Democratic candidate took 68.9 percent, 100 percent, 100 percent, 64.8 percent, 97.2 percent, 64.2 percent, 100 percent, and 64.3 percent of the general election tally.[47] In 1992, the Democrat, Blanche Lambert, outspent the Republican eleven to one.[48] Only 31 years old, Lambert received 69.8 percent of the vote in her first bid for public office, leaving the Republican less than one third of the vote.[49] Yet the hapless Republican challenger who, unlike Forbes, had never collected *any votes* in any public election, was invited by AETN to debate.

In the Second Congressional District debate, AETN invited not only the "popular incumbent," Democratic Congressman Ray Thornton, but also "long-shot Republican challenger Dennis Scott," who "filed at the last minute to run, saying [']no incumbent should get a free ride.[']"[50] Another first-time candidate, Scott was able to raise only $5,724—less than what was raised by Forbes, who collected $9,754.[51] Congressman Thornton trounced Scott by a three-to-one margin, collecting 74.2 percent of the vote to Scott's 25.8 percent.

Although Democrat-Republican debates in presidential elections are sacrosanct, it often seems obvious at the time who is going to lose. Think of Barry Goldwater's quixotic run against President Johnson in 1964 or George McGovern's 1972 candidacy against Richard Nixon. In 1996, at the time when the CPD was branding Perot unelectable, Republican nominee Robert Dole had himself been described by the Beltway establishment as "toast,"[52] and his campaign "dead meat."[53] Albert Hunt said: "This election has been over at least since August," and Sam Donaldson remarked: "This election was over last February."[54] But the viability standard always presumes that Democratic and Republican candidates are, by definition, "viable" no matter how hopeless their chances.

To be sure, it may be said that the viability test could not have been applied to Dole or the sacrificial-lamb Republicans in Arkansas because, without them, there would have been no debate at all. But this argument proves too much. It suggests that the point of candidate debates is to have a dialogue of different political perspectives regardless of whether participants have a good chance to win. If that is true, then all ballot-certified candidates should be included.

Actually, if the viability standard were to be applied neutrally, there would be precious few debates, because challengers are rarely "viable" against incumbents. The U.S. House reelection rate, for example, is over 93 percent, and the vast majority of House districts can be reliably assigned to either the Democratic or Republican columns (or Independent in Vermont).[55]

The vast majority of House races are won every election by a victory margin of over 20 percent, "the traditional definition of a political landslide."[56] Most Democratic and Republican challengers are simply never "viable" in the pinched and myopic terms of AETN: they lose by a landslide against an incumbent of the district's majority party. In this functional sense, of course, we have not a two-party system in most congressional districts, but a one-party system.

But even if we can guess how a campaign is going to come out most of the time, is there any way to truly know every time? Are there political clairvoyants out there? Because the whole point of campaigns is to *change* public opinion, and because we have a secret ballot, the history of politics includes great surprises and reversals of fortune, massive shifts of public sentiment at the last minute, late-breaking scandals, and sudden decisions to drop out, not to mention overnight candidate illnesses and deaths.[57] Campaigns are characterized by a fluidity wholly incompatible with the idea of taking a snapshot of the electorate at one moment, superimposing that image on a hypothetical Election Day, and then invoking that distorted image to cut off debate in the present. The state, by excluding candidates from debates because it thinks we will not want to vote for them, wears "our expectations like an armored suit," in the words of the rock group R.E.M.

Third-party and Independent candidates *can* win, especially if given the chance to debate. Vermont gives us the refreshing examples of an Independent House member, socialist Bernie Sanders, and an Independent senator, Jim Jeffords, elected as a Republican but likely to be reelected as an Independent. Consider Minnesota governor Jesse Ventura. A giant, bald, former all-pro wrestler derided as frivolous and unelectable, Ventura challenged the two-party system as the Reform Party candidate in 1998. On September 20, he was at 10 percent in the polls and thus would have been excluded from the debates had the CPD been running things. But he was invited to participate in every debate. On October 18, after the debates began, he was up to 21 percent in the polls, and by October 30 his numbers had risen to 27 percent.[58] On Election Day he won and has since said he would have lost had he been excluded from the debates.

In *Forbes*, AETN's judgment that Forbes was not viable was pure guesswork. The CPD now at least relies on polling, which seems superficially scientific. But polls fluctuate madly—at best, they capture the present moment but tell us nothing reliable about the future. If AETN had sponsored a debate for candidates in the U.S. Senate Democratic primary in

Wisconsin in 1992, it would have excluded the eventual winner of the election, Russ Feingold, because a major poll showed him at 10 percent of the vote, compared to 42 percent for Congressman Jim Moody and 40 percent for businessman Joe Checota.[59] Yet Feingold went on to overcome his rivals less than three weeks after this poll was taken, collecting 69 percent of the vote to 14 percent each for Moody and Checota. Feingold then went on to defeat the incumbent Republican Senator Bob Kasten, in the general election.[60] No mainstream pollster ever predicted Governor Ventura's victory, because polling vastly understates first-time and Independent voters. And, according to the *New York Times*, the vast majority of contacted voters in public opinion polls simply hang up on pollsters or refuse to participate. Response rates have fallen to 20 percent in some cases.[61]

Elections Serve Purposes Broader than Certifying the Candidate with the Most Votes on Election Day

The basic problem with the "viability" screen is that it misunderstands what an election is and what a campaign is. In the continuing public dialogue that is democracy, an election is more than a mechanical contest over who will take office. It is democracy's way of promoting rippling concentric circles of political debate which offer up new priorities on the public agenda.[62] Losing Socialist Party candidates for president and Congress in the early 1900s ran dynamic campaigns that led to the progressive income tax, woman suffrage, the forty-hour workweek and many of the progressive reforms of the last century.[63]

Winning isn't everything. Candidates often run to establish legitimacy for their politics and to position themselves for a future race. Sometimes a defeat can propel a candidate's political career, as was the case not only with Abraham Lincoln but with former President Bill Clinton, who (like Ralph Forbes) lost his first race for the House in Arkansas's Third Congressional District (in 1974) but went on to be elected attorney general of Arkansas two years later.[64] Many politicians have faced multiple losses before finding success with the voters. For example, Robert Casey "made a second career out of running for Governor" in Pennsylvania, where over the course of twenty years from 1966 to 1986, he continuously ran for and lost the democratic nomination before finally winning in 1986. He narrowly won in the general election and was reelected to a second term in 1990 with 68 percent of the vote.[65] Another Pennsylvania politician, Arlen Specter, waged an unsuccessful bid for mayor in 1967, lost his reelection campaign for district attorney of Philadelphia, and piled up back-to-back losses in the 1976 Senate primary and the 1978 gubernatorial primary before succeeding in his bid for Senate in 1980.[66]

Given declining party allegiance in modern American politics,[67] and a decade-long "surge of interest in independent and third-party candidates,"[68] a demand well documented in Micah Sifry's perceptive book about third parties, *Spoiling for a Fight*,[69] third-party candidates today can affect electoral outcomes decisively. Whatever one thinks of Ralph Nader, his candidacy undeniably had a potent effect on the 2000 presidential election. Debate exclusion is never a neutral journalistic act, as AETN would have it, nor is it a neutral public policy judgment, as the CPD suggests. It is always an aggressive interference with the course of a political campaign.

The Cacophony Alibi

The more serious argument made for exclusionary debates is that if government debate sponsors are not allowed broad discretion to pick and choose participants, they will be "faced with the prospect of cacophony," as Justice Kennedy put it, and "might choose not to air candidates' views at all. . . . In this circumstance, a [g]overnment-enforced right of access inescapably dampens the vigor and limits the variety of public debate."[70] Justice Kennedy's conclusion parallels AETN's argument before the Court that huge numbers of candidates might flood nonexclusive debates, and "public broadcasters would abandon the effort."[71]

There is no empirical basis for saying that opening up debates to all balloted candidates would produce "cacophony." In the second half of the twentieth century, in 25 straight general elections for the U.S. House of Representatives, there was on average *one* Independent or minor-party candidate running in each of America's 435 congressional districts.[72] The idea that government debate sponsors could not handle them is preposterous, and many sponsors, such as the League of Women voters, already do include them.[73] The 1992 House races in Arkansas illustrate the national pattern: Ralph Forbes was the only Independent running for Congress in the state, and his inclusion in AETN's debate would have been easy.

Indeed, given that the incumbent reelection rate floats way above 90 percent, it is often difficult to get a second candidate to run in most districts, much less a cacophonous crowd, witness the weak major-party challengers in districts neighboring Forbes's. With our stringent ballot-access laws, built-in incumbent advantages, and money-skewed elections, third-party and Independent candidates are already discouraged to the point of despair.

The idea that multicandidate debates would dissolve into white noise contradicts our experience with nationally televised debates in the Democratic and Republican presidential *primaries*, which regularly feature more than two candidates. For example, in the 1992 presidential primary season, there was a Democratic primary debate in St. Louis with Bob Kerrey, Jerry Brown, Bill Clinton, Tom Harkin, Paul Tsongas, and Douglas Wilder.[74] In the 1988 season, six Republicans squared off in New Hampshire, including George Bush, Pete duPont IV, Alexander Haig, Jr., Bob Dole, Pat Robertson, and Jack Kemp.[75] In recent years, we have been treated to large televised party primary debates that include long-shots such as Morry Taylor and Alan Keyes. No one was injured during any of these debates, and no chairs were thrown. Far from seeing multicandidate debates as cacophony, the voters see them as *democracy*.

Even if we hypothesize that debate sponsors will have many candidates in a race, the whole concept that government can restrict the speech rights of citizens in order to prevent "cacophony" offends the First Amendment norm that all citizens enjoy an equal right to speak. In its 1971 *Cohen v. California*[76] decision, the Supreme Court showed better perspective on the democratic necessity of multiple voices:

> [The] constitutional right of free expression is powerful medicine in a society as diverse and populous as ours. It is designed and intended to remove governmental restraints from the arena of public discussion, putting the decision as to what views shall be voiced largely into the hands of each of us, in the hope that use of such freedom will ultimately produce a more capable citizenry and more perfect polity and in the belief that no other approach would comport with the premise of individual dignity and choice upon which our political system rests.
>
> To many, the immediate consequence of this freedom may often appear to be only verbal tumult, discord, and even offensive utterance. These are, however, within established limits, in truth necessary side effects of the broader enduring values which the process of open debate permits us to achieve. *That the air at times seem filled with verbal cacophony is, in this sense not a sign of weakness but of strength.* We cannot lose sight of the fact that, in what otherwise might seem a trifling and annoying instance of individual distasteful abuse of a privilege, these fundamental societal values are truly implicated. (Emphasis added)

Speculation that major-party candidates will pull out of debates if third-party candidates are allowed to participate is pernicious. To exclude some candidates because their presence may cause others not to come is, in effect, to impose a prior restraint on their speech based on the long-discredited "heckler's veto." It is like saying public parks should not desegregate because white families may choose to stop coming. That result would be unfortunate, but it would be their choice. We don't deny some citizens their rights because it might influence others to decline to exercise theirs.

Nor is it permissible to suppress some political speakers in order to give other political speakers more airtime. As the Court famously remarked in *Buckley v. Valeo* in the course of striking down limits on campaign expenditures: "the concept that government may restrict the speech of some elements of our society in order to enhance the relative voice of others is wholly foreign to the First Amendment. . . ."[77]

If cacophony were ever to become a real problem, government debate sponsors have alternatives available far more democratic and efficient than exclusion. A debate sponsor should decide in advance how many candidates the voters can tolerate without losing focus: Is it five? Six? In any event, it must be a specific number the sponsor cannot alter for the purposes of major-party primary debates. If there are more candidates than places, the debate sponsor could add a second debate and randomly divide the candidates up between the two events. If time is so scarce that there is only time for a single debate, but there are nine candidates, and the judgment is made that only six candidates can participate, then names should be drawn out of a hat and each candidate given an equal chance to be one of the included. This is surely the solution suggested by the Supreme Court in *Rosenberger v. University of Virginia*, where Justice Kennedy stated that: "government cannot justify viewpoint discrimination among private speakers on the economic fact of scarcity" and declared it "incumbent on the State, of course, to ration or allocate the scarce resources on some acceptable neutral principle. . . ."[78]

Of course, if the Democratic and Republican candidates in the Third District wanted to debate without Forbes being present, they had every First Amendment right to arrange an independent private meeting of their own.[79] In such an event, everyone would know that the meeting was sponsored by the two candidates. But as a government actor, AETN had no right to set up and pay for their private debate while excluding Forbes, who met every requirement of candidate seriousness set by Arkansas and had a right to be treated as an equal in the government's forum.

Similarly, I have no quarrel with Vice President Gore and then-Governor George W. Bush devoting their own campaign resources to sponsor an exclusive private debate between the two of them. Everyone would know that the debate was their idea and reflected their strategic interests and bargaining terms. But it is something else altogether for the two parties to concoct an allegedly "non-partisan" corporation called the Commission on Presidential Debates to raise tens of millions of dollars from business corporations and then send the official-sounding message to the American people that their nominees are the only legitimate candidates and all others "unelectable."

Corporate Democracy: What Is to Be Done?

Reformers used to invoke the phrase "corporate democracy" to refer to the movement to give shareholders more control over management of private corporations. Today, it can be said to apply with more force to structural changes in the political economy of our electoral process. Our presidential debates experienced a hostile corporate takeover in the 1980s when the CPD brutally replaced the League of Women Voters, a nonpartisan civic force and the major enduring institutional legacy of the Nineteenth Amendment, which doubled America's political citizenry by granting women suffrage. The nouveau corporate democracy exists at the sufferance of the Federal Election Commission and an indifferent federal judiciary, which cannot find anything wrong with corporate-funded two-party system debates on television airwaves owned by the people.

We need America's much-vaunted but underutilized "civil society" to recapture presidential and other debates from the electoral-industrial complex. The League of Women Voters should return to challenge the CPD's continued "hoodwinking" of the American people. It should be joined by uncorrupted parts of the nonprofit sector, labor unions, and other popular associations. Universities have a special role to play in defending democratic values, since it is at least theoretically easier for academics to remain free of partisan blinders and to stay committed to procedural fairness in politics. We need an independent citizens' debate commission, outside the direct control of the two-party system and major corporations, to structure debates around fair invitation and speech protocols.

What form might fair debates take? In the spring of 2000, the Appleseed Project on Electoral Reform convened a Citizens' Task Force on Fair Debate to study the problem of debate gerrymandering and develop plausible alternatives.[80] The task force recommended that the CPD or a substitute organization extend an invitation to any presidential candidate who is on a sufficient number of state ballots to be able to win 270 votes in the electoral college and who 1) registers at 5 percent in national public opinion preference polls, or 2) registers a majority (50 percent or more) in polls asking eligible voters (not likely voters) which candidates they would like to see included in the debates. This is a sensible standard for debates that take place after the very first one, but the first debate should include all presidential candidates on the ballot in enough states theoretically to win. In each of the last several elections, this group would have included between four and six candidates.

The tricky question of who participates is the most prominent but certainly not the only issue compelling broader analysis than the loyalists of the two-party system can render. Who asks questions? Where should the debates be held? What format? What opportunities for public participation? The issue soon reduces to the logically prior question: Who decides all these things? Right now the CPD has ten commissioners selected for their loyalty to two parties. There are no Independents, no Greens, no Libertarians. At least one-third of the public has no representation. A citizens' debate commission, either set up by Congress under its powers over federal elections or organized independently, could impanel from at large an old-fashioned American grand jury of 23 citizens chosen to deliberate these issues and invite presidential candidates to debate. The jurors could also choose the moderators and questioners, who certainly need not be journalists. Why not union leaders, university presidents, businesspeople, historians, artists? A truly popular and nonpartisan commission could choose the host cities and towns. After all, why should Anheuser-Busch get to dictate the site of our presidential debates?

If there is any hope of derailing continued corporate and bureaucratic stifling of political debate, the American people must demand much more meaningful and free-flowing political dialogue. This, in turn, will require spreading the art and discipline of political debate far more widely, a project being undertaken by the Open Society Institute's important Urban Debate Program, which brings debate leagues and tournaments to inner-city public high schools. Given the proper techniques and training, poor kids from the city have been beating wealthy suburban teams in policy debates. This exciting development suggests a growing national constituency for replacing today's bipartisan sound-bite commercials with a learned and artful political dialogue.

One of the striking aspects of the Lincoln-Douglas debates was the direct spirited interaction between the candidates and also between the audience and the candidates. It is a key sign of our disempowerment today that the people are completely passive spectators in our debates, consumers of a choreographed spectacle that offers us an illusion choice between "competitors" sponsored by the same private corporations, just like those other two great Anheuser-Busch rivals, Budweiser and Bud Light. We are increasingly like the citizens Simon and Garfunkel alluded to in their melancholy 1968 song "Mrs. Robinson": "Sitting on a sofa on a Sunday afternoon/going to the candidates debate./ Laugh about it, shout about it:/ When you've got to choose, Every way you look at it, you lose."

CHAPTER SEVEN

Schooling for Democracy

Education, of course, is not among the rights afforded explicit protection under our Federal Constitution. Nor do we find any basis for saying it is implicitly so protected.

—Justice Louis Powell, *San Antonio Independent School District v. Rodriguez* (1973)

The Democracy of Everyday Life

It is a mistake to think of democracy only as a set of voting institutions. Democracy is a larger *principle* by which we strive to link the people with the power to govern society. It is the real-life *activity* of the people actually taking and using power in everyday life. And it is an historical *process* by which the objects and victims of government become its subjects and authors.

Any large democratic society faces a problem preserving democratic relationships. We can divide up sovereign political power vertically through federalism and horizontally through the three branches of government. Yet, to accomplish collectively chosen purposes, society must operate through "intermediate" institutions: schools, workplaces, business corporations, the military, shopping malls, prisons and so on. These institutions further decentralize power and keep the state from becoming totalitarian, but they can also threaten to become microtyrannies by trampling democratic liberty in their own internal operation. Michel Foucault showed us that in the hidden channels of the body politic, in these dense institutional transfer points of hierarchy and dominance, power can be turned cruelly against the bodies and minds of citizens.

Conservative theorists assert that, to fulfill their functions properly, the institutions of civil society must exist outside of the force-field of constitutional democracy. In the conservative image, democracy is not the continuing historical project of uniting people with power but only the periodic practice of conducting elections to select government leaders. What goes on underneath in society's everyday institutions is deemed an internal affair not connected to larger political values or struggles. This meager vision is sometimes candidly called "elite democracy." As spelled out by Joseph Schumpeter and most recently by Judge Richard Posner, democracy simply means rival groups of political elites competing for the public support they need on election day to capture public office and administer the macroframework of government over a society of philistines. What goes on in the institutional subculture of society is left to the will of relevant "authorities" and "traditions."

This hollowed-out vision is an affront to the project of progressive democracy, a dynamic ethos against which we must judge the character of all of society's institutional practices. Undemocratic institutional structures are justified only if, and only to the extent that they are truly necessary to accomplish democratic social purposes. We may have to run a prison like a prison, for example, but we do not have to run a school like a prison. We may have to run the army like an army, but we do not have to run the rest of society like an army. The abstract explanations for school censorship of student speech ("reasonable pedagogical objectives"), the nearly unbridled power of corporate officers to enrich themselves and control social resources ("market freedom"), the official stifling of new political ideas and candidates ("the two-party system"), and executive secrecy and lack of consultation with Congress in foreign policy ("national security interests"), to choose some important examples, look a lot like the Emperor's New Clothes to progressive democrats. It is the historical assignment of progressives to speak democratic truth to hierarchical power and unveil the human meaning behind political and technocratic ideologies.

In American life, the indispensable democratic institution is the old-fashioned local American public school. Our schools are not representative institutions; they are what we might call *presentative* institutions. Whoever shows up on the first day—even children of undocumented aliens[1]—is invited to join in the process of education, which the Warren Court recognized as the most important public function of our local governments.[2]

Ideally, schools have democratic purposes that cross the horizons of past, present and future. Looking ahead, they seek to educate children for effective citizenship, competent adulthood and a broad, tolerant humanity to last a lifetime in a diverse society. Looking backward, schools mean to instill in children an appreciation for our nation's past, the political, cultural, social and economic roots of our common life. In the present tense, schools both teach and embody democracy by creating a working and coherent community of teachers, students, administrators and parents. This was the point insisted upon by pragmatist John Dewey, who wrote in his magnificent book *Democracy and Education* that "the school becomes a form of social life, a miniature community. . . ."[3]

This minicommunity becomes an excellent barometer of the health of democracy. Over the last several years in Washington, D.C., and Maryland, I have gotten to know a bit of the character of American public education through my work with the Marshall-Brennan Fellows, a group of sixty upper-level law students who teach a "constitutional literacy" course four or five days a week in twenty urban and suburban public high schools each year. My colleague, Steve Wermiel, and I lead the fellows in a weekly seminar and make visits to the schools where they teach. As a group, we discuss the progress of the fellows' classes, their teaching problems and breakthroughs, bureaucratic obstacles they face, and the coaching of their students as we prepare the high schoolers to participate in our moot court, essay, creative arts and poetry competitions.

The enthusiasm and creativity of young people are always inspiring, and we have been awed by the ability of young people to grasp constitutional language and play with constitutional ideas. But the strong impression we receive is that American public schools have little or no consciousness of being part of a coherent democratic project. Although they have turned the modern Civil Rights movement into a kind of distant holy shrine, the schools remain riven by the unspoken and unanalyzed contemporary injuries of race, class, geography and money. Many (though certainly not all) schools in poor and predominantly African-American and Hispanic communities are training students for a lifetime of intellectual boredom and emotional indifference; bureaucratic rudeness, drudgery and meanness in the workplace; and second-class expectations. Many schools (though not all) in wealthier and more-white areas focus on testing, test preparation and zero-sum-game competition. Everyone is caught up in "teaching to the test," cycles of misbehavior and discipline, and urgent demands for "zero tolerance" policies, which turn out to be very blunt and illiberal instruments indeed.

The problems of the public schools undoubtedly are owed to many different sources. We have seen the exhaustion and resignation of underpaid teachers. We have learned of the terrible effects students suffer from broken homes, dysfunctional families, sexual abuse, bad diets, television

mind-poisoning, undiagnosed learning disabilities and the lack of structured hope. At school, we witness constant bureaucratic interruptions of
class time with silly assemblies, fire drills, stupid announcements, home-
coming pep rallies, and unexpected teacher absences. We see curricula
completely adrift and useless. And we see in some schools an obsessive
fixation on high-stakes testing, ruthless competition and social hierarchy.
There is no shortage of commission reports describing different aspects of
these educational problems. There are bookshelves bursting with them.

But at the broadest national level, the place where large social meanings and purposes are inscribed for all Americans to see, the Supreme Court
has repeatedly failed to articulate a working democratic ethos for our public schools. This failure parallels its refusal or inability to articulate a working
democratic ethos for our political process. But while almost everyone is
blamed for the problems of the schools—parents, students, teachers—no
one connects the school system's chronic problems with the Supreme
Court's double failure to defend either liberty or equality in the schools.
Rather than setting a pattern of great expectations for our common schools,
the Court has consistently undermined the democratic project in public
education.

As with the right to vote, things could have turned out differently on the
Court with respect to schooling. The Warren Court spelled out a democratic
educational project in two stirring decisions: *Brown v. Board of Education*,[4] which tried to confront, however imperfectly, the damage wrought
by racism and to proclaim the idea of equality in education, and *Tinker v.
Des Moines School District*,[5] which coherently reconciled the play of liberty and democracy in schools and public institutions generally.

Instead of building on these landmark decisions, the Rehnquist Court
(and its predecessor, the Burger Court) has ripped them to shreds and left
them twisting in the wind as fading memories of what might have been.
They have been replaced by decisions that motivate white flight to the suburbs, uphold unequal funding of schools based on property taxation, and
indulge bureaucratic control over thoughtful student expression. The Court
has thus squandered the promise of education for democracy and left us
with the fractured, crisis-prone educational landscape we inhabit today.

Just as we need to recapture the lost democratic momentum of our political life from a Court that has decreed that we have no right to vote, we
must recapture the lost democratic momentum of American public education from a Court that has decreed that young people have no right to
education. We need to turn once again to the Constitution and put it in

writing: a constitutional amendment establishing a right to receive and participate in a public education for democratic citizenship.

West Virginia v. Barnette, Tinker v. Des Moines School District and the Right to Think for Yourself in School

Like other public institutions in democracy, schools should be structured to allow their participants—students and teachers—to express themselves freely. This is a foundational democratic right that should be bounded only by the school's obligation to educate. A student may not engage in an hour-long filibuster on the evils of school vouchers during algebra class nor may students express themselves by ridiculing and harassing other students trying to learn. But when student expression is not actually disruptive, but just challenging or uncomfortable, it may not be censored. The social project of public education must itself be defined in a way that incorporates, rather than excludes, the First Amendment value of open dialogue and debate. This was the incipient meaning of the Supreme Court's seminal 1943 ruling in *West Virginia v. Barnette*[6] and its triumphant and visionary decision in 1969 in *Tinker v. Des Moines School District.*[7]

In the *Barnette* case, the Court struck down a compulsory flag salute and Pledge of Allegiance ritual that the West Virginia Board of Education had adopted for students and teachers as part of its general civics curriculum. The plaintiffs were Jehovah's Witnesses who objected on religious grounds to being forced to participate in the Pledge.

Justice Robert Jackson's magnificent opinion defined the anti-authoritarian premises of American democracy with more clarity and vigor than any other Supreme Court Justice had ever before. Taken seriously, his words make the First Amendment the guardian of the possibility of a perpetual revolution in social consciousness:

> There is no mysticism in the American concept of the State or of the nature or origin of its authority. We set up government by consent of the governed, and the Bill of Rights denies those in power any legal opportunity to coerce that consent. Authority here is to be controlled by public opinion, not public opinion by authority.[8]

Justice Jackson then laid down a kind of secular anti-establishment principle, the citizenry's right to be sovereign over its own consciousness. This idea is the soul of progressive democracy:

If there is any fixed star in our constitutional constellation, it is that no
official, high or petty, can prescribe what shall be orthodox in politics, nationalism, religion, or other matters of opinion or force citizens to confess by
word or act their faith therein. If there are any circumstances which permit
an exception they do not now occur to us.[9]

In democracy, the highest office in the land is that of citizen. No one tells
a citizen what to think or what to say.

In hindsight, and in comparison to what was to come in *Tinker*, *Barnette* seems like an easy case. The Jehovah's Witness students were playing
defense against a school system threatening to expel them and even have
them sent to a reform school for refusing to say the Pledge. But in *Tinker*,
the Supreme Court considered the suspension of thirteen-year old junior
high school student Mary Beth Tinker, a Quaker and precocious activist
who wore a black armband to school on December 16, 1965, to protest
the Vietnam War in defiance of her principal's order.[10] From the school
system's perspective, what was at stake was the principal's duty and ability
to maintain good order and discipline.

But Justice Abe Fortas found for the majority that Mary Beth's "symbolic act" was "closely akin to 'pure speech'" and thus deserving of First
Amendment protection.[11] "It can hardly be argued," he wrote, "that either
students or teachers shed their constitutional rights to freedom of speech
or expression at the schoolhouse gate."[12] Democracy pours over the walls
of the schoolhouse. By linking the speech rights of students and teachers, Justice Fortas established that students and teachers form part of a
single educational community rather than opposite ends of a bureaucratic
hierarchy.[13]

The challenge for the Court was to determine at what point a school
can forbid student speech that it sees as opposed to its educational mission.
The Court found that a school could not censor speech simply because of
a "mere desire to avoid the discomfort and unpleasantness that always
accompany an unpopular viewpoint."[14] Rather, a school must be able to
show that the student's speech will "materially and substantially interfere
with the requirements of appropriate discipline in the operation of the
school," which means "material[] disrupt[ion] of classwork, substantial disorder or invasion of the rights of others. . . ."[15]

Of course, a school might claim—as Mary Beth Tinker's did—that a
student's expressed opposition to the nation's war will be "disruptive."
But Justice Fortas held that government may not define disruption in an

infinitely elastic way, nor may it define education in a way that forecloses expression of dissent:

> In our system, state-operated schools may not be enclaves of totalitarianism. School officials do not posses absolute authority over their students. Students in school as well as out of school are "persons" under our Constitution. They are possessed of fundamental rights which the state must respect, just as they themselves must respect their obligations to the State. In our system, students may not be regarded as close-circuited recipients of only that which the state chooses to communicate. They may not be confined to the expression of views that are officially approved.[16]

Thus, a school must have a compelling interest—what one of my students, Marshall-Brennan Fellow David Mikhail, called a "damn good reason"— for shutting up a student. The "undifferentiated fear or apprehension of disturbance" will never be "enough to overcome the right to freedom of expression."[17]

Now, it might be asked why Justice Fortas's approach should be considered a democratic one. After all, the principal overruled by the Court was appointed by a superintendent who was appointed by an elected school board. From this vantage point, adopted by Justice Frankfurter in his rather cloying dissent, anything an elected body or official does is, by definition, democratic.

But surely this cannot be right.

Democracy must be read to include centrally the right of the people to freedom of consciousness and freedom of expression; these freedoms are not in tension with democracy but essentially constitutive of it. Expressive freedom is a fundamental constitutional purpose that may sometimes conflict with present-day institutional purposes, but Justice Fortas gave us the right way to think about that conflict. If democracy means that whoever holds state power can act however he or she wants, then what we have is not democracy but a continuing succession of elective tyrannies. The Court should allow expressive freedoms to be pushed aside only if our institutions, which are themselves the product of constitutional powers, will actually be thwarted in their work. Otherwise, there is nothing undemocratic about denying a principal or an elected school board the authority to censor the nondisruptive speech of a student. That student is a citizen under the Constitution, armed with democratic rights of speech and expression.

Justice Fortas's defense of liberty at school implies a democratic theory of education. Mary Beth Tinker is not to be the "close-circuited" recipient of information drilled into her mind by the school board but rather an active participant in her own education and that of her peers. Education is not something the school system does to the student. It is what takes place when the community forms and investigates how the world should be understood. Each student has something unique and precious to offer this inquiry. Thus, as Justice Fortas stated, the principle of free expression "is not confined to the supervised and ordained discussion which takes place in the classroom," but rather spills over to the whole school day, including athletic, extracurricular, and informal events:

> The principal use to which the schools are dedicated is to accommodate students during prescribed hours for the purposes of certain types of activities. Among these activities is personal intercomunication among the students. This is not only an inevitable part of the process of attending school; it is also an important part of the educational process.[18]

Justice Fortas's emphasis on mutual education registers a powerful echo of John Dewey's democratic pragmatism. The essence of true education, Dewey observed in 1916, was a student's "vital energy seeking opportunity for effective exercise."[19] He insisted that students learn from both the "formal" curriculum and the "informal" education generated in the interstices of the school days, where bureaucracy, banter, jokes, laughter, gossip, social interactions and discussion of current events acquaint the student with the world.

The spirited political imagination and conviction displayed by Mary Beth Tinker evoke the true spirit of education. A good teacher would have picked up on Mary Beth's armband to teach about everything from war powers to the First Amendment to post–World War II American foreign policy. There is no reason to fear blurring the boundaries between school and the outside world, because "learning in school should be continuous with that out of school."[20] Rather than punishing Mary Beth's independence of mind, the school should have welcomed it. Dewey wrote: "A progressive society counts individual variations as precious since it finds in them the means of its own growth."[21] The important thing is obviously not that all students agree or even that all feel comfortable in every context but rather that all feel empowered to think, act and speak for themselves: "all education which develops effectively the power to share in social life is moral."[22] Mary Beth's principal and teachers had no sense of *democratic improvisation* in the learning process.

The *Tinker* principle was not only the zenith of the Supreme Court's defense of civil liberty at school but its finest articulation of how to think about the place of democratic free expression in self-contained social institutions. In following decades, the Court's commitment to the *Tinker* principle unraveled, leaving student rights to expressive liberty vulnerable and the underlying principle of democratic freedom in our social institutions in peril.

The problems began in the Burger Court, which was friendly to local authority and unfriendly to the rights of the young. In 1986, a young man named Matthew Fraser, a popular student and known class "cutup" from Bethel High School in Pierce County, Washington, gave a nominating speech for a fellow student running for student government.[23] The theme of Fraser's unfortunate speech was a protracted and sophomoric sexual metaphor:

> I know a man who is firm—he's firm in his pants, he's firm in his shirt, his character is firm—but most ... of all, his belief in you, the students of Bethel, is firm ... Jeff Kuhlman is a man who takes his point and pounds it in. If necessary, he'll take an issue and nail it to the wall. He doesn't attack things in spurts—he drives hard, pushing and pushing until finally—he succeeds. . . .[24]

Fraser's apparent conceit was that he could get away with this silly macho innuendo because the speech contained no profanity. But the school reacted strongly nonetheless, citing its *Tinker*-like disciplinary rule that banned conduct "which materially and substantially interferes with the educational process," including "the use of obscene, profane language or gestures."[25] After five teachers wrote letters of complaint, Fraser was suspended for three days (he served two) and had his name removed from the list of potential graduation speakers.[26] Fraser went to federal court alleging violation of his First Amendment rights, and won damages against the school. Amazingly, he gave the student graduating address after winning this honor as a write-in candidate.[27] In his apparently clean commencement speech, he reflected on what he had learned about the balance of democratic rights and responsibilities.

Writing for an eight-person majority in *Bethel v. Fraser*, Chief Justice Burger reversed the lower court's decision and upheld Fraser's discipline as a reasonable exercise of the school's power to teach students the "boundaries of socially appropriate behavior."[28] The school district was "entirely within its permissible authority in imposing sanctions upon Fraser in response to his offensively lewd and indecent speech."[29] Justice Thurgood Marshall dissented, arguing that under the *Tinker* standard it had not been shown that Fraser's remarks were disruptive.[30] Justice Marshall showed true wisdom here. Fraser's show-offy bawdiness has long antecedents in Western literature and oratory, and educators should help students grow out of their immature ways, not punish them. But in his concurring opinion, Justice Brennan argued that there was no reason to carve out a separate juridical category for unprotected "lewd and indecent speech" since Fraser's speech had, within the meaning of *Tinker*, substantially disrupted the school's pedagogical mission to teach mature public advocacy.[31]

While Fraser's loss could be cordoned off as a discrete "lewdness" exception to the *Tinker* principle, the Rehnquist Court's 1988 decision in *Hazelwood School District v. Kuhlmeier* inflicted heavy frontal damage.[32] In *Hazelwood*, Principal Robert Reynolds censored two articles from *Spectrum*, the school newspaper written by students in the Journalism II class.[33] One article concerned the impact of parental divorce on students at the school, and the other was about the problem of teen pregnancy as seen through the experiences of three students.[34] The principal thought that the discussions of sex and birth control in the latter story were "inappropriate for some of the younger students" and that the former story was unbalanced.[35] Under *Tinker*, of course, these articles were pure protected speech, not disruptive of education, and also not lewd or indecent within the meaning of *Fraser*. The students were writing in a mature and thoughtful way about serious problems affecting their generation. But, like Mary Beth Tinker's principal, the principal at Hazelwood East simply thought that talk of these topics was too hot and might invite controversy. A Court serious about freedom would have rejected this censorship in an instant.

But the Rehnquist Court reads the Constitution through the prism of authority and tradition rather than democratic freedom. The Court found that while *Tinker* might govern the voluntary independent speech of students, far more latitude must be granted to the "educators' authority over school-sponsored publications, theatrical productions, and other expressive activities that students, parents, and members of the public might reasonably perceive to bear the imprimatur of the school."[36] Since the *Spectrum* newspaper was school-sponsored and implicated the name of the school, the principal could censor it for any reasonable educational purpose that was viewpoint-neutral. According to Justice White, educators can exercise "editorial control over the style and content of student speech in school-sponsored expressive activities as long as their actions are reasonably related to legitimate pedagogical concerns."[37] The Court promptly found Principal Reynolds's censorship reasonable and justified.

Dissenting Justices Brennan, Marshall and Blackmun held up the bedraggled banner of the Court's *Tinker* decision.[38] They began by noting that the school's journalism class had committed to publishing all articles that do not "materially and substantially interfere with the requirements of appropriate discipline." (It is indeed interesting to note how many schools after *Tinker* quickly embraced its intuitive free-speech formulation.) But the dissenters' main point was that mere political disagreement between students and administration should never be sufficient constitutional grounds for censoring a student's message.[39] Public schools must embrace intellectual diversity and political debate as an integral part of their mission, rather than suppress and sideline them.

Of course, educators can require students to learn the information and techniques being taught in a course, but this truism is "the essence of the *Tinker* test, not an excuse to abandon it."[40] The dissenters agreed that Hazelwood East would not have to publish student articles that are "ungrammatical, poorly written, inadequately researched, biased or prejudiced," but stated that "we need not abandon *Tinker* to reach that conclusion, we need only apply it."[41] There is nothing wrong with teaching grammar, syntax, spelling and the like and grading (partially) on these bases, but school officials cannot act as political or sexual " 'thought police' stifling discussion of all but state-approved topics and advocacy of all but the official position."[42] If the school did not like the articles about teen pregnancy and the impact of divorce, it had every right to publish an institutional answer or disclaimer in the newspaper.

Hazelwood has led to stepped-up censorship and control of school newspapers, yearbooks, magazines and theatrical productions.[43] Administrators now view themselves like private property owners who get to control who says what and when on school grounds. This judicial unleashing of censorship in the schools revives an old property-based notion of public property. Before landmark "public forum" cases in the 1930s, such as *Schneider v. Irvington* and *Hague v. CIO*, declared that people must have free access to streets, sidewalks and parks to engage in speech and protest, the Massachusetts Supreme Judicial Court in *Commonwealth v. Davis* had ruled that the officers of a municipal corporation, such as Boston, could exclude speech they disfavored from public areas, such as the Boston Common.[44] Mayors were treated like owners and bosses. Under *Hazelwood*, principals enjoy some of that unbridled power. Technically, they cannot discriminate against speech based on political viewpoint, but they enjoy very wide sway to regulate the flow of ideas and words.

If the *Tinker* principle has lost some of its definitiveness, Mary Beth Tinker herself has not. Today Mary Beth is a union organizer for the Service Employees International Union and an eloquent champion for human rights, including the rights of students at school. She does not separate the struggle for student liberties within the school from the struggle for integration, equal spending and academic excellence for all students. Addressing the Marshall-Brennan Fellows Awards Ceremony at American University in April 2001, she told a crowd of hundreds of high school students and law students: "In my mind, the patriotic thing to do is to try to make this a country where people have the right to speak up, people are treated equally and fairly, where everyone has good schools and the things that are important to a good life on this earth. I want you students to feel very powerful and strong. I want you to feel you can go out there and make the kind of changes we need so badly in this country and in the world. You deserve to be part of a strong, vibrant democracy." The magnificent spirit of the *Tinker* decision lives in Mary Beth Tinker, even if no longer on a democracy-impaired Supreme Court. It is up to the students of America to recapture her vision.

The Lost Promise of Integration and Equality:
Plessy, *Brown*, and Beyond

For 86 years, between July 9, 1868, when the Fourteenth Amendment was ratified, and May 17, 1954, when *Brown v. Board of Education* was decided, the Supreme Court interpreted the Fourteenth Amendment's promise of Equal Protection to be perfectly consistent with the practice of Jim Crow racial apartheid in public schools. For the past 48 years, it has taken the formal position that "in the field of public education the doctrine of 'separate but equal' has no place."[45]

But the belated recognition that segregation of schoolchildren is incompatible with Equal Protection has been systematically undermined by more recent Court decisions that have pulled the plug on effective desegregation efforts and upheld the traditional financing of public schools on the basis of local property taxes. The Court has abandoned the national commitment to excellent integrated education. It has decided instead that education is not a fundamental constitutional right but, like the vote, a state-granted privilege. The tenuous claim to education is subject to white flight, local political whim and the injustices and cruelties of wealth inequality.

Constitutionalizing Custom: *Plessy v. Ferguson*

The Court's post–Civil War indifference to official race segregation was formalized in 1896 in *Plessy v. Ferguson*, which upheld a Louisiana statute that required "equal but separate accommodations for the white and colored races" on railway train cars.[46] The plaintiff, Homer Plessy, who was "seven-eighths Caucasian and one-eighth African blood," challenged the statute on Fourteenth Amendment grounds, alleging that "he was entitled to every right [of] the white race."[47]

Writing for the majority, Justice Henry Billings Brown rejected Homer Plessy's argument, stating that while the "object" of Equal Protection "was undoubtedly to enforce the absolute equality of the two races before the law," nonetheless "in the nature of things, it could not have been intended to abolish distinctions based upon color, or to enforce social, as distinguished from political, equality."[48] Answering the argument that if a state can segregate people based on race or skin color, it could do the same with respect to hair or eye color, national origin or alienage, and could even make people of different races paint their houses different colors or wear different clothing, Justice Brown stated that "every exercise of the police power must be reasonable, and extend only to such laws as are enacted in good faith for the promotion of the public good, and not for the annoyance or oppression of a particular class."[49] An affluent New Englander who went to Yale College and Harvard Law School, Justice Brown simply did not view apartheid on the trains in Louisiana as oppressive to black citizens.

How did Justice Brown and the Court formally determine what was "reasonable" under the Fourteenth Amendment? The answer is crucial, because it not only decided the fate of public education for the next sixty years but set the standard terms for conservative arguments on the Court against robust enforcement of civil rights. "In determining the question of reasonableness," Justice Brown wrote, "[the state] is at liberty to act with reference to *the established usages, customs, and traditions of the people*, and with a view to the promotion of their comfort, and the preservation of the public peace and good order."[50] He then noted that: "Gauged by this standard, we cannot say that a law which authorizes or even requires the separation of the two races in public conveyances is unreasonable, or more obnoxious to the Fourteenth Amendment than the acts of Congress requiring separate schools for colored children in the District of Columbia, the constitutionality of which does not seem to have been questioned, or the corresponding acts of state legislatures."[51]

A challenge to a segregationist Southern state law on the grounds that it violated Equal Protection was thus refused by the Court on the grounds that the law reasonably codified the customs and traditions of white people. But surely this is the wrong test, since the whole purpose of Equal Protection was to overthrow repressive local traditions and majority customs that no longer fit our collective constitutional sense of the rights of the people. Indeed, the whole purpose of our democratic-rights Constitution is to replace undemocratic institutions and illiberal practices with the constitutional politics of democratic freedom.

Justice Brown finished his opinion with a series of makeweight arguments that are equally essential for understanding the deep rhetorical structures of racism that have infused our history.[52] The "underlying fallacy" of Plessy's argument, Justice Brown observed, was "the assumption that the enforced separation of the two races stamps the colored race with a badge of inferiority. If this be so, it is not by reason of anything found in the act, but solely because the colored race chooses to put that construction upon it. . . ."[53] In other words, racism is a psychological construct by the victims, not the perpetrators: it's all in their heads, so just get over it. "If the two races are to meet upon terms of social equality, it must be the result of natural affinities, a mutual appreciation of each other's merits, and a voluntary consent of individuals. . . ."[54] In other words, the law cannot change human nature and racial feelings are natural; let's wait and see how things evolve without using law to try to change nature. "Legislation is powerless to eradicate racial instincts, or to abolish distinctions based upon physical differences, and the attempt to do so can only result in accentuating the difficulties of the present situation."[55] Progressive attempts to integrate and create one society will just make matters worse by aggravating racism. "If the civil and political rights of both races be equal, one cannot be inferior to the other civilly or politically. If one race be inferior to the other socially, the constitution of the United States cannot put them upon the same plane."[56] Our racial conditions reflect human nature and there is nothing that our Constitution can do to serve black citizens. This trope just barely updates the Court's statement in the *Dred Scott* case that "[the black man] had no rights which the white man" is "bound to respect."[57] Blacks are part of the Constitution, Justice Brown was saying, but there is still essentially nothing in it for them.

Justice Harlan, of course, did much better in his dissent, which introduced the juridical idea of color blindness, but even this doctrine of formal equality was permeated with assumptions of white supremacy that we are still struggling to overcome today. Justice Harlan described the white race as "the dominant race" and predicted "it will continue to be for all time, if it remains true to its great heritage, and holds fair to the principles of constitutional liberty."[58]

Although Justice Harlan's anticaste rhetoric introduced a progressive counterprinciple, against the unabashed racism of his colleagues, his sterile image of "color blindness" prefigured the racial formalism of modern conservatives who well understand the perfect compatibility of juridical color blindness with the social reality of white supremacy.

Integrated Learning: *Brown v. Board of Education*

The path to *Brown v. Board of Education* was blazed by the creative and methodical litigation strategies of Charles Hamilton Houston, Thurgood Marshall and the NAACP, and the political struggles of black Americans all over the country.[59] The decision did not spring spontaneously from the mind of the Supreme Court. The movement to dismantle Jim Crow laws was a long-running social project. When *Brown* was decided, the Court's unanimous decision invalidating segregated schools in Kansas, South Carolina, Virginia and Delaware produced a watershed effect on public consciousness, but the Court's opinion left something to be desired and actually contained within it the seeds of its own progressive erosion over time.[60]

Chief Justice Warren's opinion in *Brown* is just a few pages long and written in plain, nonincendiary terms. The crux of the opinion is that segregation causes psychological and educational problems for black students: "To separate them from others of similar age and qualifications solely because of their race generates a feeling of inferiority as to their status in the community that may affect their hearts and minds in a way unlikely ever to be undone."[61] He quoted a Kansas decision on the same theme:

" 'A sense of inferiority affects the motivation of a child to learn. Segregation with the sanction of law, therefore, has a tendency to [retard] the educational and mental development of Negro children and to deprive them of some of the benefits they would receive in a racial[ly] integrated school system.' "[62]

This is fine and coherent as far as it goes. But the Warren opinion leaves at least three dimensions of the Equal Protection violation unarticulated. The first point is that, leaving aside its effects on African-American children, racial segregation of the schools must be unconstitutional because the whole purpose of segregating schools is to keep African-Americans subordinate, unfree and unequal. As later decisions have found, the linchpin of Equal Protection analysis is the so-called "purpose requirement,"[63] and here it is clear (if unstated by Chief Justice Warren) that the purpose of dividing black and white children in school is to perpetuate over time the system of educational, economic, social, political and legal white supremacy.

The second point is that, while the negative effects of segregation are indeed relevant and important, since purposes and effects are always connected, the Court never considered the effects of segregation on white children. If it had, Chief Justice Warren might have written something like this instead:

> To separate white and black children from others of similar age and qualifications solely because of their race generates a feeling of inferiority in the black children *and a feeling of false superiority in the white children* that may affect their hearts and minds in a way unlikely ever to be undone. *Both groups of children have a right to grow up without the psychological deformities caused by racism and to enjoy the rich and diverse experiences offered by growing up with children of all backgrounds.*

According to this approach, we would understand that desegregation is not a favor rendered to black students but rather a democratic imperative for *all* children of *all* backgrounds, who face profound educational obstacles and neurotic distortions because of the mythologies and irrationalities propounded by racism. The informal educational lesson offered to white students in all-white schools is that they exist apart from other children and do not share with them a collective destiny. This is madness. In the Marshall-Brennan program, we also often hear Hispanic and Asian-American students taking exception not only to the white racial assumptions of *Brown*, but also the Court's binary racial dichotomy which makes vanish centuries of life under white supremacy experienced by Mexican Americans, Chinese Americans and Japanese Americans, to name a few minority groups not mentioned in *Brown*.

The final missing point in Chief Justice Warren's analysis is that if the experience of segregation demoralizes children and retards their educational growth, it should make little difference whether the segregation is engineered by the state (*de jure* segregation) or the mere accidental result of purely voluntary decisions (*de facto* segregation). After all, the difference between the two surely escapes most elementary schoolchildren. But *Brown* is limited to *de jure* discrimination. In the past few decades, many school districts have been declared "unitary," free of the taint of original legalized segregation, and therefore desegregated by law even if not in fact. What this means is that these school districts need no longer worry about judicial desegregation orders because there is no continuing obligation to integrate. In many parts of America, there are 100-percent-white suburban schools and 100-percent-black or minority schools, and they are all perfectly lawful because the segregation is not commanded by the state. But why should it make any difference, if we are concerned about the injuries to children? We should view an integrated education as a matter of essential distributive justice for everyone and not as a punitive remedy for past discrimination.

This question is more than a bit academic since even the Court's lowkey effort to take on *de jure* segregation provoked a furious reaction among Southern whites. With the Confederate battle flag flying across the Deep South, elected officials from school boards to statehouses denounced *Brown* and the Warren Court and vowed "massive resistance" to desegregation. The governor of Georgia, Herman Talmadge, proclaimed in 1954 that "[b]lood will flow in the rivers" and Alabama Governor George Wallace stood in the schoolhouse door. In 1958, in *Cooper v. Aaron*, a unanimous Court shut down the Little Rock, Arkansas School Board's procrastinating suspension of desegregation, invoking the Supremacy Clause and finding that the "constitutional rights of [the children] are not to be sacrificed or yielded to the violence and disorder which have followed upon the actions of the Governor and Legislature."[64] These Southern politicians were not constitutional patriots but racist enemies of American democracy. Their opposition to *Brown* prefigured the massive white flight to the suburbs that would leave the promise of desegregation an empty shell without further strong action by the courts.

Justice Collapsing: *Milliken, Rodriguez, Freeman,* and *Jenkins*

By the 1970s, a profound desegregation fatigue had set in on the Burger
Court, reflecting the nation's exhaustion with the race issue. The Court was
in no mood to test further the patience of whites. One stunning decision
that rolled all over an already battered *Brown* was the 1974 "white flight"
holding in *Milliken v. Bradley*.[65] In *Milliken,* the federal district court found
that actions and policies of the Michigan legislature, the Michigan State
Board of Education and the Detroit Board of Education combined to
create massive *de jure* segregation in the city of Detroit.[66] Stating that a
Detroit-only plan would fail, the district court ordered a comprehensive
regional desegregation plan that involved more than fifty nearby suburban school districts as well as the city.[67]

Chief Justice Burger overturned this relief, holding that a "multidistrict
remedy" was unacceptable in a case like this since the neighboring districts
were not at fault for segregation in Detroit and the "boundary lines" of the
suburban school districts were not necessarily drawn for racist ends.[68] Thus,
desegregation orders must presumptively be limited to individual municipal districts themselves, a ruling that treats integration like a form of local
punishment and gives aggressive judicial impetus and imprimatur to the
processes of white flight, which are taken to be natural and unavoidable.

Justice White, joined in dissent by Justices Douglas, Brennan and Marshall, pronounced himself "mystified how the Court can ignore the legal
reality that the constitutional violations, even if occurring locally, were
committed by governmental entities for which the State is responsible
and that it is the State that must respond to the command of the Fourteenth Amendment."[69] Justice Marshall, also dissenting and joined by the
same group, stated that "the Court's answer" to segregation in Detroit "is
to provide no remedy at all [thus] guaranteeing that Negro children in
Detroit will receive the same separate and inherently unequal education
in the future as they have been unconstitutionally afforded in the past."[70]
Significantly, he did not see the dynamics of white flight as unrelated to
prior governmental decision-making. "[Having] created a system where
whites and Negroes were intentionally kept apart so that they could not
become accustomed to learning together, the State is responsible for the
fact that many whites will react to the dismantling of that segregated system by attempting to flee to the suburbs."[71]

This judicial validation of racial segregation across municipal boundary lines reinforced the Court's profoundly undemocratic 1973 decision in

San Antonio Independent School District v. Rodriguez, which found that states have no obligation to spend equal amounts of money per capita for students across county, municipal or school district lines.[72] In *Rodriguez*, Mexican-American parents with children in the Edgewood Independent School District, a poor urban school district in San Antonio, challenged as violative of Equal Protection a school funding system based to a large extent on property taxes.[73] The plaintiff school district, which was 90 percent Mexican-American and 6 percent black, ended up with a total of $356 spent per pupil each year.[74] By contrast, the most affluent school district in the San Antonio area, Alamo Heights, which was 81 percent white, spent $594 per pupil, nearly double the amount.[75] Yet Edgewood, the poorer district, actually taxed itself harder, at an equalized tax rate of $1.05 per $100 of assessed property, than Alamo Heights, which had an equalized tax rate of $.85 per $100.[76] But because of property values, the poorer district ended up with much less money for its children. If it kept raising taxes even higher, it would just drive more people away, worsening the dynamics. State law, in any event, limited how high it could go, making it literally impossible to catch up. The Rodriguez family believed that the state of Texas could not discriminate against children living in poorer neighborhoods in this way.[77]

The *Rodriguez* majority did not impose "strict scrutiny"[78] on the property-tax based system of school funding that produced these humiliating inequalities. It rejected the claim that poorer citizens harmed by this system were in fact members of a class being disadvantaged on the basis of wealth. Justice Powell emphasized that wealth was no suspect classification and that in those few cases where wealth was the basis for subjecting government action to strict scrutiny—poll taxes for voting, for example—poorer citizens had been *absolutely* deprived of the government benefit.[79] Things were different here, according to Justice Powell, because the argument "is not that the children [are] receiving no public education; rather, it is that they are receiving a poorer quality education [than] children in districts having more assessable wealth."[80] Poor children have no grounds to complain because they do receive some kind of education, even if not an equal one.

Furthermore, the plaintiffs' attempt to invoke strict scrutiny by asserting that education is a fundamental right also failed. Justice Powell wrote: "Education, of course, is not among the rights afforded explicit protection under our Federal Constitution. Nor do we find any basis for saying it is implicitly so protected."[81] Justice Powell was not moved by the plaintiffs' argument that education must be "a fundamental personal right because it is essential to the effective exercise of First Amendment freedoms and to intelligent utilization of the right to vote" and "the right to speak is meaningless unless the speaker is capable of articulating his thoughts intelligently and persuasively."[82]

Justice Powell did not exactly contradict these powerful claims about the relationship of education to democracy, but he demoted them far below the values of federalism and deference to state power:

> We need not dispute any of these propositions. [Yet] we have never presumed to possess either the ability or the authority to guarantee to the citizenry the most effective speech or the most informed electoral choice. That these may be desirable goals [is] not to be doubted. [But] they are not values to be implemented by judicial intrusion into otherwise legitimate state activities.[83]

The dissenting justices perceived the willingness of the majority to consign millions of poorer children to second-class educations and second-class citizenship.[84] Although he did not need to reach the issue because he saw no "rational basis" for the Texas system at all, Justice Brennan would have imposed strict scrutiny on the regime because "education is inextricably linked to the right to participate in the electoral process and to the rights of free speech and association guaranteed by the First Amendment."[85]

Justice Marshall assailed the majority's "retreat from our historic commitment to equality of educational opportunity" and "unsupportable acquiescence in a system which deprives children in their earliest years of the chance to reach their full potential as citizens."[86] He also emphasized the relationship between education and democracy: "Education directly affects the ability of a child to exercise his First Amendment interests both as a source and as a receiver of information and [ideas]. Indeed, it has frequently been suggested that education is the dominant factor affecting political consciousness and participation."[87]

The one-two punch of *Milliken* and *Rodriguez* knocked the wind out of *Brown*. The Court's toleration of racial and economic segregation across municipal and suburban boundary lines has helped to produce a broken educational landscape. As we begin a new century, "the American South is resegregating, after two and a half decades in which civil rights law broke the tradition of apartheid in the region's schools." As a general proposition, the country is turning more diverse than ever but "whites are remaining in overwhelmingly white schools even in regions with very large non-white enrollments."[88]

Yet, the current Court is running as fast as it can away from the project of *Brown*. In *Freeman v. Pitts*,[89] the Rehnquist Court, obviously trying to shed its irksome desegregation docket, found that federal district courts could partially withdraw jurisdiction over "discrete categories" of issues—such as student population, transportation, facilities—in live desegregation cases. As the original legal violation fades and schools become "unitary" in character, the courts can check out, even if some parts of the schools, such as "teacher and principal assignments, resource allocation and quality of education," continue to bear the marks of *de jure* segregation.[90] Justice Kennedy stressed that "returning schools to the control of local authorities at the earliest practicable date is essential to restore their true accountability in our government system."[91]

Here, desegregation is taken to be a form of local social punishment to be lifted as soon as new administrators can show their hearts are pure. It is certainly not a constitutional commitment and imperative that the whole "government system" must work continuously to achieve for children. "As the de jure violation becomes more remote in time and these demographic changes intervene, it becomes less likely that a current racial imbalance in a school district is a vestige of a de jure system," Justice Kennedy observed. "The causal link between current conditions and the prior violation is even more attenuated if the school district has demonstrated its good faith."[92] Justice Scalia was even more blunt about his belief that the segregation we see today is not the product of government but of natural private forces—custom and tradition, you might say: "[Since] a multitude of private factors has shaped school systems in the years after the abandonment of de jure segregation—normal migration, population growth . . . , 'white flight' from the inner cities, increases in the costs of new facilities—the percentage of the current makeup of school systems attributable to the prior, government-enforced discrimination has diminished with each passing year, to the point where it cannot realistically be assumed to be a significant factor," declared Justice Scalia.[93] So why not let bygones be bygones and allow neutral private phenomena—things like the costs of new facilities and white flight—take their course?

The conservative majority on the Court displayed its hostility to the ideal of desegregation in an even more dramatic way in *Missouri v. Jenkins*,[94] an eighteen-year old desegregation case from Kansas City, Missouri, decided in 1995 when the lower federal district court, frustrated by the failure of prior efforts and the state's continuing delays and excuses, finally took strong equitable action to make the constitutional promise of equality real in Kansas City. Chief Justice Rehnquist tells the story nicely for the majority in this five-to-four decision:

> [T]he District Court has set out on a program to create a school district that was equal to or superior to the surrounding [suburban districts]. This remedy has included an elaborate program of capital improvements, course enrichment, and extracurricular enhancement not simply in the formerly identifiable black schools, but in schools throughout the district. [The] District Court's remedial order has all but made the Kansas City, Missouri School District itself into a magnet district [designed] to attract nonminority students from outside the KCMSD schools.[95]

Great news, and what high praise for a model program from the Chief Justice of the United States, right? Read on:

> But this interdistrict goal is beyond the scope of the intradistrict violation identified by the District Court ... the District Court's order [of] across-the-board salary increases for instructional and noninstructional employees [and its] order requiring the State to continue to fund the quality education programs because student achievement levels were still 'at or below national norms at many grade levels' cannot be sustained.[96]

Thus, just as *Milliken* forbade the judicial redrawing of school district boundaries to cut across municipal lines, *Jenkins* invalidated judicial efforts to radically upgrade and improve urban schools on the suspicion that they might attract suburban white students and this would become an "interdistrict" remedy! How quickly things fall apart.

Justice Thomas goes even further in *Jenkins* by essentially calling into question whether *Brown v. Board of Education* was rightly decided. He denounces the district court for taking "it upon itself to experiment with the education of the KCMSD's black youth."[97] Does he mean that all federal district court remedial orders are illegitimate efforts to "experiment"? Has he forgotten that there is a constitutional right at stake here? Perhaps. For Justice Thomas announces his opposition to the "theory that black students suffer an unspecified psychological harm from segregation that retards their mental and educational development."[98] This is, of course, the essence of *Brown*, a decision that Thomas believes relies not only "upon questionable social science research rather than constitutional principle" but also on "assumption of black inferiority."[99] He declares his opposition to the Court's practice of allowing "federal courts to exercise virtually unlimited equitable powers to remedy this *alleged* constitutional violation. The exercise of this authority has trampled upon principles of federalism and the separation of powers and has freed courts to pursue other agendas...."[100]

Therefore, in the name of denying "black inferiority," Justice Thomas voted to overturn a program of major improvements in the Kansas City public schools, apparently striking a blow for the principles of "federalism and separation of powers." These same principles had less of a pull on Justice Thomas's attention in *Richmond v. Croson*, where he enthusiastically voted to strike down Richmond, Virginia's minority set-aside plan for public contracting, or *Shaw v. Reno* and *Miller v. Johnson*, where he voted to strike down state legislation that produced majority-African-American districts. How fascinating that Justice Thomas, champion of the virtues of *de facto* segregated all-black schools, considers integrated majority-black districts "Bantustans" and a type of racial apartheid. Why are all-black schools praiseworthy but majority-black congressional districts unconstitutional?

After decades of retreat from *Brown* and the implications of *Tinker*, we need a constitutional amendment that makes clear a principle denied by the Court but implicit in the belief system of American democratic culture: that young people have a fundamental right to receive and participate in an equal and integrated education for democratic citizenship. Consider the following language:

> All children in the United States have a right to receive an equal public education for democratic citizenship.

Such an amendment would allow us to overcome the forces of social, racial and fiscal conservatism that impede efforts to redress school funding disparities. It would allow the Court to reverse *Rodriguez* and establish the necessity of parity in school funding. And it would make explicit the connection between education and democracy that our greatest jurists, teachers and philosophers have insisted upon. There can be no effective democracy unless the citizenry is educated, and there can be no effective education unless we have a democratic society committed to the life success of all.

A National Movement for Constitutional Literacy

The problems that we face in our schools cannot be resolved without the active involvement of young people themselves. Democracy teaches us that people must work to solve their own problems or the solutions won't stick. Teachers, parents and others can help, but we need a national student movement in this century to revitalize public education.

Yet as a society, we are not giving students the intellectual equipment they need to confront issues such as school vouchers, prayer in the classroom, "zero-tolerance" discipline, testing mania, the Pledge of Allegiance "under God," and mandatory drug-testing of students in extracurricular activities.

I first learned that we were falling down in the transmission of essential constitutional values and knowledge in the fall of 1996 when I received a phone call from Andrea Stuart and Andrea Merriam, high school seniors who represented a group of distressed students at Montgomery Blair High School in Montgomery County, Maryland. They were in a communications class that produced a monthly television debate-format news show called *Shades of Gray* for the school system's cable channel. But the channel had e-mailed them to say it was refusing to broadcast their October show, a debate between two conservatives and two liberals about whether gays and lesbians should be allowed to marry. Could anything be done to help them get their show aired?

I told the students that the school system's refusal to broadcast was deeply suspect on First Amendment grounds but that we needed more to go on. I suggested they e-mail the official in charge to ask precisely what was wrong with the debate. On October 23, 1996, the program director sent an e-mail reply explaining the decision:

> We ... felt that the gentleman who was a guest on the show [Dr. Frank Kameny] brought up the issue of religion and God in a very heated and controversial manner. . . . We both felt it would be inappropriate to air the program for that reason alone.

In a First Amendment case turning on motivation, this statement is as close to a smoking gun as you might hope to find: a government official admitting that speech had been censored because of its content, viewpoint and form of expression—"for that reason alone."

The officials objected to a segment of the debate in which the student moderator asked the guests what motivated their different positions on the issue (which is a fascinating question, never asked on network talk shows). One of the conservative guests, Paula Govers, of Concerned Women for America, introduced religion into the discussion:

> GOVERS: The Concerned Women for America believes that marriage is an institution sanctioned by God, licensed by the state, specifically between one man and one woman, and specifically for the purpose of procreation and should be a covenant between two people that should be a lifetime commitment.

This comment prompted Dr. Frank Kameny, of the Washington, D.C., Gay and Lesbian Activists Alliance, and Judith Schaeffer, of People for the American Way, to respond:

> KAMENY: Paula, you said that the First Amendment guarantees us freedom of religion, and we all have our own views of God. My God gave us homosexuality as a blessing to be enjoyed to its fullest.... My God sanctifies same-sex marriage even if your God does not, and we are both American citizens and both Gods deserve equal recognition from our— not your—*our* government.
>
> SCHAEFFER: That's exactly what the First Amendment requires. The government cannot legislate religious beliefs.
>
> KAMENY: If you don't want to enter into a same-sex marriage, don't. But don't tell us just because your God doesn't sanctify it, my God is to be ignored.
>
> GOVERS: Dr. Kameny, you said that your God does sanctify these unions. So your religious beliefs would say it's a good thing and our religious beliefs would say it's not. Why does your view get to trump ours?
>
> KAMENY: It does not. If you believe that, you have an absolute right not to enter into a same-sex marriage.
>
> KRIS ARDIZONNE [the other conservative guest and legal director of the Eagle Forum]: But my taxpayer dollars go to pay for the institution of marriage. And we don't believe in it.
>
> KAMENY: And so do the tax dollars of gay people go to pay for marriage as well....

To my mind, the spirited debate on this show remains the most thoughtful examination of the subject I have ever seen. The class teacher, Christopher Lloyd, said that it "dealt with a contemporary and controversial topic in a superb fashion." But as a high-ranking school system official would foolishly tell the *Washington Post,* giving us even more damning evidence of the system's attempt to suppress public debate, the show was simply "too hot ... it raises lots of issues that I'm not sure the mainstream is comfortable hearing about."

I told the students I would gladly take their case *pro bono.* The show was being censored because of the government's opposition to a speaker's religious views, in direct violation of the Supreme Court's 1995 decision in *Rosenberger v. University of Virginia.* Striking down the University of Virginia's practice of subsidizing all student journals but religious ones, the Court in that case emphasized that speech on public affairs from a religious perspective enjoys the same constitutional protection as secular viewpoints. The Court stated: "The government must abstain from regulating speech when the specific motivating ideology or the opinion or perspective of the speaker is the rationale for the restriction."[101]

I wanted to go to federal court right away for an injunction, but the students felt strongly that the censorship should be lifted by the school superintendent or, if not by him, then the board of education. They wanted to fight the censorship internally. So we prepared an administrative appeal and planned to rally the community.

The decision to fight inside rather than sue proved to be an excellent one on the students' part. Their teacher was an ally from the beginning. After we met with the Blair principal, Phil Gainous, and showed him the censored show, he also championed the students' cause. In short order, I helped the students draft a constitutional analysis of the controversy, which they used to pick up resolutions of support from parent-teacher associations (PTAs), high school student councils across the county, elected officials, and prominent Blair alumni such as the famed *Washington Post* reporter Carl Bernstein. Soon there were supportive articles in the *Post* and community newspapers and full-blown debates on National Public Radio. We even won positive coverage in the conservative *Washington Times,* which focused on the school system's selective determination to censor speech about religion. There was excitement in the community as the many underground copies of the censored tape we produced were passed around. The initial anxiety people had when hearing about a show on gay marriage vanished when they saw a bright student moderating a debate in a drab room among well-mannered people sitting around a table.

At the appeal hearing, the superintendent's examiner decided against us, as expected, but the moronic superficiality of bureaucratic process stunned the students. When we appealed to the Board of Education, the students activated hundreds of people to support free speech in general and provocative journalistic speech in particular. Going into the vote, I had not only the sense that we were going to win but the amazing sense that we had *already* won, that whatever took place in the vote, the students and community had experienced a powerful constitutional education. Truth be told, more people had seen the show *Shades of Gray* during this controversy than ever before. The board voted that night four-to-three to reverse the superintendent and to air the tape—not once, as originally scheduled, but six times. The controversy also led to the revision of the general policy governing student expression on the system's cable channel. The students wrote their college application essays about the experience, and I learned two things that would profoundly change my scholarly agenda as a professor of constitutional law.

The first thing I saw is that high school students are fascinated by Supreme Court decisions, constitutional law and history, and the principles of democratic government. Yet the students I represented, well-schooled kids in suburban Maryland, had never read or learned about the Court's decisions in *Tinker v. Des Moines School District, Hazelwood v. Kuhlmeier, Goss v. Lopez* or *Vernonia School District v. Acton,* to mention just a few of the landmark cases relevant to their lives. I saw that we had been missing an extraordinary opportunity to educate young people about the character and functions of democratic society by teaching them about the Supreme Court's treatment of cases and controversies arising in public schools. Indeed, when you look through the prism of these cases, it is impressive how much of our basic free speech, religion, search and seizure, racial justice, sex equality and privacy jurisprudence has been worked out in the context of the American public school. But the students themselves are unaware of this rich history.

But I also came to see from this controversy that "constitutional law" is neither simply nor exclusively nor primarily a matter of what the Supreme Court does. The vast majority of conflicts about rights take place and are worked out in the ordinary course of institutional events. They never become legal cases, much less the infinitesimally small percentage that become Supreme Court decisions. (The Court decides to hear appeals in fewer than one percent of the cases brought to its attention.)

Thus, in a democratic society, constitutional law should not be seen as the esoteric province of lawyers and judges but rather as a field of contested meanings that maps all of our social interactions. In this sense, constitutional law governing education is not just the structure of case doctrine relevant to America's schools; it is the pattern and practice of relationships among students, parents, teachers and administrators as they negotiate the difficult terrain of community, authority and individual freedom. What we are missing today is an organizing idea for America's massive educational establishment. That idea should be rooted in the text of the Constitution. We should amend it to say that all children have a right to receive an equal public education for meaningful democratic citizenship.

CHAPTER EIGHT

Democracy and the Corporation

The State need not permit its own creation to consume it.
   —Justice Byron White, *First National Bank of Boston v. Bellotti*[1]

In progressive constitutional democracy, participatory values—to various degrees but always to a great extent—must stay alive in all of society's institutions. This is the *Tinker* principle. Without it, we run the risk of preserving the ritual forms of democracy in the electoral dream life of society but imposing hierarchy and injustice in the everyday experiences of people.

But where does this principle leave the central institution of the American economy, the "private corporation"? Corporations are owned by shareholders, who elect boards of directors, which appoint management to conduct the affairs of the business. Neither the larger political community nor the employees of corporations have any formal say in their decision-making or administration. Does constitutional democracy therefore stop at the borders of the private corporation? Must government defer to all corporate decisions as the free exercise of "private" contractual and property rights? Is the state indeed the realm of coercion and the corporation a realm of freedom? Does democratic liberalism forbid regulatory intervention in the corporate economy?

There is an equally pressing obverse problem. Because of the legal advantages they have, corporations amass huge amounts of wealth and power. To what extent can they turn around and use their wealth and power to influence democratic processes and institutions? After we ask whether democratic power must halt when it reaches the borders of the private corporation, we must ask whether the political power of the private corporation must stop at the borders of public institutions. These are critical problems that will define the character of our economic and social life.

Are Private Corporations Private?

Once upon a time, corporations were just plain corporations, all of them chartered by the states or Congress to engage in specific functions. The strong division between *private* corporations and *public* corporations (such as municipalities) came about in the nineteenth century. The key Supreme Court decision lending energy to this development was the *Dartmouth College* case.[2] There, Chief Justice John Marshall held for a conservative, pro-Federalist majority that the New Hampshire legislature had violated the Contract Clause of the Constitution, Article I, Section 10, when it amended Dartmouth's royal charter of 1769 to replace the entrenched conservative Board of Trustees and bring the college under greater public scrutiny and control.[3] If Dartmouth were a public corporation like a town, it is clear that the state could change its governance structure. But Marshall treated Dartmouth as a privately owned corporation, rather than a publicly owned one, and the college's original royal charter as a binding contract.[4] The state law revising the organization and composition of the corporation impaired the state's obligation under the Contract Clause to respect the vested property and management rights of the controlling members of the Board.[5] This decision validated the emerging division between public and private corporations and helped to rope off private corporate power from democratic oversight and regulation.

But we still have no historically stable consensus about what a corporation really is or whether the private corporation should be considered "public" or "private." Surely the Legal Realists were right that these questions are of an essentially metaphysical nature. When we ask whether a private corporation is public or not, the critical issue is why we want to know. Is it because the state wants to regulate the wages and hours the corporation pays employees and the corporation thinks it unconstitutional? Is it because the corporation wants to pour treasury money into the congressional candidacy of one of its directors or political allies? Is it because employees who lost money in corporate pension funds as a result of corporate malfeasance now want to recover personally from executives? Issues like these have concrete legal answers that reflect social choices. These choices may, in turn, inform our sense of whether corporations are "public" or "private" but they cannot give us any kind of authoritative natural-law definition of what a corporation is.

From the standpoint of progressive democracy, it should be obvious that private corporations are, in most significant respects, public entities. They are chartered by the state, which defines for them their internal structure and meticulously governs the interaction of shareholders, the board of directors and the management. The Delaware Code, hundreds of pages long, details the mandatory and permissible functions of the various actors in the corporation from proxy elections to distribution of dividends to board meetings. The state, especially the judiciary, invests enormous amounts of time and energy attempting to rationalize corporate behavior and adjudicate the dynamics of greed, faction and power that make corporations such dynamic and costly economic institutions.

Beyond public regulation of internal corporate processes, there is an elaborate structure of state subsidies and ground rules that underwrite the modern corporation. Corporate shareholders have "limited liability," which means that in the event of a terrible corporate accident, say an oil spill or a mass toxic tort, shareholders are liable only up to the point of their stock investment and cannot be sued personally for recovery of damages. This is, of course, not the case with respect to individual owners of property and businesses, who can face huge tort liabilities in the event of such disasters. The "perpetual life" of the corporation permits assets to grow in perpetuity, which is another distinctive institutional advantage. Corporate bankruptcy protection minimizes the risks of investment. For private corporations that have "gone public" and sold stock on the open markets, the Securities and Exchange Commission enforces a vast legal regime in the securities laws to give stockholders collective confidence in the securities markets. It is the government that (theoretically) makes Wall Street safe for investment. The "business judgment rule" protects corporate executives in a very broad range of decision-making against most restitution suits charging waste. And so on.

Thus, when corporations want to be considered private, it is obviously not with respect to the risks of capital investment where they have done everything in their power to socialize the risks of corporate liability. They want to be wholly "private" with respect to profit, accountability and decision-making but not with respect to risk and loss, where they want their productive social character to stay uppermost in our minds. The much-trumpeted "free market" that protects their privacy is actually a massive political construction of public charters, licenses, subsidies, incentives, protections and entitlements. So do we need to accept this powerful corporate desire to be free from the operation of society's democratic norms and democratic will?

We have said of society's public institutions that they must accept all the democracy that is consistent with the basic integrity of their mission: the *Tinker* principle. This principle should also govern private corporations whose mission is to turn profit for their shareholders. Profit-making can be a perfectly fine and socially useful agenda, but it must fit in, anthropologically speaking, with the other values of society and not totally supplant and subordinate them. Thus when profit-seeking corporations operate on such a grand and powerful scale that people's democratic rights are threatened by them, the prerogatives of private property must yield to the rights of the people.

The modern Supreme Court once briefly shared this vision and gave primacy to democratic rights over corporate power. The seminal case involved the free-speech claims of a Jehovah's Witness, Grace Marsh, who was arrested and jailed for passing out religious literature in a company-owned town.[6] The Court, deciding her case in 1946, articulated a First Amendment principle subordinating the rights of corporate property to the rights of citizenship. However, the Court subsequently lost all of its democratic nerve in assessing the rights of citizens in private contexts like shopping malls. Today, the property rights of corporations are far more powerful than the political rights of the people.

The Politics of Public Space: *Marsh v. Alabama*

Grace Marsh was a Jehovah's Witness of modest means living in Alabama in the 1940s.[7] At that time, members of her religion faced intense hostility throughout the country for refusing to salute the flag and for their unorthodox theology. In Alabama, Witnesses endured the violent wrath of the Southern Baptist majority and were often hounded by mobs and arrested for proselytizing in public. In the *Watchtower* newspaper, Marsh described how she was jailed in "a filthy, cold cell for 11 days" for conducting a Bible study in a private home.[8]

One day Marsh ventured 30 feet off the public highway into the "business block" of a suburb of Mobile called Chickasaw, where there were a number of stores and shops and a U.S. post office. Standing on the sidewalk to catch the foot traffic, she offered pedestrians the *Watchtower* newspaper and other religious materials.[9]

It turned out that Chickasaw was a "company town" privately owned by the Gulf Shipbuilding Corporation. Soon a town police officer, deputized by the Mobile County Sheriff but paid by Gulf, appeared to tell Marsh that she was trespassing and had to leave.[10] She said that she was exercising her rights under the First Amendment and refused to leave.[11] She was arrested, prosecuted by the county, and convicted of criminal trespass.[12] She appealed her conviction all the way to the Supreme Court, where she found a more sympathetic audience than in Alabama.[13]

Writing for the majority, Justice Hugo Black observed that had Chickasaw been a public municipal corporation, it could not "bar the distribution of literature containing religious or political ideas on its streets, sidewalks and public places...."[14] With startling democratic perception, he asked why a privately owned corporation operating a town in the interests of its owners should have more power to deny the speech rights of the people than a municipal corporation that represents everyone:

> [I]t is clear that had the people of Chickasaw owned all the homes, and all the stores, and all the streets, and all the sidewalks, all those owners together could not have set up a municipal government with sufficient power to pass an ordinance completely barring the distribution of religious literature.... Can those people who live in or come to Chickasaw be denied freedom of press and religion simply because a single company has legal title to all the town?[15]

Turning the tables on Alabama, which had hinged its argument on the public-private distinction, Justice Black reformulated the difference between municipal corporations and private ones as the difference between state-chartered institutions that represent all citizens and state-chartered institutions that represent small groups of them.

Justice Black found that the "corporation's property interests" under state law could not "settle the question" of Grace Marsh's federal constitutional rights.[16] Ownership does not constitute "absolute dominion."[17] Stated Justice Black: "The more an owner, for his advantage, opens up his property for use by the public in general, the more do his rights become circumscribed by the statutory and constitutional rights of those who use it."[18]

Significantly, the majority looked at the uses to which the property was actually being put rather than to the character of the corporation's formal invitation to the public. The majority was not beguiled by the fact that the Gulf corporation had posted signs throughout stores on the block stating, "This Is Private Property, and Without Written Permission, No Street, or House Vendor, Agent or Solicitation of Any Kind Will Be Permitted."[19]

Ultimately, Justice Black found, it makes no difference whether "a corporation or municipality owns or possesses the town," because "the public

in either case has an identical interest in the functioning of the community in such manner that the channels of communication remain free."[20]
Like all of the "[m]any people in the United States" who "live in company-
owned towns," the citizens who live and work in Chickasaw, Justice Black
noted, "are free citizens of their State and country."[21] They have a right to
go into public spaces to interact with other citizens. The fact that a private corporation owns title to the town cannot justify "the State's permitting
a corporation to govern a community of citizens so as to restrict their fundamental liberties. . . . Insofar as the State has attempted to impose criminal
punishment [on Grace Marsh] for undertaking to distribute religious literature in a company town, its action cannot stand."[22]

The majority's decision provoked an outraged dissent by conservative
justices, who perceived the radical implications of a First Amendment right
to trespass on corporate property for expressive purposes.[23] If the holding
were not going to be chained exclusively to the company town, the obvious question would arise over the next few decades as the post–World
War II suburbanization of America accelerated: Would Americans win
speech rights on the millions of acres of land that have been turned into
shopping malls?

Democracy Gives Way to the Perfect Shopping Environment: The Shopping Mall Cases

In the 1968 Supreme Court ruling of *Amalgamated Food Employees Union
v. Logan Valley Plaza, Inc.*,[24] it looked like the answer was going to be yes.
In *Logan Valley*, the Court overturned a Pennsylvania state court injunction preventing a grocery workers' union from picketing a nonunion
supermarket in the store's parcel pickup area.[25] The state court had proceeded on standard common-law notions of the rights of private property
ownership and treated the unwanted union pickets as trespassers.[26]

But Justice Thurgood Marshall, writing for the majority, extended the
logic of *Marsh v. Alabama*, finding that the "shopping center here is clearly
the functional equivalent to the business district of Chickasaw. . . ."[27] He
held that "the State may not delegate the power through the use of its
trespass laws, wholly to exclude those members of the public wishing to
exercise their First Amendment rights on the premises in a manner and for
a purpose generally consonant with the use to which the property is actually put."[28]

Here, in Justice Marshall's decision, we find all of the ingredients we need to develop a theory of the democratic uses to which corporate property can be put in the age of the shopping mall. Corporations must be willing to surrender their property to the exercise of democratic rights to an extent congruent with their true invitation to the public and the social uses to which their property is put. The state, therefore, may not criminalize through the trespass regime citizens' exercise of constitutional rights on privately owned corporate property that has an essentially social character. In trying to figure out exactly what the dimensions are of such a right of democratic speech on corporate property, the barometer is that the speech activity must be "generally consonant" with the legitimate commercial purposes for which the property is being used. Yet in general, citizens may not be reduced to robotic consumers responding to market stimuli.

Had the Court's shopping mall jurisprudence continued to evolve along these lines, America would today have hundreds of thousands more acres of social space available for face-to-face political dialogue. But the Court stopped this line of reasoning dead in its tracks in 1972 in *Lloyd Corp. v. Tanner.*[29] In that case, opponents of the Vietnam War were repeatedly threatened with arrest for passing out their antiwar flyers in Portland Oregon's Lloyd Center Mall, a 25-acre mall with dozens of stores, restaurants, movie theaters, gardens, an auditorium and a skating rink.[30] To establish their rights, they went to federal district court, which determined on the authority of *Logan Valley* that this giant mall was "the functional equivalent of a public business district" and the picketers therefore had a right to speak and petition there.[31]

But the Supreme Court majority swung sharply away from this approach. Justice Powell distinguished *Logan Valley* by observing that the union picketers in that case had been specifically addressing the patrons of the supermarket in the shopping mall, whereas the antiwar activists in *Lloyd Corp.* were addressing a general public audience.[32] The antiwar activists, therefore, "could have distributed these handbills on any public street, on any public sidewalk, in any public park, or in any public building in the city of Portland."[33] In other words, for the purpose of their message, they did not really need to be in the mall. Noting that "this Court has never held that a trespasser or an uninvited guest may exercise general rights of free speech on property privately owned,"[34] Justice Powell found that, while the mall had been opened for certain community meetings and events, the purpose of that narrow invitation was "to bring potential shoppers to the Center, to create a favorable impression, and to generate goodwill."[35] There was simply no "open-ended invitation to the public to use the Center for any and all purposes, however incompatible with the interests of both the stores and the shoppers whom they serve."[36]

The *Lloyd Corp.* ruling inverted the basic premises of *Logan Valley* and created untenable doctrinal instability. The Court had invented a foggy content-based rule to determine when speech at shopping malls would be allowed. If the speech were deemed sufficiently related to the business of the mall, then the Court might find reason to allow it; if it concerned something ostensibly unrelated, like foreign policy or animal rights, the speakers would have to go elsewhere. This cut against the general First Amendment doctrine that speech rights in essentially public places do not depend on the content of what we plan to say. Grace Marsh, after all, was not in Chickasaw to talk about the Gulf Corporation's environmental record but her private religious beliefs. Yet Justice Powell removed the democratic bite from the *Marsh* principle by finding that the general free-speech rights we carry into malls depend not on the actual social character of the property but on the formal character of the corporate invitation.[37] Thus, if the mall wanted to invite boy scout meetings and church choir practice but ban antiwar pickets and animal rights activists, then this would be the corporation's prerogative in order to bring "potential shoppers to the Center, to create a favorable impression, and to generate goodwill."[38] The Constitution should not interfere with the business of consumer capitalism by changing the mood of the buying environment.

By reviving absolutist private property conceptions, the *Lloyd Corp.* decision led the Court in 1976 flatly to overrule *Logan Valley* in a case called *Hudgens v. NLRB.* There, the Court held that union picketing in a shopping mall did not enjoy any First Amendment protection at all.[39] The majority observed correctly that "the reasoning of the Court's opinion in *Lloyd* cannot be squared with the reasoning of the Court's opinion in *Logan Valley.*"[40] Either all speakers have rights in the malls, or none do. The majority chose door number 2, returning to a conservative public-private distinction and explicitly denying that the "large self-contained shopping center" is "the functional equivalent of a municipality."[41] *Marsh* was left standing alone on the sidewalk in Alabama, a discrete and lonely case about company-owned towns. Dissenting, Justice Marshall asked the Court to remember the democratic insight of *Logan Valley*: "that the owner of the modern shopping center complex, by dedicating his property to public use as a business district, to some extent displaces the 'State' from control of historical First Amendment forums, and may acquire a virtual monopoly of places suitable for effective communication."[42] But there was no going back.

In the wake of *Hudgens*, a handful of state high courts, such as California's and New Jersey's, have found that citizen free-speech rights in shopping malls are protected by their state constitutions, and the Supreme Court has allowed this state-based enlargement of civil liberty.[43] But in the vast majority of states, corporate-owned shopping malls are not free-speech zones but speech-free zones. To be more precise, they have speech within them but only the speech that is authorized by corporate management, which can decide to let in all speakers, no speakers, or just those who are friendly to the managers or share their views. The First Amendment sinks beneath the power of corporate managers to shape the perfect consumer environment. As we can see through the *Marsh* decision, the short-lived *Logan Valley* holding and the California and New Jersey rulings, there was nothing inevitable about this outcome. We could still restore communicative political democracy to its proper place in the hierarchy of social values, certainly above the corporate desire to design the perfect mood enhancements for loosening consumer inhibitions.

Why Laissez Isn't Fair: *Lochner v. New York* and the Hidden Assumptions of Libertarianism

The rampant corporate fraud and criminality that have surfaced in the new century should not be read only as a morality tale about individual avarice and hubris. We have something crucial to learn from episodes like the Enron and the WorldCom scandals about the nature of the corporate sector and the relationship between private corporations and democratic values. Private corporations obviously play a central role in economic growth and wealth creation. But corporate ideology invites us to believe that the private corporate sector is, in its essence, the realm of freedom and public power the realm of tyranny. In this ideological frame, all public regulation of private corporations represses human freedom. But we saw in *Marsh* and the shopping-mall cases how corporate freedom from government does not necessarily advance the political freedom of citizens to communicate. What about the more general proposition? Does public regulation of contractual relationships in the market economy, by definition, interfere with human liberty?

This is the central claim of the political ideology that goes, somewhat unfairly, by the name of "libertarianism" today. Libertarians, such as

University of Chicago professor Richard Epstein or the late Harvard
Philosophy professor Robert Nozick, want principally to keep government
small and out of the way of business corporations. In *Anarchy, State and
Utopia*, Nozick famously endorsed a "minimal state" that is "limited to the
functions of protecting all its citizens against violence, theft, and fraud,
and to the enforcement of contracts ..."[44] Nozick, whose political philosophy class I took in my freshman year of college, loved to argue that
the state never had cause to interfere with "capitalist acts among consent-
ing adults."[45] Thus libertarians seek a "laissez-faire state" that zealously
protects the untrammeled common-law rights of those who own and control private and corporate property: corporations, landlords, employers.
What matters is that the government refrain from interfering with property rights and faithfully enforce business contracts.

This political creed has little to do with democracy, since the public will
and general welfare barely enter the picture. But it is also hard to see why
it merits the rather upbeat and appealing designation of "libertarian." After
all, if liberty is the central human good and the state is defined categorically as the enemy of liberty, then true libertarians should all be anarchists.
They should oppose the existence of the state for any purpose at all. Under
conditions of true statelessness, there will be freedom, and presumably
whatever happens will happen for the best.

But today's libertarians are not anarchists. On the contrary, they insist
on the existence of a very strong government for select purposes that they
see as essential to freedom. But the moment they allow for the existence
of a state in this way, they concede that democratically organized public
power *can* work to advance human liberty. This means that human liberty has a positive content and dynamic history of its own that is analytically
distinct from the simple absence of government coercion.[46] From this perspective, there is no such thing as a laissez-faire state: there is either a
state or there is laissez-faire, but not both. Laissez-faire in the American
state today is the idiosyncratic political rhetoric of those who like what the
government has done historically to promote the interests of propertied
classes but would stop it now from doing anything to benefit people who
have historically been the victims of state coercion and people whose principal property lies in the labor of their bodies.

If we are going to be intellectually honest in our libertarianism rather
than ideological about it, once we grant that there is going to be government to help produce liberty, the relevant questions become which public
purposes are essential to freedom, *how* government should work to advance

liberty and *whose* liberty should be advanced. The class-bound "libertarian" answer, typified by the work of the Cato Institute today, is that the state can advance liberty by protecting private property through the police power and the criminal justice system and by enforcing contracts. But what reason do we have to suppose that these are the only ways or the best ways to advance liberty? Perhaps creating a system of fine public schools to equip everyone with the civic literacy and professional skills they need to succeed in life is the best way to promote freedom. Perhaps protecting the rights of workers to organize unions in the workplace is the best way to safeguard liberty for most people. We cannot decide these matters in an abstract and deductive way, which is to say ideologically: they must be resolved democratically, through political dialogue and the people's lived experience of freedom and unfreedom in society.

But even if we grant the rather narrow premise that the protection of private property is the *sine qua non* of protection of liberty, we must ask the question that working-class people have posed for more than a century: Why should the democratic state have the power to act in defense of the property that some citizens maintain in their business investments but not in defense of the property that other citizens maintain in the labor of their bodies and minds?

Consider the famous *Lochner* decision,[47] where the Supreme Court in 1905 struck down the New York state legislature's enactment of a sixty-hour workweek for bakery employees as a violation of the "substantive due process" liberty interests of employers and employees freely to contract as they will. In *West Coast Hotel v. Parrish*,[48] the Supreme Court would come to reverse this line of authority as a constitutional mistake, but it is important to consider the logical fallacy that lies at the heart of *Lochner*, the fallacy that today's libertarians at the Cato Institute, like the indefatigable Roger Pilon, seek to revive in constitutional law.

The bakery owners and libertarians of the day (then they were just called conservatives) took the position that the number of hours worked by bakery employees was a matter of contract law between the bakery owners and their employees. If the owners wanted to have their employees work eighty hours a week for one dollar an hour, the employees receiving such an offer would be free to take it or leave it. As employees at will, they could walk off the job if they disliked the offer, or they could attempt a counteroffer.

But assume that bakery owners and workers have bargained back and forth and now stand at an impasse. Because of economic conditions, the employers want their employees to work eighty hours a week. Employees want to spend more time with their families; they want a sixty-hour work-week and they refuse the employers' offer. But they cannot walk off the job since they are poor and they face an uncertain future outside a job where they have invested many years of their lives. They are also afraid that their employers will blackball them in the industry. They view the employers' bargaining intransigence as a form of duress, but this is their collective experience of the contractual process and not a legal description that can do them any good in a court operating under "laissez-faire" contract notions, which allow for hard bargaining.

Frustrated, the employees now take the rhetoric of a free market seriously. They decide to freely "sit in" at work and explain to the employer and management why eighty-hour weeks are too long, why wages are too low, and why breathing flour dust all day long in unventilated cellars is dangerous to their health. At this point, the employer will invoke not contract but "property" rights and call the police, who will arrest the sitting-in employees as "trespassers," take them to a public jail, and have them prosecuted by taxpayer-supported district attorneys and tried before a judge and jury in a public courthouse. They may be convicted and jailed, deprived of their liberty and belongings, and ordered not to return to their former workplace.

From the perspective of the employees, it is hard to see what is "libertarian" or "laissez-faire," much less democratic, about such a governmental system. The state has not been neutral between the two concerned parties; it has mobilized all of the criminal-justice resources of government to terminate the dialogue taking place inside the bakery and have the employee-protestors removed, arrested and perhaps incarcerated. The employees become criminals. What could be legitimate about this arrangement?

But the conservative libertarian answers that the state's intervention *is* legitimate, neutral and "laissez faire" because the state defends property against trespassers in *all* cases, without regard to the owner's identity. The fact that the owners of the bakery invoke their property rights and the workers are arrested is a contingent and provisional fact. If the management sent company-paid goons to invade union headquarters, the police would arrest them for trespass as well. Government categorically defends Lockean property entitlements as they exist.

It is a dubious factual claim in light of the history of the labor injunction and police interference on behalf of management, but let us accept the argument that the arrest and prosecution of workers who "occupy" their workplaces is a natural result of a neutral property regime. Now consider this possibility, where the actual history of the *Lochner* case takes over.[49] Employees seeking a shorter workweek but not willing to face criminal prosecution decide to organize bakery employees statewide in New York to lobby for wage-hour legislation. They get unions and newspapers interested in the plight of bakery employees. They communicate the hardship of their lives to their fellow citizens. The New York legislature now unanimously approves a sixty-hour workweek and a ten-hour day for the bakery workers.

But it is not over yet. The owners challenge the law's constitutionality. A free-market-minded Supreme Court strikes it down as a Due Process violation under the Fourteenth Amendment. Justice Peckham writes: "There is no reasonable ground for interfering with the liberty of person or the right of free contract, by determining the hours of labor, in the occupation of a baker."[50] According to the majority, the sixty-hour workweek law "is not, within any fair meaning of the term, a health law, but is an illegal interference with the rights of individuals, both employers and employees, to make contracts regarding labor upon such terms as they may think best...."[51]

The *Lochner* Court thus constitutionalized the rule that the democratic state could use law to defend capital investments that owners have in their businesses but not labor investments that workers have in their bodies. To put it more graphically, the state could use the police power to protect the absolute control of corporate owners over their workplaces but not to protect the health and dignity of employees. But the Thirteenth Amendment, which abolished slavery and involuntary servitude, emancipated labor and essentially established in our Constitution that each person's labor was not only his own property but the basis of his civil and political liberty.[52] How can it be right in a democracy that the people can decide to use the machinery of the state to defend the security of corporate property in material things but not the security of property and liberty that the majority of working people have in their own labor?

After President Roosevelt's much-maligned Court-packing plan, the Court would come to overrule the whole *Lochner* ideology, which inscribed a sharp class bias into the interpretation of Fourteenth Amendment "liberty." The *Lochner* period obviously marked an aggressive attack on the democratic rights of free labor. Where the state has acted vigorously over time to enrich and protect certain corporate classes—and if you think this history is over, look no further than the Enron and WorldCom scandals—the political rhetoric of "laissez" to destroy regulation isn't remotely fair.

Corporate Power, Human Freedom, and Anti-Discrimination Law

We should keep in mind that resurgent Lochnerian efforts today to confine the state to enforcing property and contract rights are motivated by neither liberty nor democracy but agendas of class privilege and class power. Democratic counter-pressure must be allowed to cross over into the sphere of private corporate power to promote majoritarian regulatory agendas, such as the forty-hour workweek, workplace safety rules and laws against race or sex discrimination.

Each of these progressive agendas faces corporate argument that public regulation is illegitimate, inefficient and an assault on private freedom. Consider, for example, sexual-harassment law under Title VII of the Civil Rights Act of 1964. Because of the pathbreaking work of Professor Catharine MacKinnon, it is illegal sex discrimination today not only to impose *quid pro quo* sexual demands on employees in the workplace, but also for employers to encourage or tolerate a "hostile workplace environment" in which women (or men) are forced to endure pervasive and severe sexual ridicule, banter, insult, displays and humiliation. A dramatic example of such a workplace is captured in Clara Bingham's and Laura Leedy Gansler's vivid and gripping book, *Class Action*, which tells the gruesome story of a hostile work environment—complete with centerfolds, public masturbation, groping, fondling, name-calling, pornographic cartoons, vulgar graffiti and an endless gauntlet of humiliation—at the Eveleth Corporation in the Minnesota Iron Range that led to the case of *Jenson v. Eveleth*.[53]

Now, many people have maintained that the free-speech rights actually at stake in hostile workplaces are those of the women terrified by the license for sexual abuse created by corporate managers. This is the argument made powerfully by Professor Suzanne Sangree.[54] But there are many law professors, such as UCLA's Eugene Volokh,[55] as well as corporate lawyers and right-wing pundits, who claim that sexual harassment law today violates the First Amendment rights of male employers and employees to speak freely in the workplace. As part of their argument, it is important for them always to try to minimize the hostile character of workplaces when corporations get sued under Title VII. Professor Deborah Epstein has done a fine job refuting the factual mystifications and legal obfuscations of this grim project.[56]

But it is important to see what is conceptually flawed about the conservative attack on Title VII sexual-harassment law as a violation of the First Amendment. As an exercise of Congress's Commerce Clause powers, federal civil rights laws are not a regulation of speech but a federal regulation of the permissible uses of private (or public) property in the stream of interstate commerce. The sexually harassing vulgarities and insults that create actionable Title VII claims probably do belong to the class of protected speech when they are uttered in private homes, at parties and in the streets. What is different about the public or private workplace in the stream of interstate commerce is that Congress has power to regulate such property under its Commerce Clause authority. This was established in the Supreme Court's 1937 decision in *NLRB v. Jones & Laughlin Steel Corp.*, upholding the National Labor Relations Act and its ban on employer discharges of workers for talking union.[57]

The First Amendment argument is thus wholly out of place. The background common law presumption about private corporate property is that workers have no First Amendment rights there since the property belongs to the owners. (We have seen how the Court has whittled the *Marsh* case down to a tiny exception.) Indeed, all of the conservatives complaining about the "chilling effects" of harassment law would be the first to argue that employees in private businesses have no First Amendment rights at work. Thus, if a private employer wanted to impose a private sexual harassment speech code that went much further than Title VII—say by completely banning use of the word "bitch" in the workplace—it would clearly not violate the First Amendment. So Professor Volokh is not arguing that employees have constitutional free-speech rights in the workplace; he is just arguing that employers have the right not to be sued for certain kinds of speech-based harassment. But if that is the case, why aren't the following statements protected speech also, since they equally involve language: "You are fired because you are African American," "Have sex with me or you lose your job," "You're out of here because you're prounion and we're anti-union." All of these statements are instances of *verbal language* embodying particular viewpoints and agendas and yet have long been found to be evidence of illegal employment discrimination. What federal labor laws such as the Wagner Act, the Equal Pay Act or Title VII do is regulate the employer's control over private property for the promotion of other social interests that Congress has power to advance. With Title VII, the social

interest promoted is protecting a majority of America's population—
women—from tyranny and exploitation in the workplace. Nothing in
the law of property or speech stands in the way.

The Borders of Democracy: *First National Bank v. Bellotti,* the Tillman Act of 1907 and Corporate Power in Public Elections

To conservative libertarians, it is axiomatic that corporations should be
able to participate in the democratic process not only with direct political speech through media outlets but with contributions and expenditures
in public elections. At the very least, they say, if government can regulate
corporations, corporations have to get their fair say in the conduct of
government.

But this superficially appealing argument based on symmetry badly mis-
characterizes the relationship between democracy and corporations. The
democratic state *charters* the private corporation to engage in particular
purposes for the instrumental benefit of the common good. The corporation is designed to serve the broader public interest through the creation
of private wealth. But the corporation is not a democratic citizen and
should enjoy no political rights under the Constitution. It is a subordinate
entity with no independent constitutional standing outside of the individual rights of the people involved with it.

This is not the state of the law. In *First National Bank of Boston v. Bellotti,*[58] the Supreme Court in 1978 struck down a Massachusetts law making
it a crime for banks or business corporations to make political contributions or independent expenditures to influence "the vote on any question
submitted to the voters, other than one materially affecting any of the property, business or assets of the corporation."[59] The statute, passed out of
frustration with massive corporate spending to defeat initiatives favoring
progressive income taxes, defined initiatives respecting individual income
taxes as not affecting the interests of banks and corporations.[60] It would
have been cleaner and perhaps more compelling for the Massachusetts
legislature simply to ban all corporate initiative spending and contributions, but the issue was nonetheless fairly posed.

The parties to the case, the First National Bank and the Commonwealth
of Massachusetts, battled over whether corporations and banks have First
Amendment rights to spend and give money in campaigns, a right that
the Court had upheld with respect to *persons* two years before in *Buckley
v. Valeo.*[61] But the Court refused to decide explicitly whether corporations

have First Amendment rights.[62] It instead focused on whether the proposed *speech* itself was protected. Justice Powell wrote:

> The speech proposed by appellants is at the heart of the first amendment's protection. [If] the speakers here were not corporations, no one would suggest that the state could silence their proposed speech. It is the type of speech indispensable to decision making in a democracy, and this is no less true because the speech comes from a corporation rather than an individual. The inherent worth of the speech in terms of its capacity for informing the public does not depend upon the identity of its source, whether corporations, association, union or individual.[63]

Justice Powell's move here was pure metaphysics. Speech does not exist in the abstract, hovering in midair, waiting for the opportunity to express itself. Speech has an irreducible material basis in the speaker, without whom the speech would have no content, meaning or existence. So the whole issue was precisely whether corporations chartered by the Commonwealth of Massachusetts had a First Amendment right, in explicit opposition to Massachusetts law, to spend money from corporate treasuries to influence ballot-question campaigns. Recall that there was nothing stopping individual corporate and bank executives, shareholders and directors from expressing their personal views hostile to the progressive income tax initiative by spending their own money to try and stop it. The issue was whether they could take corporate treasury money to spend for these political purposes.

Since the speech affected was of the highest value, the Court determined to use strict scrutiny to examine the state's two suggested interests in the law. If the interests were not sufficiently compelling and the law not narrowly tailored to advance them, the Court would strike the law down.[64]

The first interest was protecting democracy itself. The Court here agreed that "preserving the integrity of the electoral process, preventing corruption, and 'sustaining the active, alert responsibility of the individual citizen in a democracy for the wise conduct of government' are interests of the highest importance."[65]

But the problem with the state's democracy argument was that it depended on the assumption that corporate spending "would exert an undue influence on the outcome of a referendum vote, and—in the end—destroy the confidence of the people in the democratic process and the integrity of government."[66] If these fears "were supported by record or legislative findings that corporate advocacy threatened imminently to undermine democratic processes, thereby denigrating rather than serving First Amendment interests, these arguments would merit our consideration,"[67] the majority stated, but "there has been no showing that the relative voice of corporations has been overwhelming or even significant in influencing referenda in Massachusetts, or that there has been any threat to the confidence of the citizenry in government."[68]

This analysis seemed to leave open the possibility that states could indeed ban corporate spending in campaigns if they showed that the corporate voice was "overwhelming" or even "significant" and threatened popular democracy.[69]

But the Court then quickly and, paradoxically, observed that: "To be sure, corporate advertising may influence the outcome of the vote; this would be its purpose. But the fact that advocacy may persuade the electorate is hardly a reason to suppress it."[70]

This is perfectly incoherent. The Court says at once that corporate speech might lose protection if it were to become at some point too effective and overwhelming and then, in the next breath, that its effectiveness could not be the basis for regulating it.[71]

The Court's embarrassing confusion on this point follows from its refusal to reckon seriously with what a corporation actually is. And this failure becomes obvious in its consideration of the second major interest invoked by Massachusetts to defend its law: its interest in "protecting the rights of shareholders whose views differ from those expressed by management on behalf of the corporation."[72] The majority rejected this alleged interest in protecting dissenting shareholders because the statute was "both underinclusive and overinclusive" for these purposes.[73] The law did not go far enough because it tolerated corporate lobbying to defeat or pass state legislation that certain shareholders might also disagree about and it did not ban corporate spending on public issues that were not the subject of a public referendum.[74] It also failed to target other associations such as unions and business trusts for the same treatment. Conversely, it swept too far because it prohibited "a corporation from supporting or opposing a referendum proposal even if its shareholders unanimously authorized the contribution or expenditure."[75] Justice Powell noted that shareholders who truly object can use the "procedures of corporate democracy" to register their dissent or can bring a "derivative suit to challenge corporate disbursements alleged to have been made for improper corporate purposes...."[76]

Justice White, in his superb dissenting opinion, joined by Justices

Brennan and Marshall, stated that "the issue is whether a State may prevent corporate management from using the corporate treasury to propagate views having no connection with the corporate business."[77] He set forth the "artificial entity" view of the corporation, a venerable understanding that goes all the way back to Chief Justice John Marshall:

> Corporations are artificial entities created by law for the purpose of furthering certain economic goals. In order to facilitate the achievement of such ends, special rules relating to such matters as limited liability, perpetual life, and the accumulation, distribution and taxation of assets are normally applied to them. States have provided corporations with such attributes in order to increase their economic viability and thus strengthen the economy generally.[78]

But Justice White pointed out the danger that these economic advantages could be converted into political power which could, in turn, be used to perpetuate special privileges:

> It has long been recognized ... that the special status of corporations has placed them in a position to control vast amounts of economic power which may, if not regulated, dominate not only the economy but also the very heart of our democracy, the electoral process.[79]

Justice White conceded that *Buckley v. Valeo* rejected any public interest in "equaliz[ing] the financial resources available to candidates," but argued that Massachusetts's interest was quite different:

> It is not one of equalizing the resources of opposing candidates or opposing positions, but rather of preventing institutions which have been permitted to amass wealth as a result of special advantages extended by the State for certain economic purposes from using that wealth to acquire an unfair advantage in the political process, especially where, as here, the issue involved has no material connection with the business of the corporation. *The State need not permit its own creation to consume it.* Massachusetts could permissibly conclude that not to impose limits upon the political activities of corporations would have placed it in a position of departing from neutrality and indirectly assisting the propagation of corporate views because of the advantages its laws give to the corporate acquisition of funds to finance such activities. . . .[80]

The only problem with Justice White's opinion was that he character-ized the state's democratic insistence on abolishing corporate influence over elections as a social "interest" to be weighed against corporate free-speech rights rather than a logically prior definitional principle that, under our Constitution, *corporations are not citizens.*

In his perceptive dissent, Justice Rehnquist essentially got that point. To begin with, he seemed to doubt the solidity of the ominous 1886 deci-sion of the Supreme Court declaring that the business corporation is a "person" within the meaning of Fourteenth Amendment Equal Protec-tion.[81] He emphasized Chief Justice John Marshall's statement in the Dartmouth College case that a "corporation is an artificial being, invisi-ble, intangible, and existing only in contemplation of law. Being the mere creature of law, it possesses only those properties which the charter of cre-ation confers upon it, either expressly, or as incidental to its very existence."[82] While Justice Rehnquist correctly defended the Court's prior findings that chartered media corporations have First Amendment freedoms and all prop-ertied corporations have a right not to have their property confiscated without due process of law, he strongly doubted whether ordinary busi-ness corporations should be construed to have constitutionally protected political rights. He could not see why "liberties of political expression" are "necessary to effectuate the purposes for which States permit commer-cial corporations to exist. . . . Indeed, the States might reasonably fear that the corporation would use its economic power to obtain further benefits beyond those already bestowed."[83]

Justice Rehnquist and the other dissenters had a much stronger hold on what a corporation really is and how democratic majorites have con-ceived of its role in our politics. After a series of scandals involving corporate looting not unlike the current wave, Congress categorically banned cor-porate contributions in federal election campaigns in 1907 in the famous Tillman Act,[84] a prohibition that has been continued uncontroversially in federal law ever since. If it is the case that the political speech that corpo-rations want to promote in ballot-issue campaigns is constitutionally protected, as the majority determined in *Bellotti,* [85] it is hard to see why the long-standing ban on corporate contributions to federal candidates is constitutional. It cannot be because an unusual danger of *quid pro quo* cor-ruption exists within the meaning of *Buckley v. Valeo.*[86] After all, if a reasonable limitation of $1,000 suffices to regulate "the reality or appear-ance of corruption"[87] for individual contributions, why not corporate ones?

Why not allow corporations to write candidates checks for up to $1,000 to candidates from their treasuries?

The answer takes us back to the political and legislative history of the Tillman Act of 1907. Adam Winkler has written a fine article explaining that, contrary to received judicial and academic wisdom, the "primary purpose of the ban on corporate campaign contributions" in the Tillman Act and parallel state laws was not to limit corporate political power generally, but more specifically "to prevent corporate managers from using stockholders' money to finance electoral politics."[88] Winkler associates the extraordinary early–twentieth century political controversy over corporate and insurance company campaign contributions with the profound anxieties caused by "the separation of ownership and control" in the modern corporation.[89] Political reformers of the time "sought to ban corporate contributions primarily because such contributions were seen to be a serious misuse of 'other people's money.'"[90] Thus the "political danger of corporate campaign financing" was not so much to the rest of democratic society but "to the members within the corporate organization, in particular the stockholders." [91] It was their money being used without their consent or knowledge and often against their own actual political interests, positions and values.

Winkler relates how several nationally publicized examples of life insurance companies secretly pouring corporate treasury funds into national Republican Party political campaigns provoked widespread public outrage.[92] The scandal of New York life insurance company corruption led to an investigation by the New York legislature's Armstrong Committee which, according to Upton Sinclair, "shook the nation to its depths."[93] The investigation revealed a pattern of corporate managers taking the money of "widows and orphans"[94] out of the corporate treasury to bankroll politicians who wrote laws favorable to the managers' own power in the corporation. According to the *Nation*, the Armstrong investigation, which would propel a little-known corporate lawyer and law professor named Charles Evan Hughes to the governorship of New York and ultimately a seat on the Supreme Court, focused on "the corrupt alliance of insurance companies with great speculators and powerful politicians."[95] In the Tillman Act and similar state laws, Americans resolved to stop corporate managers from using "other people's money"—"the money stolen from men and women who toiled and slaved and saved pennies to pay premiums"[96]—to advance the managers' personal and corporate political agendas.

Most Americans instinctively understand the *external* threat that corporate wealth and power pose to democratic institutions, but the logic of the "internal" threat to the rights of shareholders and employees has largely escaped us in recent times—at least until the Enron and WorldCom scandals broke. Perhaps these heartbreaking assaults on the financial security of tens of thousands of people will help us to reunite the "external" and "internal" dimensions of the critique of corporate political participation. Top executives at Enron deployed their control over the corporate assets of the shareholders to spread very large soft-money campaign contributions around both major political parties.[97] Top Enron and Arthur Anderson executives also gave direct hard-money contributions to a large group of key politicians, including 51 out of 56 members of the House Energy and Commerce Committee and 49 out of 70 members of the House Financial Services Committee.[98] In the decade before Enron's collapse, its leaders pumped nearly $6 million into federal campaigns and the two-party system to guarantee effective application of the principles of "deregulation."[99]

The corporate managers' resulting pervasive political influence in Congress and in the Republican Party, which went all the way to President George W. Bush and the White House,[100] shielded them from meaningful official scrutiny and accountability and allowed them to entrench their power with respect to the shareholders. Enron executives thus used other people's money not only to enrich themselves beyond belief but to ingratiate themselves with politicians and insulate their lawless power from public accountability. When the company ultimately went bankrupt, the shareholders, many of them Enron employees, were left holding the bag and saw their life savings disappear.

If anything positive can come from this kind of disaster, it will be a total ban on corporate soft-money and other political contributions to national and state political parties, political committees and candidates. What is at stake is not just the rights of "dissenting shareholders," for this phrase trivializes the structural transgression. Dissenting or not, citizen-shareholders in democratically chartered corporations have a right not to have their money, which is invested for economic reasons, put to partisan political uses. Society has a corresponding right not to have the corporation, endowed with so many government blessings, exploited by incumbent managers to perpetuate and enlarge their own political power. What is at stake is the unjust enrichment and self-aggrandizement of a class of corporate managers who have been historically tempted to use "other people's money" to buy themselves greater political power and freedom from public oversight and accountability.

Bellotti should be overruled, and must be if the new McCain-Feingold ban on corporate "soft money" contributions to the parties is to be upheld by the Court. We need to create a wall of separation between private corporations and public elections as high and thick as the wall of separation between Church and State. This proposed wall of separation is already a fact when it comes to federal election campaigns: private corporations have been prohibited from giving to candidates since passage of the Tillman Act of 1907,[101] and no one seems to question the constitutionality of this ban. The *Bellotti* Court held that a state had an interest in banning corporate contributions to candidates, but not referendum campaigns, on the theory that candidates can be corrupted in a way that ballot questions cannot.[102] This point seems dubious. In the first place, the *Buckley* Court had already upheld "reasonable" limits on candidate contributions,[103] so it is hard to see why such caps would not already prevent corruption by corporate candidate contributions. Secondly, the idea that corporate spending on initiatives cannot corrupt seems suspect in light of the fact that many candidates have been attaching themselves to initiatives and referenda and then riding them to public fame and popularity. In any event, even if it were true that corporate contributions to ballot-issue campaigns could not corrupt, it has nothing to do with the logically prior issue of whether corporations have a right to engage in political speech in the first place, the point Justice Rehnquist and White emphasized.

The wall of separation between public elections and corporations is also something we already accept when it comes to municipal corporations. In a revealing case called *Anderson v. City of Boston*,[104] the Supreme Judicial Court of Massachusetts in 1978 stopped the city of Boston from spending money to support a campaign for a progressive taxation "classification" proposal that was on a statewide referendum election ballot. Significantly, the municipal corporation of Boston wanted to spend this money to counteract private corporations, which were spending lavishly to defeat the measure. The Court doubted whether "the First Amendment has anything to do with this intra-state question of the rights of a political subdivision."[105] Yet even assuming that this kind of municipal corporate political speech is protected, the Court found that Massachusetts had shown a "compelling interest in assuring the fairness of elections and the appearance of fairness in the electoral process" which justified its implicit ban on any municipal expenditures in a statewide referendum campaign.[106] The Court emphasized how fairness was advanced by keeping the city from "using public tax revenues to advocate a position which certain taxpayers oppose,"[107] precisely the interest that the *Bellotti* Court dismissed when it came to private shareholders. The Anderson Court characterized Boston's view as suggesting that "the Commonwealth is apparently powerless against political entities of its own creation," precisely the terms in which Justice White castigated the arrogant argument of private corporations and banks in *Bellotti*.[108]

The current state of the law leaves us with an indefensible asymmetry: private corporate managers can spend to the heavens in pursuit of their political objectives, while municipal corporations can spend nothing even if, as in the *Anderson* case, the elected representatives of the people on the city council authorize and approve it. This imbalance swells the power of private corporations and leaves municipal corporations at their mercy. It probably makes sense to view municipal corporations as not having free-speech rights since they are artificial entities that should effectuate the public will and not try to shape it. On the other hand, in a statewide election, if private corporations are going to campaign for or against ballot issues and spend other people's money involuntarily on such a campaign, then surely municipal corporations with specific regional and political commitments should be able to make the same choice, especially since the democratic accountability of cities is stronger and their voices are needed to offset the political power of large private corporations. But the best solution would be for the Court to recognize that no corporation, public or private, has a constitutionally protected right to spend or contribute money in electoral politics. Political rights should belong to voters and their voluntary membership groups and associations.

Democracy, Union Elections, and Corporate Speech

Democracy's relationship to the corporation took its most radical turn in 1935 with passage of the National Labor Relations Act (the Wagner Act),[109] which guaranteed all private-sector employees a statutory right to engage in concerted activity and to join unions without reprisal. The Wagner Act, pushed by national labor militancy, marked an important moment in the progress of American democracy because it essentially declared that private corporate workplaces were not to be vacuumed free of the kinds of rights of free political expression and organization that employees enjoy and expect as citizens under the First Amendment. What *Marsh v. Alabama* did for petitioners on the premises of company towns, the Wagner Act did for workers in factories, on shop floors, and in secretarial pools. But the structural change caused by the Wagner Act was, of course, even more fundamental because it protected the right of employees not only to speak but to form and elect democratic unions that would engage over time in collective bargaining with employers.

Corporations challenged the constitutionality of the Act when it was first implemented on the grounds that Congress was not actually regulating "commerce" within the meaning of the Constitution, but regulating industry and manufacture. The Court rejected this precious distinction.[110] It would have been equally plausible, and more democratically defensible, for Congress to define its protection of union organizing in the Wagner Act as an exercise, not of its Commerce Clause powers, but of its powers and duty under the Republican Guaranty Clause to guarantee to the people of the states a Republican form of government. To have huge numbers of Americans employed as lowly wageworkers by state-chartered corporations operating in authoritarian and unaccountable ways is to jeopardize democratic liberties and the political sovereignty of the American people. Congress was acting not only to regulate commerce in the interests of justice but to restore democratic relationships torn asunder by the rise of concentrated and autocratic corporate industry.

During the early decades of the Wagner Act's existence, an energized labor movement organized nearly 40 percent of the private-sector workforce.[111] Today, the unionized sector is less than 15 percent of the total private workforce, and the labor movement must contend with an aggressively hostile corporate opponent backed up by a sophisticated antiunion consulting industry, a lethargic National Labor Relations Board and seething hostility in the federal courts. Much has gone wrong, both externally and internally, for the labor movement's capacity to organize, but perhaps the central problem pervading this malaise is that the law does not embody a coherent democratic vision of labor organization or collective bargaining.

Consider, for example, the Wagner Act's tortured and incoherent rules governing the central problem of employer speech during union elections. Section 7(c) of the Act permits any employer speech to workers during a union campaign so long as it "contains no threat of reprisal or force or promise of benefit."[112] Thus the corporation that owns the property, controls the management, hires and fires, promotes and demotes, gives raises or pay cuts, and regulates every aspect of the workplace, and even determines the place and manner of the union election also has a right to intervene in the election to campaign against the choice of a union, to herd workers into closed "captive audience" meetings about the horrors of unions, to show slick anti-union videos, and to try to persuade employees to vote no, just so long as it makes no *explicit* threats or promises.

Section 7(c) doctrine has developed in predictably pro-management ways. In *NLRB v. Gissel Packing Co.*, the Court developed a distinction between forbidden "threats" by employers to close down operations and perfectly acceptable objective "predictions" by employers of disaster in the event of unionization.[113] This silly distinction permits employers to dress up threats in objective and dispassionate language, giving the threat the added vice of being board-certified and authoritative. Experience has shown that an employer can get away with saying almost anything, as long as its tones are subtle and fatalistic rather than harsh and mean-spirited.

However, rather than obsess on hopeless metaphysical questions such as whether an employer's statement that "we're on the financial edge now, and the smallest economic shock could push us over" is a threat or a prediction, we should reconsider the statutory rule itself. Why should employers have *any* right to participate in the employees' union election decision? They are not members of the bargaining unit electorate, they cannot become members of the union or contributors to it, and their interests are structurally adversary. Employees enjoy no corresponding right to participate in meetings of management or the corporation's board of directors and, in their capacity as employees, have no say in proxy fights or the election of the corporate board of directors. In other words, the union representative election is a sovereign democratic election *among employees* in which managers ought to have no more right to participate than anyone else not part of the bargaining unit.

The law should call for the strict neutrality of management in a union election. Any departures from this neutrality through expression of an official position for or against unionization should constitute an unfair labor practice. Rather than asking whether a particular anti-union statement or communication is a threat or a prediction, we would need only ask whether it constitutes an effort to interfere in the union election. If it is employer interference in the free democratic choice of the workers, it is an unfair labor practice.

Now, it will surely be asked why this is not a violation of the First Amendment. After all, the Supreme Court has simply assumed, at least since the *Gissel* decision in 1969, that the "employer's free-speech right to communicate his views to his employees is firmly established and cannot be infringed."[114] But this is a flawed paradigm for analyzing the speech of corporations, which are state-created artificial entities, and speech generally in the private workplace, which is galaxies away from being a public speech forum. Employers don't want employees talking union and organizing on work premises during work hours, and they presently forbid pro-union publicity on the principle that "work time is for work." Fair enough, but the same should then hold true for them as well. If "work time is for work" for workers, then work time should be for work for managers as well; they should have no special right to campaign on work premises during work hours in order to persuade workers to oppose (or support) a union. Surely individual managers and owners have full-blown citizen speech rights to speak freely off-premises after hours in their private capacities, but the corporation as a corporation has no constitutional right to intervene in the workers' process of democratic will formation—and it should no longer have a statutory right to do so either. Just as union officers who run for reelection are barred by the Taft-Hartley Act from using any union resources or staff to campaign, so corporate officers and managers should be strictly forbidden to use corporate resources and staff to campaign against the union.

It is hard to know whether restoring the integrity of union representative elections would revitalize the labor movement, but it would certainly renew our vision of what citizens organizing in the workplace are doing. A union election is not a contest between the union and the management akin to a contest between the Democratic and Republican parties in another ideologically closed two-party system. Rather, a union election constitutes the exercise of sovereign democratic power by citizens in their workplace, where they spend as much time as they do at home with their families. While a corporation receives a state charter to engage in business, a union is a voluntary group of citizens recognized under federal law who have made a choice to bind themselves together for the purposes of contract negotiations and political self-empowerment. Our law should make our unions at least as strong and viable as it has made our corporations.

CHAPTER NINE

Unflagging Patriotism
The People, the Flag, and the Constitution

The United States themselves are essentially the greatest poem.
—Walt Whitman, introduction to *Leaves of Grass*

The hideous terrorism of September 11, 2001, and the magnificent heroism of our firefighters, police officers, service members and rescue workers that followed, have not only reaffirmed our profound love of country but revived debate about patriotism. What does love of country ask of us? What should we do with it today?

In his essay "Notes on Nationalism,"[1] George Orwell argued that love of country can take the form of patriotism or nationalism. Patriotism, Orwell explained, means "devotion to a particular place and a particular way of life, which one believes to be the best in the world but has no wish to force upon other people."[2] It contrasts with nationalism, which he said is "inseparable from the desire for power. The abiding purpose of every nationalist is to secure more power and more prestige, *not* for himself but for the nation or other unit in which he has chosen to sink his individuality."[3] Nationalism, patriotism's troublesome twin, has often drawn on the darker subterranean impulses of human nature: ethnocentrism, paranoia, racism, bigotry, sadistic hatred of the other.

Americans responded to 9/11 in a deeply patriotic way: donating their blood, giving their money to funds for families of victims, volunteering their time to deal with the many crises following the attacks. But many politicians and columnists have been eager not only to embrace the patriotism we all feel but to promote a militant and haughty nationalism that can be turned to dubious ends.[4]

But the best impulses in American history and culture are indeed patriotic, in Orwell's terms, not nationalistic: they focus on democratic community and individual liberty, not "national superiority" and military triumphalism. After centuries of social struggle, we stand unified as Americans today not by one racial or gender hierarchy, one ethnicity, one religion, one language, one ideology or one political party, but by one Constitution that establishes democratic processes and rights to protect (in theory at least) everyone's freedom and equality. Beyond painting the horizon of our democratic aspirations, the Constitution gives us the "public space" through the First Amendment, and the institutional suppleness, through the separation of powers, to challenge and transcend political tyranny and social injustice.[5]

It is a passionate faith in this system of constitutional values that, borrowing a page from Jürgen Habermas, I will call "constitutional patriotism."[6] Habermas has used this term to mean, I think, not love of a body of technical rules but a profound respect for the foundational and binding constitutional processes that structure a self-governed community. I will try to stretch Habermas's somewhat dry sense of constitutional patriotism to include a love of the constituting *ideals* of the nation. As the world's first written-down constitutional democracy,[7] we have been defined by a transcendent commitment to our constitutional system, which has been both the framework and instrument of progressive democratic inclusion.

In these terms, our greatest constitutional patriots were people who challenged us to translate the grand promises of the Declaration of Independence and the lofty ideals of the modern Constitution—equality, liberty, democracy, rejection of cruelty—into better political and social realities on the ground. In the face of injustice, these patriots held America to its *constituting* promises.

Reverend Martin Luther King, Jr. is a towering example. In his transcendent "Promised Land" speech before a crowd of hundreds in a Memphis church the night before his death, he argued that "the greatness of America is the right to protest *for* right."[8] With this stunning phrase, Dr. King linked the legal concept of *a* right with the moral concept of *the* right and placed the freedom of expression at the heart of American constitutional patriotism.

Dr. King had gone to Memphis to march with striking sanitation workers in defiance not only of water hoses and German shepherds but of what he called an "illegal, unconstitutional" injunction by a state court. There could be no justice for the garbage collectors earning poverty wages unless they could exercise their right to petition for redress of grievances. Because the Jim Crow state defended racial oppression with police repression, the right to protest for right would have to be vindicated by nonviolent civil disobedience. Like Dr. King, the authentic patriots of our history, whether minutemen, abolitionists, populists, suffragists, or SNCC workers in Mississippi, have done what is necessary to secure this original democratic right of protest and then held America fast to its highest self-proclaimed ideals. As Dr. King thundered in Memphis that night: "All we say to America is, 'Be true to what you said on paper.' "9

If the highest form of military patriotism is service in active combat abroad against the enemies of American democracy, the highest form of civilian patriotism at home is working actively to realize and deepen the democracy that we may justly defend. This means sometimes holding the country to constitutional principles that are being flouted, and sometimes changing the Constitution to conform to commonsense democratic understandings. Today, constitutional patriotism requires that we add imperfectly realized rights to American democracy: the citizen's right to vote, the majority's right to elect the president, the political party's right to compete by having fair access to the ballot and to candidate debates, the right of young people to receive an equal and integrated first-class public education for democracy, and the right of citizens to work and organize unions at the workplace.

The Cosmetic Patriotism of the Flag Amendment

Many conservatives have a sharply different vision of what patriotism requires today and how to revise the Constitution. The amendments they seek are of a symbolic and even supernatural character. They favor amendments upholding the Ten Commandments in public places, reinstating organized school prayer, making marriage off-limits to gays and lesbians and making English our official language. Most of their amendments represent an assault on freedom of consciousness and expression. But the one they press with the most passionate seriousness would overturn the Supreme Court's decision in *Texas v. Johnson* (1989)10 and authorize the federal government to arrest, prosecute and jail people who "desecrate" the flag of the United States.

This proposed amendment reads: "The Congress shall have power to prohibit physical desecration of the flag of the United States."11 It is crucial to examine this amendment up close as a polar counterpoint to a progressive constitutional agenda. It is important as a mater of civic respect to take it seriously.

The flag amendment has passed overwhelmingly in the House of Representatives several different times, always clearing the constitutional two-thirds requirement, but has regularly fallen just two or three votes shy of the required 67 votes in the Senate. Given that the flag amendment is only a couple of votes in the Senate away from being sent to the states for ratification, it is important to analyze how much democratic liberty it would subtract from the Constitution.

This proposed constitutional amendment would be the first since Prohibition designed to send people to jail—not, in this case, for drinking evil spirits, but for thinking evil thoughts. Contrary to popular assumption, flag desecration does *not* mean flag-burning. Federal law today affirmatively *recommends* flag burning as the proper mode of flag disposal.[12] This is why tens of thousands of patriotic Boy Scouts and Girl Scouts burn the flag every year. Under the new amendment, the suddenly revived federal criminal flag code will thus not make it a crime simply to burn a flag but to burn a flag (or to paint one, wear one, display one, or rearrange its design elements) *in a context that suggests a political message critical of a government official or some other nearby authority figure.* To "desecrate" means to strip something of its sacredness: the government will use its police powers to tell us when it believes someone has impaired the *sacredness* of the flag. The essence of the flag amendment is political thought control.

In a society where the American flag is ubiquitous and accessible, the amendment would have a sweeping effect on popular culture. If the government enforces current flag law, it could prosecute people for making or using flag clothing, flag swimsuits, flag boxer shorts, flag linen, flag napkins, campaign signs and posters that use the flag, political bumper stickers that use the flag, or any use of the flag for commercial advertising purposes. The federal flag code effectively neutralized by *Texas v. Johnson* would criminalize the use of flags as dress, costume, apparel and in everyday profane activity.

The flag amendment would make the government the effective owner of exclusive trademark rights in the flag design. It would have the power and presumably the duty to police all unauthorized political, artistic, literary, theatrical and cultural uses in which the image of the flag appears. Given that a "flag of the United States," for desecration purposes, means not the regulation flag but "any flag of the United States, or any part thereof, made of any substance, of any size,"[13] the amendment would invite and provoke all of the antics, tomfoolery, and brain-teasing provocations that people develop to subvert thought-control regimes. We would see burning of 49-star flags or red-white-and-*turquoise* flags, the melting of hot wax on flag birthday cakes, the virtual desecration of flags on the Internet, and all manner of taunting red-white-and-blue semiotic mischief.

Traveling down this road is so unnecessary as to be absurd. America is not suffering from political flag cruelty. On the contrary, our nation, from sea to shining sea, is swept up in a vivid demonstration of love of country through spontaneous and beautiful flag display, much of which, ironically, would be made illegal under the new regime. For example, at the 2002 Super Bowl half-time show, rock star Bono of U2, after singing two songs and displaying the names of the victims of terrorism on September 11, flashed the inside of his leather jacket lapel to show a partial fragment of an American flag. The crowd went wild for this classy gesture, but it would have been a crime if the Amendment were passed and today's sleeping flag laws were revived. The moribund flag code makes *any* use of the flag in dress or apparel unlawful.

The flag amendment would fundamentally change the meaning of the Constitution by loading it down with a principle of political content and viewpoint discrimination. It would also change the relationship between the people and our flags, since the present universally accessible stars-and-stripes color scheme would now become the exclusive intellectual property of the government. The amendment would distort patriotism by shifting our emotional focus away from popular freedom to the deified symbol of the nation-state. It would transform the flag itself from a symbol of boundless freedom to an icon of statist thought control. The flag amendment is a dangerous departure from real constitutional patriotism, which calls on us to expand not the police powers of the government to regulate expression but the people's rights of democratic participation.

Political Repression and the "Living Flag" Fallacy

The flag amendment forces, led by the Citizens' Flag Alliance, want us to revive treatment of the flag as a "living thing," in the words of federal law held in abeyance by *Texas v. Johnson*. But this is both a logical fallacy and a glaring factual error. The flag is a powerful symbol but it is not a living thing with feelings. It is not a sentient being. What we call "the flag" is, in reality, an appealing three-color design scheme that can be reproduced in almost any medium, from cloth to nylon to birthday cake to bikini wear to newspaper to bow tie. Individually produced regulation flags are inanimate objects. Anyone who would save an innocent American flag in danger of being destroyed over the life of an innocent human being in danger of being killed has chosen to rescue an inanimate object over a human being, a thing over a person. This would be an awful moral confusion. (Of course, some soldiers have courageously risked their own lives to save an American flag, but surely their loved ones would prefer they not do so since flags are replaceable while people are not.)

What is important about the flag is not the physical "signifier"[14] itself, its dimensions or fabric specifications, but its significations: what it means to us as a political community. It is obviously "polysemous": it has multiple available meanings. People see different things in the flag. When I look at it, I read into it the story of the social struggle and moral progress of America from the Revolution forward: democracy over royalty, liberty over power, individual mobility over hereditary privilege, freedom over slavery, national reason over local tyranny, liberalism over totalitarianism, justice over inequality, democratic inclusion over snobbery and human rights over hierarchy. I see the boundless, magnificent promise of inclusive popular democracy. Other people see other things: I saw a truck in Louisiana that had on its bumper both a Confederate flag sticker and an American flag sticker, as though the driver were blissfully ignorant that armies clashed in brutal combat under these two symbols.

The flag amendment aims to freeze some unarticulated positive meaning of the flag and protect it with the might of the criminal justice system. This impulse to treat the flag as a living thing with rights of its own has a strong hold on the nationalist imagination and a not altogether contemptible history. Prior to the Civil War, the American flag "played a very minor role in the political, or even in the decorative, life of the United States," but the war against slavery "transformed the flag into a genuinely popular, and frequently displayed symbol of the nation, or, more precisely, of the North, in its struggle to maintain the Union against the Confederacy, which, of course, had its own flag."[15] During the war, it was a serious criminal offense to show contempt for the Union flag or to display a Confederate flag. After the Civil War, as Americans grew determined to put the Confederacy in its place and bolster a newfound sense of national identity, many states passed laws to treat "disrespect" of our flag as if it were physical assault on a person. The flag became the favored symbol of those fighting for egalitarian and inclusive democracy. As one senator put it, it was the government's duty to "see that no man who had voted for the flag should be under the feet of him who had insulted it."[16]

Unfortunately, the Reconstruction effort to redistribute wealth and power did not last, but the official treatment of the American flag as a holy and living thing did. This conceptual confusion led to the states incarcerating hundreds, perhaps thousands, of American citizens for misusing their flags over the years. Until its landmark First Amendment decision in *Texas v. Johnson* in 1989, the Supreme Court was implicated in a very cruel and irrational political repression.

The first target of the flag-protection movement—led by patriotic-hereditary organizations such as the Daughters of the American Revolution and veterans' groups, such as the Grand Army of the Republic—was commercial desecration, the widespread use of the flag design in business and advertising. In 1895, the flag-protection movement identified more than 120 types of commercial flag uses in Chicago alone, including the flag-based decoration or advertising of belts, breweries, burlesque shows, ballet dresses, doormats, pool halls, saloons, brothels, chewing gum, toilet paper, fireworks, the shorts of prizefighters, paper used to wrap cheese and ham, cigars, soap and urinals.[18] Some 31 states passed criminal flag desecration laws between 1897 and 1905, and other states followed suit soon thereafter.[19]

The constitutionality of criminal punishment of commercial flag desecrators came before the Court in 1907 in *Halter v. Nebraska*,[20] when Nebraska convicted two businessmen for selling a bottle of "Stars and Stripes" beer which had a little flag emblem on it. The businessmen argued that the state's anti-desecration law interfered with their constitutionally protected property rights, specifically their right to pursue a lawful calling (which shows you how substantive due process "right to contract" arguments were considered more viable in the Court than free-speech arguments during the *Lochner* era).

But the Court rejected the businessmen's appeal, embracing Nebraska's argument that it could impose criminal "penalties upon those who do not observe a decent respect for the patriotic, moral and religious sentiments and feelings of others." The Court made it clear that it would uphold all laws against commercial desecration because "it is a matter of common knowledge that the use of the flag for advertising purposes offends the sensibilities of a large portion of our people," and that "[a]dvertising usage of the flag tends to degrade and cheapen the flag in the estimation of the people."[21]

After the *Halter* decision upheld repression of flag-based commercial speech early in the twentieth century, World War I shifted the gaze of the flag-protection movement. The point was no longer to keep the flag design off beer cans and underwear but to suppress perceived mistreatment of the flag by radicals, anarchists, and anti-war activists.[22] According to historian Robert Goldstein, "by 1920 the focus of the flag protection movement" was "overwhelmingly centered upon left-wing political dissent."[23] Between World War I and the start of the Vietnam War, there were 45 reported flag-desecration convictions at the state or federal level, almost all of a political or artistic nature, and hundreds more unreported.

Some of the stories are striking. During World War I, a man named E.V. Starr in Montana was prosecuted for desecrating and insulting the flag when in public he called it "nothing but a piece of cotton" with "a little paint and some other marks" on it. He was sentenced to between ten and twenty years of hard labor in the state penitentiary and handed a $500 fine. The judge called Starr's sentence "horrifying" but said that he had no choice under the statute.

In 1930, two young mothers who ran a left-wing summer camp for children were sentenced to jail for ninety days for refusing, at the behest of a mob, to lift and kiss a flag that was on the ground. The judge that sentenced them said the harsh sentences were intended "as a warning to communists all over the United States that they could not trifle with the American flag or teach un-christian doctrines." During World War II, hundreds of children of the Jehovah's Witness faith were expelled from school for refusing to salute the flag, and two adults were sentenced to prison for two to ten years for passing out a flier denouncing compulsory flag salutes. (This struggle would lead to *West Virginia v. Barnette*.[24])

During the Civil Rights movement and the Vietnam War, with protest on the rise, Congress passed its first flag-desecration statute and dozens of others passed in the states. Many anti-war protestors and hippies went to jail for burning flags, placing peace signs on them, writing "stop the war" on them, having flag patches on their knees or on their rear ends, wearing a flag vest, poncho, or cape, or flying the flag upside down. Meanwhile, conservative and clean-cut people who put a flag decal on their cars with "Nixon-Agnew" printed over it, wrote "America: Love it or Leave it" on their flags, or wore flag T-shirts that said "Burn this one, asshole" on them, were simply left alone by the police and prosecutors. A 1971 article in *Art in America* found that those arrested for flag desecration "are invariably critics of national policy while patriots who tamper with the flag are overlooked."[25] By the end of the Vietnam War, there had been more than a thousand criminal prosecutions, including the following:

- In a 1970 Dallas case, nineteen-year-old Gary Deeds went to jail for four years—and served every day of his sentence—for burning a piece of flag bunting that actually had on it only 21 stars and 8 stripes. Robert Goldstein quotes Deeds's lawyer John Nelms as saying: "If Deeds had done almost anything else, possession of drugs, stealing a car, burglarizing a house ... he would have gotten probation. I never dreamed at anytime ... that there was even a remote possibility he would go to prison." He said that it was the "biggest shock that I've had as a trial lawyer. I've tried over 500 cases in jury trials and I couldn't believe it."[26]
- In the same year in Cambridge, Massachusetts, a high school senior who burned a flag was sentenced to carry a large, fifteen-pound American flag on a three-mile march through Cambridge or do six months in jail. She chose the three-mile march and was surrounded by police officers and a screaming mob. The president of the local ACLU likened her sentence to "the pillory and the stocks of 250 years ago."[27]
- In Albuquerque, New Mexico, in 1970, a "hippie" wearing a flag headband was arrested and sentenced to six months in jail.[28]
- In a 1971 case called *Joyce v. U.S.*,[29] the United States Circuit Court for the District of Columbia upheld a one-year jail sentence imposed on an anti-war protestor at Richard Nixon's inauguration. The protester had pulled out a miniature American flag, removed it from its staff and torn off a piece of it to wrap around his finger so that he could make a red-white-and-blue peace sign. Judge MacKinnon (the father of Professor Catharine MacKinnon!) held that "a little American flag is entitled to the same protection as a large one," and emphasized that this was no innocent act but a deliberate attempt to "disrespect" and "disgrace" the flag.[30] Amazingly, the arresting police officer brought a miniature flag replica to the trial and reenacted the entire crime for the benefit of the jury by tearing off a piece of the flag and wrapping it around his finger. No arrest was made despite the fact that this was not a narrative description of the "crime" but a precise reproduction of it.[31] It would be as if a testifying police officer killed someone to show a jury how a murder happened.

Ironically, the original post–Civil War flag protection movement also wanted to stop political disrespect of the flag, but its target was the rampant partisan use of the flag by mainstream political candidates on campaign signs, posters and brochures. For example, in the 1896 presidential campaign between Republican William McKinley and Democrat-Populist William Jennings Bryan, the "McKinley campaign enveloped itself in flags and clearly suggested, both by slogans and symbols, that the Bryan forces were out to crush 'the American way of life.'"[32] McKinley's campaign manager Mark Hanna gave out buttons containing a replica of the American flag with McKinley's name on it and produced literally millions of flags for use at Flag Day rallies he organized in McKinley's personal honor. The leader of the flag protection movement at the time complained that the flag's "sacredness" had been "encroached upon" by "the great political parties ... and crafty politicians, who turn it into a campaign banner for rival political clubs, a mop for the floor of political barrooms and other despicable uses."[33]

But while the anarchists, socialists and anti-war agitators of later periods would end up behind bars, McKinley and Hanna proceeded to take over the country, road-testing and perfecting the modern Republican formula of corporate money and nationalist flag-waving to defeat the Populist candidate. While it is easy to foresee the new flag amendment resulting in imprisonment of radicals, it is impossible to imagine mainstream politicians going to jail for using the flag for self-interested partisan or demagogic purposes.

How the Court Defined Democratic Rights against Flag-Based Thought Control

It was a transforming moment in the history of political freedom when the Supreme Court recognized that flags were not living things and that putting people in jail for hurting flags was in effect—and let us not mince words here—to make political prisoners. The Court took its first giant step away from the 1905 *Halter* decision in 1943 when it struck down compulsory participation in public school flag-salute ceremonies in *West Virginia v. Barnette*.[34] Although it did not deal explicitly with desecration, the *Barnette* decision essentially established that the state could not fix official meanings of the flag and then criminalize departure from rules of proper respect.

In *Barnette*, the West Virginia Board of Education had ordered students to join in a daily Pledge of Allegiance ritual. The board modified its original plans after the Boy Scouts and Girl Scouts protested that its hand salute was "too much like Hitler's."[35] But the board declined to accommodate Jehovah's Witnesses, who objected that complying with any salute of the American flag would require their children, at the pain of being expelled and declared delinquent, to salute a "graven image" and practice a kind of idol worship forbidden by their religion.[36] The Board's position was that the Jehovah's Witnesses' interpretation of the flag salute was wrong and that the flag salute was a reasonable secular policy that could not be read to interfere with their religious freedom.

But Justice Jackson essentially found that the meanings of symbols were in the realm of opinion and argument such that the state could not impose politically correct interpretations on the public. The compulsory pledge required students to affirm a belief and a specific "attitude of mind" that they did not hold, violating the First Amendment right not to speak against conscience.[37] Only a grave security emergency—a "clear and present danger"—could justify compelling the Jehovah's Witnesses to profess a belief they did not hold.[38]

Justice Jackson refuted the claim, which the Court had embraced in 1940 in *Minersville School District v. Gobitis*,[39] that the flag ritual was acceptable because "national unity is the basis of national security."[40] Calling forth the ghosts of totalitarianism and genocide, he stated: "Those who begin coercive elimination of dissent soon find themselves exterminating dissenters. Compulsory unification of opinion achieves only the unanimity of the graveyard."[41]

Urging the nation to celebrate "intellectual individualism and the rich cultural diversities that we owe to exceptional minds," Justice Jackson wrote that the "price" of tolerating dissent "is not too great" in this case. But even where society finds the price to be a high one, he stated, "freedom to differ is not limited to things that do not matter much. That would be a mere shadow of freedom. The test of its substance is the right to differ as to things that touch the heart of the existing order."[42]

And then, Justice Jackson gave us the central principle of democratic freedom in our Constitution:

> If there is any fixed star in our constitutional constellation, it is that no official, high or petty, can prescribe what shall be orthodox in politics, nationalism, religion, or other matters of opinion or force citizens to confess by word or act their faith therein. If there are any circumstances which permit an exception they do not now occur to us.[43]

Barnette set the table for the Court's later treatment of criminal convictions arising from the crime of "flag desecration." Of course, a finding that children may decline to salute a flag did not mean that adults had a constitutional right to destroy one. Indeed, for decades after *Barnette*, and especially through the turmoil of the Vietnam War, the Court continued to allow the conviction and punishment of flag desecrators.

Yet on April 21, 1969, the Court in a five-to-four decision[44] took another step in a libertarian direction when it overturned the criminal conviction of a flag-burner charged under New York's flag desecration statute forbidding the casting of contempt upon the flag "either by words or act." The defendant, Sidney Street, a 47-year-old African-American bus driver from Brooklyn who had collected a Bronze Star for heroism in World War II, was sentenced to a year in jail for burning a flag after he learned of the shooting death of Civil Rights activist James Meredith at a march in Mississippi. Street said at the time of the protest that, "if they let that happen to Meredith we don't need an American flag."[45] The Court's slender majority found that the statute created the possibility that Street had been found guilty based only on his words, which it could not do short of demonstrating that he had incited imminent violence. Justice Harlan made it clear that the Court was not confronting the constitutionality of the whole ban on physical mistreatment of the flag since this narrower ground for decision was available.[46]

Texas v. Johnson

The key test of the state's power to make physical desecration a crime came in 1989, when the Court heard the case of Gregory Johnson, a youth member of the Revolutionary Communist Party who burned an American flag at the 1984 Republican National Convention in Houston. The Court in *Texas v. Johnson*[47] struck down Johnson's conviction for violating a state law making it a crime to "deface, damage or otherwise physically mistreat" the American flag "in a way that the actor knows will seriously offend one or more persons likely to observe or discover his action."[48]

Writing for a five-to-four majority in *Johnson*, Justice Brennan found that "Johnson's flag-burning was 'conduct' sufficiently imbued with elements of communication to implicate the First Amendment."[49] Because "speech" and "nonspeech" were mixed together in the flag-burning, Justice Brennan followed the Court's *O'Brien* standard, which requires government to show a "sufficiently important governmental interest in regulating the nonspeech element" in order to justify any "incidental limitations on First Amendment freedoms."[50] However, as Justice Brennan emphasized, the asserted "governmental interest" itself must be "unrelated to the suppression of free expression."[51] The problem for Texas was that its asserted interest "in preserving the flag as a symbol of nationhood and national unity" was precisely related to political expression. The state wanted to control the symbolic uses of the flag to prevent anti-government messages.

Justice Brennan picked up the thread that had been woven into the fabric of free speech law by Justice Jackson:

> If there is a bedrock principle underlying the First Amendment, it is that the Government may not prohibit the expression of an idea simply because society finds the idea itself offensive or disagreeable. We have not recognized an exception to this principle even where our flag is involved.... [If] we were to hold that a State may forbid flag-burning wherever it is likely to endanger the flag's symbolic role, but allow it wherever burning a flag promotes that role—as where, for example, a person ceremoniously burns a dirty flag—we would be saying that when it comes to impairing the flag's physical integrity, the flag itself may be used as a symbol only in one direction. We would be permitting a State to "prescribe what shall be orthodox."[52]

It is hard to resist the logical force of this analysis, which is why the dissenters in *Texas v. Johnson* rounded up strikingly irrational and mystical arguments. Chief Justice William Rehnquist's dissent, joined by Justice Byron White and Justice Sandra Day O'Connor, quoted at length dense and flowery passages of poetry and prose extolling or mentioning the American flag, including Ralph Waldo Emerson's "Concord Hymn," the lyrics of Francis Scott Key's National Anthem, and John Greenleaf Whittier's poem, "Barbara Frietchie." These extraconstitutional literary sources were mobilized to show that "the American flag has occupied a unique position as the symbol of our Nation, a uniqueness that justifies a governmental prohibition against flag burning in the way Johnson did here."[53] The fact that the First Amendment contains no exception for government censorship of speech about "unique" literary symbols did not faze Justice Rehnquist, since "millions and millions of Americans regard it with an almost mystical reverence...."[54] The reverent millions can turn mystical and jail other Americans for their patriotic incorrectness.

In his dissent, Justice John Paul Stevens, ordinarily lucid and well grounded in the First Amendment, also favored suspending the conventional rules of constitutional analysis: "Even if flag burning could be considered just another species of symbolic speech under the *logical* application of the rules that the Court has developed in its interpretation of the First Amendment in other contexts, this case has an *intangible* dimension that makes those rules inapplicable."[55] Justice Stevens likened the claimed right to burn flags in political protest to "a federal right to post bulletin boards and graffiti on the Washington Monument."[56] The problem with this analogy, of course, is that we have only one Washington Monument, and all of it is public property; if it is defaced, it is ruined for everyone for all time. But we have tens of millions of flags, and almost all of them are private property: they belong to citizen-owners who can do with them what they will without harming their fellow citizens' enjoyment of their own flags or the government's control of its own flag stable. Government-owned flags are protected by laws forbidding destruction of public property.

The *Johnson* decision provoked not only weepy panegyrics to the flag by dissenting Justices but a storm of political protest. President George Bush, Sr., originally unhysterical about the decision, met with his political advisers and did an about-face, calling for a constitutional amendment to reverse it. Soon thereafter, spurred by liberal Democrats eager to avoid voting on a constitutional amendment but afraid to stand up for free speech, Congress passed the Flag Protection Act of 1989, which made it a crime for any person "knowingly to mutilate, deface, physically defile, burn, maintain on the floor or ground, or trample upon any flag of the United States."[57] The government maintained that this law was structured to protect "the physical integrity of the flag under all circumstances" without referring to political viewpoint and therefore did not impermissibly "target expressive conduct on the basis of the content of its message."

However, in *U.S. v. Eichman*,[58] a five-to-four majority once again ruled against the validity of banning flag desecration. Justice Brennan found that the whole purpose of the law was to prevent certain kinds of messages about the flag from being communicated by citizens to one another: "Although Congress cast the [Act] in somewhat broader terms than the Texas statute at issue in *Johnson*, the Act still suffers from the same fundamental flaw: it suppresses expression out of concern for its likely communicative impact."[59]

By closing the door on flag-desecration statutes, the *Eichman* decision gave birth to a powerful conservative movement to amend the Constitution to "protect the flag." In both 1990 and 1995, Congress, by the narrowest of margins, rejected the following constitutional amendment: "Congress and the states shall have power to prohibit physical desecration of the flag of the United States." The Citizens' Flag Alliance lost narrowly again in 1997 with the following amendment: "Congress shall have power to prohibit physical desecration of the flag of the United States." In 2001, this language passed overwhelmingly in the House of Representatives by voice vote.[60] The current war against terrorism has only increased the determination of the Citizens' Flag Alliance and its conservative allies to amend the Constitution.

What's the Big Deal?

In this time of war against terrorism and high patriotic and nationalist passion both, it is tempting to ask: What's the big deal? Why *not* amend the Constitution to provide a "flag exception" to the First Amendment?

But the spirit and angle of this question are way off. When we think about proposals changing the Constitution, we should ask: Why amend? rather than, Hey, why not? The Constitution is the nation's permanent governing covenant. It has the virtue of being clear, relatively brief and not weighted down by rhetoric. We should make changes to it only when the people have soberly concluded that, over time, the document is systematically neglecting basic social values or needs in a way that causes serious problems for democratic life. This is the test I have tried to use in exploring my proposed amendments on the right to vote, abolition of the Electoral College and the right to an education. Democratic citizens should keep in mind the difference between constitutional politics, which should concern problems of enduring and unavoidable national significance, and legislative politics, which concerns issues that are part of the normal push-and-pull and hurly-burly of everyday partisan maneuvering and factional struggle.

Why Do We Need a Flag Amendment?

So let us ask why Americans should want to enact the first amendment since Prohibition designed to subtract liberty from the Constitution, the first amendment to the First Amendment? What does the flag amendment accomplish?

The vague answer provided by flag-amendment proponents is that it is needed to "permit the people . . . to protect the flag," as the amendment's leading academic exponent, Harvard Law School professor Richard Parker, puts it.[61] And yet a moment's reflection discredits this reason. There is no such thing as "*the* flag," at least in the sense that we have "*the* Washington Monument" or "*the* Lincoln Memorial." We have countless millions of flags all over the fifty states and the District of Columbia. Most of them are owned privately, but hundreds of thousands are owned by government agencies, military bases, schools and so on. All of these flags are already protected from desecration, since they are property belonging to private individuals or to government. They thus enjoy all of the legal protections attendant to property. If anyone tries to take down and burn the American flag that flies on my front porch, for example, I can call the police and have the intruders prosecuted for trespass, theft, malicious destruction of property and arson. If anyone tries to take down and burn a government flag, he will face not only theft, arson and trespass charges but a charge of destruction of government property. We need no more protection for our flags in criminal law than already exists.

When the proponents of the amendment talk about "flag protection," they have to mean protecting flags from their rightful owners, specifically the minuscule handful who intend to fold, spindle, mutilate or burn them in public with a subversive point in mind. Conservative flag protectors are really calling for a nationalization of intellectual property rights in the flag—in essence the establishment of an official government trademark in any renderings of the colors red, white, and blue—in order to stop any representations that are suggestive of both flagness and seditious criticism.

Out of millions of flags waving everywhere in America, only a tiny number are ever "desecrated" by their owners: about ten a year in a nation of around three hundred million people. You have a greater chance of being hit by lightning, winning a lottery or being racially profiled than you have of encountering a flag on fire at a protest. The fact that flags can sleep so peacefully in America is due not only to the patriotism of most Americans but also to the fact that there is no incentive for even the most bitter dissidents to desecrate them, since it is perfectly lawful to do so. Since *Texas v. Johnson*, the Maoist fire starters at the Revolutionary Communist Youth Brigade have had no reason to burn flags. Since it's protected symbolic speech, the press doesn't show up to cover them, the public doesn't show up to jeer them, and flag-burners just advertise their own depressing inarticulateness. In a free country, who cares? Flag-burners have a right to make jerks out of themselves.

But if we pass a constitutional amendment to criminalize desecration,

we will pull every pyromaniac militiaman, every publicity-starved performance artist on a National Endowment for the Arts grant and every
self-dramatizing teenager reading Ayn Rand or Mao Tse Tung out into
the streets to test the boundaries of our new symbolic thought control
regime. Flags will go up in flames; they will suffer the indignity of blood
or ketchup stains; they will endure the affixing of peace signs; they will be
turned into blue jean patches for the knees or bottom; they will become
part of visual and performance art shows. America remains a freedom-
loving country; many people still pride themselves on another of our original
flag themes: "Don't tread on me."

Thus, if the purpose of the amendment is really to reduce the tiny number of flags now being destroyed in public, the amendment is the wrong
way to go. The amendment will increase substantially the incidence of
flag mutilation. If we really want to act on the deranged premise that flags
have feelings (like persons or animals) and hope to "protect" them from
cruelty and flag abuse, the most ineffective strategy I can think of is in effect
to dare people with a thought-control constitutional amendment to become
free-speech martyrs by torturing a flag.

Proponents skip over this rather obvious point because they are not
primarily interested in "protecting" the flag at all. Beyond its function as
a cheap campaign issue, the amendment has only one practical purpose:
putting people in jail.

Flag Boxers, Barbara Bush's 1988 Inaugural Gown,
and Fourth of July Napkins: What Is "Desecration"?

But why? What are the specific elements of this crime of "desecration"?
To "desecrate" means to strip something of its sanctity, to treat a holy object
in a sacrilegious way.[62] The flag amendment would essentially turn the flag
into a holy relic, our untouchable national religious idol. For many believers in the Old Testament, not just Jehovah's Witnesses, this secular idolatry
will offend not only the First Amendment but the First and Second Commandments, which forbid idol worship and graven images. For believers
in an Enlightenment Constitution that elevates reason over superstition,
the deification of the flag threatens to unleash a virus of unreason in the
Constitution.

The metaphysical crime of flag desecration will have to be defined as
physical abuse of a flag accompanied by a politically incorrect thought.
Otherwise there will be no way to separate dutiful, patriotic flag-burning

from the subversive kind. Recall that flag-burning is *not* flag desecration. Federal law right now practically *requires* flag-burning as the proper mode of flag disposal: "The flag, when it is in such condition that it is no longer a fitting emblem for display, should be destroyed in a dignified way, preferably by burning."[63] This is why millions of Boy Scouts and Girl Scouts have burned flags in public.[64]

What will distinguish a teen Boy Scout troop burning flags from teen members of the Revolutionary Communist Youth Brigade burning flags will be whether some radical political thought is perceived to accompany the act. The act itself is perfectly inscrutable. When we turn to other kinds of even more ambiguous desecrations—sewing a flag patch on a quilt or blue jeans, using the flag in an anti-war painting, making the flag part of a television ad to sell beer or bathing suits or condoms, making the flag design part of a napkin that gets bunched up with birthday cake and thrown away—lines again will necessarily be drawn by official perceptions of the character of political statements being made by the suspects.

So the flag amendment is a dagger pointed at the heart of the First Amendment, which protects unpopular, subversive and anti-establishment speech. Everything in the campaign for the flag amendment suggests that its purpose is to put people in jail for the crime of thinking negative thoughts about the government while engaging in the legally recommended mode of flag disposal. The agenda is to give police and prosecutors a hunting license to pounce on political outsiders and radicals who use their flag in officially unapproved ways.[65]

Of course, if the purpose of the amendment is not to hound political dissenters but truly to make the flag "sacred" and keep it pristine like the original parchment Constitution in the National Archives, we will have to enforce the federal criminal code in a viewpoint-neutral way that sweeps far more broadly across popular and nonpolitical uses of the flag. Consider the following kinds of things that would (and should) be made criminal under federal laws still on the books if *Texas v. Johnson* is reversed by the flag amendment and these laws spring back to life.

Any Use of the Flag for Business Advertising, Clothing, or Household Decor
Commercial flag desecration would become illegal if the amendment passes, since the sleeping federal flag statute bans all advertising uses. It states: "The flag should never be used for advertising purposes in any manner whatsoever." [66]

But society is replete with this kind of market desecration. The flag appears on ads for Speedo bathing suits, Ralph Lauren Polo sport after-shave, Tommy Hilfiger sweaters, $2,000 Perry Ellis cashmere flag-mink stoles, skimpy stars-and-bars bikinis found in *Sports Illustrated* swimsuit issues, Old Glory flag condoms and the cover of Bruce Springsteen's album *Born in the USA*. If the amendment passes, the U.S. flag code of 1942 and similar state statutes will make it a crime to sell or possess any of these materials.

But the flag also makes significant appearance in dress, fashion, costume, household goods and social life. All of this will be illegal, because the flag code provides: "The flag should never be used as wearing apparel, bedding or drapery" or "as a costume or athletic uniform."[67] It also states that the flag "should not be embroidered on such articles as cushions or handkerchiefs and the like, printed or otherwise impressed on paper napkins or boxes or anything that is designed for temporary use and discard."[68]

Here are some of the everyday uses that will therefore be made criminal: making the flag part of a quilt or owning an antique Civil War–era quilt with a flag sewn on it; wearing a flag-theme sweater; Olympic athletes wearing flag-design uniforms; sewing a flag patch on your blue jeans; wearing flag boxer shorts; Barbara Bush wearing a flag dress to her husband's inauguration in 1988; using red-white-and-blue napkins at a Fourth of July barbecue; dressing up as a flag for Halloween. The mother of one of my law students who does quilting and needlepoint sent me an e-mail explaining that her needlepoint circle is vehemently opposed to the flag amendment because many members make creative designs out of the flag scheme that will presumably be rendered illegal under the Amendment.

Patriotic and Partisan Flag Desecration
Political desecration deeply troubled the flag-protection movement a century ago. In our day, of course, the flag is used by political parties all the time, and not just the Revolutionary Communist Party. Think of the Democratic and Republican national conventions, where the convention floors are awash in a sea of red, white and blue. During the 1996 congressional campaign, the Citizens' Flag Alliance used a beautiful waving flag as a backdrop for millions of dollars of negative TV ads against U.S. Senate candidates who opposed their amendment, including Senator Paul Wellstone and Senator John Kerry, a Vietnam veteran. Surely if we are going to keep the flag sacred, these partisan uses profane and desecrate the flag, as prior generations of flag protectors understood, converting it from a symbol of the "whole people" into a symbol of "one party."[69]

It is also common practice for political candidates to write their names over flag-background bumper stickers, posters and buttons. But the federal law that will be revived by the princely kiss of the flag amendment clearly provides that the flag "should never have placed upon it, nor on any part of it, nor attached to it *any* mark, insignia, letter, word, figure, design, picture, or drawing of any nature."[70] All campaign literature with flag dress will be illegal. It will be no more permissible for some people to write "John Smith, Democrat for Senate" on a flag background than for others to put "Stop Trading with China," "America: Love It or Leave It," or "Peace Now" on their own flag designs. Recall that a "flag of the United States," for desecration purposes, means not the regulation flag but "any flag of the United States, or any part thereof, made of any substance, of any size...."[71]

Artistic and Cultural Flag Desecration

In the history of flag protection, the government has often hounded and prosecuted artists who use the flag in their works and also the people who display them. In a famous 1966 case, Stephen Radich, the owner of an art gallery in New York, was arrested for showing the anti-war art of Marc Morel, whose sculpture and paintings included flag fragments and designs. The case dragged on for eight years before his conviction was overturned.[72]

Much art and theater still incorporate flag themes. Think of the beautiful but clearly altered and "desecrated" paintings of flags done by Jasper Johns. Think of the partially burned and framed American flag that Robert Redford's character has on his office wall in the movie *Spy Game*. Think of the musical *Hair* with its flag costumes. Think of the provocative flag-on-the-floor art exhibit at the Chicago Museum of Art by "Dred" Scott Tyler in 1989. Think of Woody Harrelson starring in *The People vs. Larry Flynt* and wearing an American flag diaper (after escaping the attempt on his life). Because all of these artistic or cinematic uses run afoul of federal flag law, they would become criminal contraband and evidence of felony thought crime. If we say that no prosecutors will actually follow up on any flag desecrations from Hollywood, then we are saying that the rich and famous should have more expressive rights than everyone else.

If the flag amendment is not going to be about singling out dissident political speech, then it will ban *all* commercial, partisan, artistic and everyday desecrations of the flag. That is, the government will essentially capture the flag from its rightful owners—the American people—and create a state-owned monopoly trademark in the people's flag. We could expect to see one day an official government licensing authority that will approve or disapprove proposed citizen uses of the flag design in business, art, culture, theater and clothing.

Flag-Stamp Cancellation, Virtual Flag-Burnings, and the Magritte Flag Paradox: What Is "The Flag"?

Beyond the perplexing question of what categories of desecration are to be banned, the amendment creates headaches relating to the definition of flags and the classification of particular instances of disrespect. Like all thought-control measures, this one is doomed to paradox and absurdity. Consider the following brainteasing dilemmas destined to emerge under the new flag treason regime. Recalling that current federal law defines a flag as "any flag of the United States, or any part thereof, made of any substance, of any size,"[73] which of the following will constitute criminal desecration?

- Someone stages a "virtual" flag-burning on the Internet. (There is already a flag-burning Web site operating.) The burned flag has no fabric, but it must have some kind of physical existence in the real world, otherwise we couldn't see it!
- Someone sews, displays and then burns a 49-star flag. Criminal desecration or parody?
- Someone sews and burns a fifty-star flag but replaces the blue with turquoise. Desecration or avante-garde art?
- Someone makes a flag that is two inches too short in length, writes "This is not a flag" on it and then burns it. (This is what my friend Michael Anderson calls the Magritte flag paradox.)
- Someone gathers a bunch of old flags and burns them in opposition to the flag amendment. Criminal desecration or patriotic retirement of worn flags?
- Someone burns a flag stamp. Criminal desecration or *de minimis* exception?
- The post office cancels millions of flag stamps a year. Government saboteurs?

Where does the flag amendment end and the First Amendment begin? In freedom-loving America, people will gleefully test the boundaries of any system of thought control.

It might be said that the amendment will never be used to jail people for mere unauthorized tampering with the flag design. Perhaps its purpose is simply the high-symbolic function of expressing the sanctity of the stars and stripes. Yet if this is its purpose, it is hard to see why the existing hortatory federal statutory regime prescribing proper flag protocol and etiquette (including flag-burning!) is not already perfectly sufficient. If we do not plan to use the amendment to put people in jail, weighting the Constitution down with its first purely symbolic amendment seems like a pointless and dangerous exercise.

Why Not Ban the Confederate Flag?
Taking Treasonous Flag Semiotics Seriously

If we want to carve out exceptions to the First Amendment to get rid of flag-related offenses to the Union, why begin with the relatively trivial problem of a handful of political flag desecrations each year? The truly pervasive, taunting insult to the American nation is the Confederate flag, which symbolizes to many people slavery, secessionism, and violent destruction of the Union. It flies from porches, offices, the bumpers of pickup trucks, pom-poms and beach towels all over America.

No human perished because a handful of teen Maoists burned a flag in Dallas in 1984 at the Republican Convention, but hundreds of thousands of Americans lost their lives fighting against the Confederate battle flag and the secessionist pro-slavery government for which it stood. To many Americans, the Confederate flag communicates more of a clear and present danger than an American flag on fire. Arguably, under current Thirteenth Amendment doctrine, the Confederate flag could already be banned by Congress as a "badge and incident" of slavery.[74] Why not constitutionalize the nation's triumph over the Confederacy with the constitutional censorship of what one Union veteran and commander in chief of the Grand Army of the Republic in 1891 called "the banner of secession and treason"?[75]

I do not actually favor this idea, since it is a bad idea to use the Constitution to ban the symbolic representation of evil things. To be sure, we should use our Constitution and collective power under it to fight and denounce evil things, like slavery, fascism and terrorism and to root in principles and mechanisms of democratic self-government. But political thought control does not promote political justice. It does not work because the repressed subject inevitably returns with more force just to spite the censor: it is hard to imagine a bigger boon to racism in America than an effort to ban private display of the Confederate battle flag. Social progress takes place through active engagement with the public conscience and consciousness; this is why movement politics is necessary for change to take place. But in a democratic society, where public opinion controls authority and not vice versa,[76] the state must regulate only conduct, not thought.

The flag amendment threatens to change the character of the Constitution. It is possible, of course, that the new amendment could become a carefully defined exception that proves the rule of viewpoint- and content-neutrality. Far more likely is that it will spread like a virus through the Constitution, inviting new amendments to expressive liberty and new judicial interpretations that treat patriotic symbols and ideas as off-limits to criticism. This is a most troubling prospect since, in a democracy, the sovereignty of the people depends on their ability to criticize government and even precious symbols that government inevitably mobilizes to defend its power.

The flag amendment is unwarranted and unnecessary. The fact that people have been able to burn the flag with impunity since 1989 has probably *reduced* the incidence of flag desecration while not in the least damaging patriotism or popular love for the flag. Just look around. Americans love the flag as a visible symbol of our democracy, and we redouble that love in the face of hostility to it.

Ironically, only the amendment itself could compromise and tarnish the reputation of the American flag today. Right now the flag that flies on my front porch symbolizes a freedom so vast and so deep as to encompass even the right to purchase a flag and make it part of a sculpture, weave it into a quilt, or turn it into part of a dramatic political statement. If this amendment passes, the flag—our cherished symbol of freedom—will suddenly become a symbol of political thought control. The banner of freedom turns into a sign of repression.

By trying to sanctify the flag, its self-appointed protectors sully and cheapen it. We do not need an army of police, prosecutors and judges telling us what to do with our flags or how to feel about them. I love the flag, but I love even more passionately the boundless freedom of thought that the flag represents. Why would we amend the Constitution to undermine not only our freedom and our patriotism but the semiotic honor of the flag itself? We have a far more serious and hopeful constitutional agenda to pursue.

CHAPTER TEN

Democracy Rising

Overruling the Court, Rerighting America

When precedents fail to assist us, we must return to the first principles of things for information; and think as if we were the first men that thought.
—Thomas Paine, "The Forester's Letter IV," May 18, 1776[1]

It is indeed time to rewrite the Constitution, but not for the purpose of expanding the government's power to control expression. We should rewrite the Constitution in order to *re-right* American democracy. When the Supreme Court shrinks our civil rights by misinterpreting a federal statute, Congress can go back and amend the law to restore the original meaning, something it has done frequently in the new age of judicial reactivism. In 1982, for example, Congress amended the Voting Rights Act to make clear that the Act legislates an "effects" test for discrimination against minorities in voting and not an "intent" test, as the Court had misconstrued it in *Mobile v. Bolden*.[2] In 1991, Congress amended the 1866 Civil Rights Act to overturn the Supreme Court's pinched and narrowing construction of the statute in *Patterson v. McClean Credit Union* (1989), which found race discrimination in the performance of contracts (as opposed to their formation) to be outside the scope of the statute.[3] Practically speaking, the Court then has no choice but to live with congressional acts "overruling" its prior squinting construction of federal civil rights laws.

But Congress lacks a parallel legislative power to reverse the Court's misreadings of the Constitution. If the Court declares that there is no constitutional right to vote or to receive an education, such pronouncements are final and controlling against normal legislation. The Court becomes the final arbiter of what the Constitution means. (Although not of what the Constitution *says*.)

Sometimes when Congress simply cannot stomach the Court's constitutional vision, it fools itself by thinking that it can supply the same rights through legislation that the Court has denied in constitutional adjudication. It might work in theory but, in reality, today's activist conservative Court will promptly put Congress back in its place and chastise it for its impertinence. In 1990, for example, the Court found in *Employment Division v. Smith* (1990) that Native American Indians have no right to use peyote in religious observances.[4] The Court declared that state laws that substantially but incidentally burden religion do not trigger strict scrutiny under the Free Exercise Clause. Outrage over this holding among religious Americans led to the 1993 passage of the Religious Freedom Restoration Act (RFRA). This law gave people experiencing substantial governmental burdens on their religious practices the right to a waiver unless government could show that the offending law was necessary to advance a compelling state interest.

But in *City of Boerne v. Flores*,[5] the Supreme Court struck RFRA down, holding that Congress lacked the power to enact it under Section 5 of the Fourteenth Amendment, which gives Congress "power to enforce, by appropriate legislation," Equal Protection (and, by incorporation, other constitutional rights). The problem, according to the majority, was that the new law did not "enforce" the right of religious free exercise but redefined it. The new standard lacked "congruence" and "proportionality" with the alleged problem it was addressing.[6] For good measure, the Court sternly lectured Congress about respecting the Court's primacy in defining the meaning of the Constitution, essentially telling members of Congress not to worry their little heads about the rights of the people.[7]

If we, the people, want to overhaul the Court's impoverished constitutional vision of political democracy in America, there are no legislative quick fixes. *We must amend the Constitution.* This is the only way to outflank the new system of judicial supremacy and replace it with enduring new rights of political citizenship.

A Movement for a New Constitution

In the preceding pages, we have identified the need for constitutional amendments on the right to vote, popular election of the president and the right to an education. The language I have offered is merely suggestive, not final, and I hope that we can initiate a public debate about the content of possible constitutional changes. Already I want to take issue with the conservatism and timidity of some of my own proposals. For example, if we are going to guarantee the right to vote, why not use the opportunity to lower the voting age to 16 or 17? This would have a tremendous effect on voter registration and participation since we could register people to vote for their first elections while they are still in high school. It would also catalyze a movement for much greater civic and political consciousness among teenagers. Similarly, why don't we add a sentence to the voting amendment which declares that "the corporation is not a person within the meaning of the Constitution" to abolish the idea that corporations have political rights? This may become an urgent issue depending on what happens in the Supreme Court's consideration of the McCain-Feingold Legislation, the Bipartisan Campaign Reform Act, in the 2003 term.

These changes may take us too far afield from what is most essential and compelling right now. But the point is that we need a vigorous rational dialogue about constitutional revision. Liberals have forgotten, but constitutional politics has always been central to progressive change in America. Not only are constitutional changes more enduring and resistant to the winds of reaction than legislative acts, but constitutional movements push the whole national political and judicial spectrum in a more progressive direction.

The Reconstruction Amendments were part of an ongoing political and legislative movement to open up the Southern states to multiracial democracy. The Nineteenth Amendment gave women a national organizing force to press for equal laws and public recognition. The Twenty-Third Amendment, which gave residents of the District of Columbia the right to participate in presidential elections, created sufficient public space and political energy in the District of Columbia to lead to its modern home rule form of government and the statutory creation of a nonvoting delegate in the House of Representatives in the 1970s.

Paradoxically, outside movements for constitutional change also clearly influence the Supreme Court's understanding of the existing Constitution. For example, everyone knows that the Equal Rights Amendment in the 1970s was not ultimately ratified by enough states to pass. But the ERA mobilized a powerful movement for equal rights that changed the consciousness of the country to the point where the Supreme Court now employs "heightened" Equal Protection scrutiny of any gender-based classifications, demanding "exceedingly persuasive justification" for discrimination against women.[8] This change came about despite the fact that the authors of the Fourteenth Amendment Equal Protection Clause clearly did not have women even remotely in mind when they passed the amendment.

Similarly, the Civil Rights movement's demand for abolition of the poll tax led to ratification of the Twenty-Fourth Amendment in 1964, which banned poll taxes in federal elections. Despite the fact that Congress had considered and rejected the idea of banning poll taxes in state elections, the Court just two years later found that a poll tax of $1.50 in Virginia's elections violated Equal Protection.[9] "Notions of what constitutes equal treatment for the purposes of the Equal Protection Clause *do* change," Justice Douglas wrote in *Harper v. Virginia Board of Elections*.[10] One of the factors that clearly changed the Court's conception of the legitimacy of poll taxes was the Twenty-Fourth Amendment itself and the spirited political movement on its behalf. Far from reading the amendment as a ceiling for justice and political democracy, the Court regarded it as a floor and a new source for interpreting democratic constitutional values.

It is time for America's much-celebrated and much-trampled civil society once again to pick up the agenda of progressive constitutional politics. The League of Women Voters, which is the great institutional legacy of the movement for woman suffrage and the humming engine behind so many modern progressive voting changes, must reclaim its visionary role. Ousted unceremoniously from sponsoring the presidential debates by the bipartisan corporate alliance called the Commission on Presidential Debates, the League of Women Voters should rally America behind a constitutional agenda for full political democracy. This movement should also restore the league to its rightful historical role as sponsor of America's presidential debates.

We have other important institutions of civil society that are part of the legacy of constitutional reforms past. The organization Common Cause has been not only a leading champion of a political process liberated from special-interest money but the key mover behind the Twenty-Sixth Amendment, which in 1971 extended the vote to eighteen-year-old citizens. Under the leadership of former Massachusetts Attorney General Scott Harshbarger, Common Cause can once again be a crucial catalyst for democratic revitalization. The NAACP has been the indispensable institution fighting for interracial democracy and justice. With the great Julian Bond at the helm, it has the grassroots strength, historic legitimacy and institutional energy to put fundamental constitutional change on the agenda. The ACLU also has been a leading defender of the political rights of the people and its voice is critical to marrying the politics of democracy with the politics of civil liberty. If the ACLU can challenge campaign expenditure limits across the country for curtailing political liberty, surely it can help us to reconstitute our politics on a more democratic footing.

Labor unions, a stalwart source of democratic agitation in our history, can teach the public about the need for participatory sovereignty in all of our social institutions. John Sweeney, the president of the AFL-CIO, has promoted the idea that unions are critical to the health of political democracy generally and can help move us around a democratic agenda. Such an agenda can pour over to reconstitute labor law itself.

Universities, which are our laboratories of social thought, should lead us in a national dialogue about different ideas for constitutional change. They can bring a global perspective to the task, since many law professors have traveled abroad over the last decade to assist other nations in drafting new constitutions. It is time for them to bring their expertise home and participate in a vast constitutional conversation here. But, above all, it is students in college and law school and high school and young people generally who can provide the moral and physical energy to change our Constitution. Amy Quinn and the other young people running the Democracy Action Project at the Institute for Policy Studies and the impressive Democracy Summer embody the spirit of Tom Paine, who often said that we must not be weighted down by assumptions of the past but must think anew, as if we were the first ones ever to be confronting a problem.

Who's Afraid to Amend the Constitution?

A movement to revitalize constitutional democracy will eventually galvanize America's progressive majority. What holds us back at the moment is the fear many liberals have of amending the Constitution. They conservatively suspect that any constitutional tinkering will lead to disaster. Kathleen Sullivan, the distinguished dean of Stanford Law School, has warned against the "bad and unintended structural consequences" of amending the Constitution as well as of "mutiny against the Supreme Court."[11] But if America is a ship, the Supreme Court is not our captain; here, the people steer. Today, we need not worry about mutiny against the Court but the Court's mutiny against the people. We can no longer ignore the bad and unintended structural consequences of doing nothing in the wake of debacles such as the 2000 presidential election.

To be sure, the discourse of constitutional change has been right-wing in the last few decades: conservatives have proposed egregious amendments on subjects like flag desecration, school prayer, and term limits.[12] As the last chapter shows, it is possible to deflate these schemes with a little time and patience. But just because bad constitutional amendments are being offered does not mean good constitutional amendments should be held back. On the contrary, it makes it all the more strategically critical that we infuse the nation's constitutional politics with a progressive content and momentum.

Yet many liberals want to treat the Constitution like a sacred and untouchable religious text. They worship the Founding Fathers. This is an ironic and embarrassing position for progressives to be in, since the original document was deeply compromised by white supremacy and fear of popular democracy. Starting with the great Thomas Jefferson, progressives have always believed that we living Americans can make the Constitution better and have refused to treat it in mystical terms. Many of the 26 amendments enacted since the founding are suffrage amendments championed by progressives, including the Seventeenth Amendment (1913), the Nineteenth Amendment (1920), the Twenty-Third Amendment (1961), the Twenty-Fourth Amendment (1964), and the Twenty-Sixth Amendment (1971).

The party of hope in American history must never be afraid to engage with foundational questions. It is the *people's* Constitution, something even conservative Chief Justice John Marshall insisted on as long ago as 1819.[13] And, in an important sense, though it may not be a rough draft exactly, it is always a *working* draft. This was clearly the meaning of Lincoln's invocation of the Declaration of Independence ("Four score and seven years ago ...") as the nation's seminal document when he spoke at Gettysburg in November 1863 to commemorate the war dead. Lincoln dated the birth of the United States not to the radically imperfect Constitution of 1787 but to the Declaration of 1776, which brought forth a "new nation conceived in liberty and dedicated to the proposition that all men are created equal." The Articles of Confederation, the Constitution, the Bill of Rights and each subsequent amendment represented successive and imperfect efforts to institutionalize the commitments to equality, liberty and the "consent of the governed" that Jefferson first articulated in 1776 in the Declaration of Independence. We are thus always struggling to live up to the promises of the Declaration. It is not the personal greatness of Thomas Jefferson we are hankering after. Great though he was, he was personally flawed like us, and tortured by his participation in slavery, as Roger Wilkins has reminded us in his brilliant book *Jefferson's Pillow*. No, it is the clarity of the Declaration's vision about what America might become that anchors us and gives us a touchstone for continuing constitutional elaboration and amendment, the process which we should see not as a threat to our most cherished values but as a logical requirement of them.

A Movement for Democratic Political Reform under the Constitution

A constitutional movement organized around abolishing America's democracy deficit will unleash pent-up energies for *subconstitutional* democratic reform along the way. Three important projects will be the development of systems of proportional representation for voting in federal, state, county and local legislative elections; the development of public campaign-financing regimes at both the state and federal levels; and the adoption of noncitizen voting in local elections. I close with these thoughts to make clear that constitutional politics is never a final destination but a kind of opening dialogue with the political reforms of the future.

Representing Everyone: Proportional Representation

Most of the issues addressed in the constitutional amendments I proffer above are "first-generation" voting issues. They have to do with people being able to cast ballots and get them counted; with the people as a collective enjoying the basic right of majority rule; and with young people having a right to receive an education for democratic citizenship. The question of legislative proportional representation is a kind of second-generation structural issue, a background rule-setting question that grows in importance as we resolve the pressing first-generation problems.[14] Indeed, proportional representation is fast moving from being a curious idea to an urgent democratic imperative.[15]

Both democracy and equality tell us that public office must be open to all.[16] Beyond democracy and equal opportunity, in contemporary American politics another kind of interest compels us to hold the door of public office open: this is the political legitimacy achieved when all citizens have in government political leaders who actually represent them, their values, their lives and concerns. President Clinton spoke to this felt need in the country when he said that he wanted to build an administration that "looks like America."[17] It might improve this democratic sentiment a bit to say that we should seek a government that thinks and feels like America, although it is logical to suppose that such a government would look like America, too. But the looks of our leaders are a concern secondary to the outlooks of our leaders, who should represent all of the people in our great diversity of thoughts and values.

The Court's doctrinal mess over majority-minority districts creates a critical opportunity to push for new rules to replace the chaos and unfairness of inescapably arbitrary legislative district line-drawing. The public is about to discover the advantages of proportional representation election methods, such as instant runoff voting (which is built into the presidential election amendment), preference voting and the like. Often the case for proportional representation is cast as an argument to guarantee electoral minorities a voice. This argument, though not exactly inaccurate, is radically incomplete, because it misses the true virtue of proportional representation.

The strong argument for proportional systems, which was made by John Stuart Mill in 1861,[18] is that they empower the vast majority of people to be represented and active. Consider a state with ten U.S. House seats where 60 percent of the people belong to Party A, 30 percent to Party B, and 10 percent to Party C. Assuming an even partisan distribution of voters across the state, in an election, Party A will capture all of the House seats, meaning that 60 percent of the voters will have 100 percent of the representation, and 40 percent of the voters will get none at all. This is an especially dramatic problem when only half the people turn out to vote, which means, in this hypothetical case, that 30 percent of the electorate is winning 100 percent of the representation.

If we switch to a system of cumulative voting or preference voting, we would instead expect Party A to capture six of the state's House seats, Party B to win three of them and Party C one. Thus by overthrowing a winner-take-all single-member district regime and replacing it with proportional representation, we have actually given the entire population of the state some representative voice and agency in Congress. This brings democratic politics into line with a powerful majoritarian principle.

The clean one-party sweep of congressional delegations is no imaginary thing. In Utah, Idaho and Alaska, for example, Republicans have every Senate and House seat, meaning that Democrats, Greens, and Independents in those states have no partisan representation in Washington. Similarly, in Massachusetts and Rhode Island, Democrats have all the Senate and House seats, leaving the substantial parts of the population registered to other parties without any ascriptive partisan representation over time.

In truth, most congressional districts in America include large numbers of citizens who continue to vote for losing parties and candidates and grow increasingly disgruntled over time. The Center for Voting and Democracy can safely predict the party affiliation of the winner in more than 90 percent of U.S. House districts a year before the election because the vast majority of districts are partisan-gerrymandered and safely in the Democratic or Republican column. Those incumbents essentially get to design their own districts and then, as presumptive winners and officeholders, consolidate their huge fund-raising advantage over opponents. In 2000, 90 percent of House incumbents won by at least 10 percent of the vote and most won by substantially more than that. Political analyst Charles Cook tells us that, after the 2000 census and redistricting process, fewer than 50 out of 435 House seats are truly competitive.[19] As the Economist puts it, redistricting has become "a glorified incumbent-protection racket."[20]

It would be easy enough to cast aside this hopelessly stacked, winner-take-all, zero-sum regime by using the state's apportionment of House seats in a way to maximize the whole public's ability to see someone they support elected. If Maryland has eight U.S. House seats, these members should be elected statewide using a system of preference or cumulative voting. It would essentially take one eighth of the votes cast statewide to win, rather than 50 percent plus one in a district. This is the way most of the world does it, and it holds major advantages in terms of voter turn out and participation over single-member districts, which produce a lot of frozen-out and despondent voters over time.[21]

Indeed, although we know the decision is not supposed to have precedential effect, *Bush v. Gore* invites us to wonder whether there is an Equal Protection violation when a voter in a 60-percent bloc ends up having a partisan affinity with 100 percent of the state's delegation and a voter in the 40-percent bloc ends up with no effective representation. What about a virtual tie in a presidential election, where a few hundred votes out of millions cast make the difference between getting 25 Electoral College votes and zero? Is this really treating each vote equally? Another brewing problem which militates in favor of proportional representation arises from the fact that current one person, one vote case law requires an extremely close population equality among congressional districts within a state; in *Karcher v. Daggett*,[22] the Court refused to allow *de minimis* population disparities among districts and essentially required exactly equal populations. Yet because of standard population movement and demographic changes, there are always huge disparities by the end of a decade following a reapportionment. Thus according to Rob Richie, several districts at the end of the 1990s had more than 200,000 voters above the constitutional requirement in their states. Statewide proportional voting would prevent these inevitable departures from the otherwise scrupulous one person, one vote norm by liberating congressional elections from the vagaries of single-member districting.

There is nothing in the Constitution stopping states from choosing House members or state legislators along proportional lines in at-large elections. But federal law since 1967 has required states to use single-member districts.[23] This was, ironically, a Civil Rights measure designed to protect the Voting Rights Act of 1965 by preventing Southern states from using winner-take-all, at-large districts not to spread representation out proportionally but rather to render an effective black vote impossible. Before her defeat in 2002, Congresswoman Cynthia McKinney, an African-American representative from Georgia who favored proportional representation methods, introduced legislation to permit at-large elections in conjunction with cumulative voting, limited voting or preference voting. Such at-large elections would promote rather than undermine the representational purposes of the Voting Rights Act. There are numerous examples of successful use of proportional systems, such as Illinois's famous 110-year-run with cumulative voting and the preference voting system employed by Cambridge, Massachusetts.[24]

Notice that this more robust and expansive political representation need not be defined exclusively or primarily in racial or ethnic terms. The reflexive assumption that group representation necessarily means representation on the basis of race or ethnicity reflects the mental prison we have constructed from our racial past. People should be able to elect leaders who effectively represent their politics, moral values, ethical perspectives, social commitments, cultural attitudes, economic interests and local agendas. One of the great losses of the Clinton period was President Clinton's decision to nominate but then cut loose Professor Lani Guinier as assistant attorney general for civil rights. Professor Guinier is a leading champion of proportional political representation but was singled out and slammed by right-wingers as a "quota queen,"[25] which is outrageous since proportional representation is rooted in the idea that voters should be able to group themselves as they please. Its practice would eliminate the power of state legislators to design districts for racist purposes, incumbent self-protection or partisan manipulation. The neoconservative witch-hunt against Professor Guinier remains a disgraceful case of intellectual racial profiling.

Sometimes people's voting belief systems *will* overlap and correlate with their racial, ethnic and religious identities and those of their preferred candidates. For example, when Congressman Harold Washington, an African American, ran for mayor of Chicago in 1983, he received overwhelming support from other African Americans because they believed that he would champion the interests of citizens who had been victimized by racism and the exclusionary machine politics of the city.

In Maryland, however, overwhelming numbers of African Americans voted in 1988 and 1992 for the distinguished progressive Senator Paul Sarbanes (who is white) and feisty Senator Barbara Mikulski (also white) against ultraconservative African-American Republican Alan Keyes, who would later run for president. In Washington, D.C., a majority-African-American city, the public has elected an African-American mayor ever since modern home rule was granted in 1974, but the city also repeatedly elected a white politician, the late David Clarke, to be chairman of its council. Clarke, a committed progressive with deep roots in the Civil Rights movement, repeatedly won huge support in the black community against several African-American opponents. Today, a gay white Republican councilmember, David Catania, has strong support in the African-American community.

Thus nothing compels whites to vote for whites, African Americans for African Americans, Asian Americans for Asian Americans, Hispanics for Hispanics and so on. Such a primitive voting system appeals to the lowest common denominator, which in American society has been racism, specifically the toxic ramifications of white supremacy. Everything politically progressive in our history, from abolitionism in the 1850s to populism in the 1890s to the unionism of the 1930s to the Student Nonviolent Coordinating Committee and other Civil Rights groups in the 1960s to the Rainbow Coalition of the 1980s, has argued for interracial political coalition against balkanized, group-think racial politics. But racial polarization and organization have obviously had a powerful influence on our political development, especially given the ubiquity of single-member districts and patterns of white bloc voting in the South and elsewhere.[26] As recently as the 1980s, for example, in "the majority of southern states, not a single majority-white district elected a black legislator,"[27] and this basic pattern of racially polarized voting continues today in major parts of the country.

Professors Lani Guinier and Gerald Torres have championed the virtues of proportional representation methods over winner-take-all systems and have made a subtle argument for the use of what they call "political race."[28] By this they mean organizing people not along the lines of essentialized racial identity politics but around the lived experience of having been oppressed by race and yet influenced as well by a corresponding politics of social solidarity and community. These experiences can sustain the practical and visionary political hope for building an interracial society that addresses everyone's real needs. Understanding the risks of race-based politics, they emphasize that "use of race as a political category gains its legitimacy from its promise to increase the quantum of democracy in society and to resist unfair concentrations of wealth and power."[29] They thus embrace "the possibility of using race and politics to create an identity that resists conventional categories and supports democratic renewal."[30] Theirs is a kind of strategic democratic politics that could make a movement for broad constitutional change nationally a movement for deep social change locally.

Replacing the "Wealth Primary" with the "Clean Money" Option

The problem of campaign finance presents another significant second-generation democracy problem. It is well understood as a matter of both academic study and common sense that private wealth plays a central role in the dynamics of modern electoral politics. As the Supreme Court itself remarked in *Buckley v. Valeo*,[31] it is virtually impossible to run a political campaign for high federal or state office without raising and spending vast sums of money for television, radio, campaign literature, campaign staff, travel, telephones, fax machines and so on. This money must come from somewhere. Overwhelmingly, it comes from a disproportionately affluent, white and male segment of the population living in the ritziest zip codes and from wealthy donors affiliated with specific industries—banking, agriculture, Wall Street, military contractors—deeply interested in the business of government.

The monied interests that dominate political fund-raising in America are the decisive actors in what my friend John Bonifaz and I called, back in 1993, the nation's electoral "wealth primary."[32] The "cash constituents" decide who will have enough money to run for office; these constituents critically influence the course of campaigns and the outcome of elections; and they then define the character of resulting public policy. We argued that this tyranny of private money in public elections and government corrupts the essential democratic relationship of one person, one vote, replacing it with the market logic of everything being for sale and the highest bidder winning. In this sense, the private market in campaign contributions and expenditures is a conservative economist's utopia where the Coase Theorem is operationalized. The wealth primary practically guarantees that electoral and policy outcomes will go to those who would pay the most for them because it allows special interests to use money to influence elections and legislation and similarly allows the politicians themselves to spend money to win public office.

Whatever its appeal to free-market ideologists and public choice theorists,[33] the existing private-wealth primary—combined with handsome incumbent self-subsidies in the form of press secretaries, speechwriters, telephones, office space and so on—is in deep tension with norms of Equal Protection. This is because the exclusionary wealth primary, like the exclusionary white primary, often constitutes a "successful effort to withdraw significance"[34] from the normal voting process. Many candidates are forced out of campaigns before they even enter them because of a shortage of funds. The vast majority of people cannot even contemplate finding enough money to support themselves while running for high office, much less pay for their campaigns. Like high candidate filing fees invalidated in *Bullock v. Carter* (1972), the wealth primary thus sets up an economic gauntlet that "in every practical sense"[35] prevents less affluent candidates—"potential office seekers lacking both personal wealth and affluent backers"—from competing for high office.[36] Meanwhile, the candidates who are either independently wealthy or in proper favor with monied power compete to out-fund-raise one another and service the political agenda of organized wealth. A progressive judiciary taking Equal Protection seriously would recognize that there is a "constitutional imperative"[37] for democratically financed elections—a total public-financing option for candidates who cannot or choose not to compete in the private-wealth primary.

Needless to say, the federal courts have not embraced this indictment of the current wealth-primary regime, but a number of states have over the last decade passed "clean money" public-financing schemes in statewide initiatives. In Maine, Massachusetts, Vermont and Arizona, voters have approved plans in which candidates for state office qualify for public financing by crossing the threshold of collecting a few hundred contributions of $5 each. Once the candidate crosses the seriousness threshold by collecting the required number of qualifying contributions (in Massachusetts, it is six thousand for governor and two hundred for state representative), the state essentially writes the candidate's campaign a check for most of the costs of running a serious (albeit modestly financed) campaign. In Massachusetts, for example, a candidate for state senator will be given $72,000 for her campaign and will be allowed to raise only another $18,000 in individual private $100 contributions, for a total of $90,000. A candidate for governor will be given $2.5 million and has the right to raise another

$450,000, for a total of $3 million. If certain candidates opt out of the system and raise private money and spend more on their campaigns than the voluntary public-finance option makes available to publicly financed candidates, the laws provide for escalator matching fund increases in the public subsidy.

These systems have been vehemently opposed by incumbents averse to political opposition and by big-money interests afraid of losing their leverage and inside track. Indeed, in Massachusetts, the entrenched political class has done everything in its power to frustrate implementation of the new law, including refusing to fund it.

But where the incumbentocracy has not blocked their implementation, the clean-money laws have been remarkably successful in expanding the numbers of candidates, teasing out new voices and new choices, dislodging incumbents, diversifying the pool of candidates, and reducing the influence of special-interest cash in campaigns and the legislative process. In the 2000 state elections in Maine, the first after adoption of the clean-elections law, there was a 40 percent jump in contested primaries. In the 2000 Arizona elections, also the first post-adoption, there was a 60 percent increase in the total number of candidates running for state legislature and a 62 percent increase in contested races. Some 60 of 214 primary candidates ran as Clean Elections candidates and 44 of those 60 won. Of the 44 who ran in the general election, 16 won. Some 33 percent of challengers ran "clean," and 23 percent of the challengers who won were "clean" candidates. Only 7 percent of winning incumbents ran "clean."[38]

National groups pushing for democratic reform of campaign finance, such as Public Campaign and the National Voting Rights Institute, and the leaders of this movement, such as Nick Nyhart, Randy Kehler, Spencer Overton, Ellen Miller and John Bonifaz, have shown the nation a way to break the political-financial nexus between special-interest donors and cash-hungry politicians. They have also shown us a way to diversify the pool of political candidates.

The next logical step would be to establish a clean-money option in federal campaigns. For even if McCain-Feingold survives the onslaught in the Supreme Court, it is already clear that private money will find the most efficient channels to reach its political destinations and that the doubling of the hard-money contribution limits doubles the strength of large private donors in the wealth primary. Public financing may seem like pie in the sky in Congress today, given how difficult it was to pass the relatively modest and judicially imperiled McCain-Feingold legislation in the spring of 2002. But public financing was hugely popular after Watergate and it actually passed the House of Representatives in the 1970s. A movement to deepen constitutional democracy could put public financing for congressional elections back onto the public agenda in a way that has not been seen in a quarter-century.

Because states and House districts are so large, a critical component of a federal public-financing regime will be reclaiming the public's control over of the public airwaves. Federal candidates and parties spent more than $3 billion in the 2000 elections, most of it on media, so replacing that money dollar for dollar with a public program would be very expensive indeed. The way to make federal public financing affordable is to stop giving away broadcast licenses, a public trust and a resource worth billions of dollars, without reserving free time for the programming of political democracy.

A meaningful system of providing candidate access to the airwaves for appearances and debates would dramatically lower the costs of candidacy. The current system is illogical in that we take the precise soapbox that candidates need and give it away for free to private broadcast corporations, which then sell the time back to political candidates for huge sums of money. These candidates must, in turn, curry favor with organized special interests, including notably the broadcast industry itself, to raise the cash to buy the media time that the public actually owns! And one of the broadcast industry's key policy agendas is always to keep the public from discovering that it has the power to confer free airtime on candidates.

If Congress and the Federal Communications Commission prove to be too beholden to the current regime to reserve airtime for political debate, we can turn back to the states. There is nothing stopping the current clean money states from extending their public-finance programs from state legislative elections to federal congressional campaigns. If Congress will not abolish the wealth primaries in Senate and House races, why shouldn't the states do it? We have a fine working model now. To be sure, these programs must also remain voluntary since, if they were made compulsory, it would run afoul of the line drawn by the Supreme Court in *Buckley* with respect to public-financing programs[39] (and also potentially violate the Qualifications Clause). But creating an option for candidates to choose public financing has shaken up politics in the clean-money states.

Of course, even if we created a national clean-money option for congressional campaigns, not everyone would participate. We could expect the emergence of a bifurcated politics in which publicly financed candidates act on behalf of public agendas and public things while privately financed candidates act on behalf of private agendas and private things. This may be the best we can hope for today. Within the ranks of the public candidates would be not only the advocates of public goods such as the environment, education, workplace rights and civil rights and liberties but also businesspeople who favor truly free and fair markets and want to stop corporate rent-seeking by statist big-business industries such as military contractors, aeronautics, and nuclear power. The public campaign plan would liberate the time and energy of participating elected officials and further empower new voices and choices to emerge.

The ultimate vision of two different classes of candidates is not ideal, but it fairly mirrors our social condition. We have flourishing private schools and struggling public schools, manicured country clubs and unkempt public parks, sleek limo services and crowded subways, thriving corporate welfare and vanishing social welfare. The private for-profit sector has always paid handsomely for its politicians and will continue to do so. Isn't it time the rest of us had candidates we can call our own?

Noncitizen Voting

Noncitizens are disenfranchised in all federal and state elections and maintain the right to vote only in a handful of localities.[40] This disenfranchisement seems natural to us today, but it was not always so. When the nation began, most states allowed aliens to vote and to run for office—that is, as long as they were white male property holders over the age of 21. As the nation spread westward in the nineteenth century, new states vying for population to fill up the land extended the vote immediately to all "declarant aliens," that is, immigrants who had declared their intention to become naturalized citizens. The alien vote was so important that noncitizen voting became a divisive sectional issue prior to the Civil War. Southern politicians denounced the practice, which they saw bringing into the body politic a lot of anti-slavery Europeans. Indeed, Article I of the Confederate Constitution explicitly forbade alien voting at all levels of government. After the Civil War, the practice of alien suffrage rapidly spread across the country again, but it declined around the turn of the twentieth century with the rise of anti-immigration sentiment. All the while, however, the Supreme Court affirmed the constitutionality of states choosing to extend the franchise to aliens. Today, the practice survives in school board elections in New York and Chicago and in city council and mayoral elections in some smaller municipalities such as Takoma Park, Maryland, where I co-chaired a Share the Vote campaign in 1991. In Takoma Park, noncitizen voting that it was adopted by the city council as a charter change after a favorable citywide referendum vote.

With more than ten million permanent residents lawfully present in America today, the argument for alien suffrage makes sense again at the local level. It is not just the fact that permanent resident immigrants work, pay all kinds of taxes and shoulder the other responsibilities of "citizenship," including military conscription. Nor is it just that reciprocal noncitizen voting in local elections is now the law in the European Union or that many Americans enjoy this right living abroad. The point is that we should want all residents of cities and towns, regardless of nation-state citizenship, to participate in the public life of their communities. I have no reason to fear my Canadian or Guatemalan neighbors voting in local elections, because they have all the same interests that I have in excellent public schools, efficient garbage collection, safe streets and so on. Our interests may diverge along lines of national citizenship in federal elections, but I should have every possible reason to want them engaged in the community's well-being at the local level. Participation benefits everyone.

A majority of parents of children in Los Angeles public schools are not U.S. citizens. Can anyone seriously argue that citizens of Los Angeles will be better off by not allowing them to vote in school board elections, run for office and enjoy the status of locally recognized citizens? If we give immigrants a taste of democratic life here, many will grow hungry for more. As in the past, local noncitizen voting can become a direct pathway to naturalization and full citizenship.[41] In the future, noncitizen voting will become an important way to make the process of globalization democratic.

Conclusion: Unpacking the Court

There will continue to be very trying conflict in Congress and the nation whenever vacancies appear on the Supreme Court. This is because Americans now have two diametrically opposed approaches to the meaning of the Constitution.

Conservatives on the Court have rallied around a judicial philosophy that reads the Constitution through the prism of state power and social tradition. The organizing notion is that state governments are presumed under the Tenth Amendment to have any powers that the Constitution does not explicitly deny to them through the creation of individual rights.

Liberals interpret the Constitution as a freedom charter establishing both democratic sovereignty and the individual rights of the people. The organizing notion is that the people are presumed under Due Process, Equal Protection and the Ninth Amendment to enjoy any rights that the Constitution does not explicitly deny to them through the delegation of powers to government.

Justice Scalia is our conservative traditionalist *par excellence.* In *Planned Parenthood v. Casey,*[42] for example, he posed the question as whether "the power of a woman to abort her unborn child ... is a liberty interest protected by the Constitution of the United States." He answered plainly: "I am sure it is not." He reached this conclusion "because of two simple facts: (1) the Constitution says absolutely nothing about it, and (2) the long-standing traditions of American society have permitted it to be legally proscribed."[43] The only liberty interests that can be recognized under Due Process are those "rooted in history and tradition."[44] Thus, because there was a social tradition at the time of the Fourteenth Amendment's passage of the states criminalizing abortion, Due Process cannot be said to include a right to choose abortion.

The problem with this logic is that it completely misapprehends what a democratic constitution is. In an authoritarian society, citizens assume that anything that is not specifically authorized by the state is forbidden, but in a democratic society we assume that anything not specifically forbidden and demonstrably harmful is allowed to the citizenry. Justice Scalia wants to say that government maintains any powers that were exercised at the time when certain rights were first inscribed into the Constitution if the rights did not specifically overthrow the powers in issue. The problem with this reasoning is that it ignores that the whole purpose of the Bill of Rights in American democracy is to define the rights of the people and then create a dynamic of freedom that allows courts to elaborate and enforce them against hostile official practices.

Liberals thus uphold the Ninth Amendment over the Tenth. The Ninth provides that rights specifically enumerated in the Constitution should *not* be read to disparage or deny other rights retained by the people. This textual canon of constitutional construction cuts directly against the Scalia method.

When the Democrats came to power in the Senate in 2001 with Senator James Jeffords's principled conversion from Republican to Independent, they made it clear that they will not roll over and play dead if the president tries to stuff the courts with reactionary judicial activists. Spurred on by an energetic campaign led by People for the American Way's Ralph Neas, the Leadership Conference on Civil Rights' Wade Henderson, and the Alliance for Justice's Nan Aron, Democrats held strong in rejecting President Bush's nomination of United States District Judge Charles Pickering to the Fifth Circuit Court of Appeals in the spring of 2002.

The usual suspects, such as the *Wall Street Journal* editorial page, accused the liberal groups of "Borking" Judge Pickering and other similar judicial nominees, but liberals should take that as a compliment. Judge Robert Bork was an unreconstructed right-wing ideologue who pretended to a certain kind of confirmation conversion before being rejected by the biggest bipartisan vote in the history of the Senate's consideration of Supreme Court nominees. Unlike Lani Guinier, for example, or the 35 percent of President Clinton's judicial nominees between 1995 and 2000 who never received a vote on the floor of the Senate, Judge Bork had a full and fair hearing in the Judiciary Committee, where he discussed his belligerent views for hours on end, and then a full-blown debate and vote on the floor of the Senate. If Borking means thoroughly exploring the records and views of right-wing judicial appointees, then the Democrats should bring it on.

Future Supreme Court confirmation clashes will undoubtedly feature a struggle between the traditionalist and progressive democratic understandings of the Constitution. The conservatives will describe themselves as advocates of judicial restraint and opponents of "judicial activism." But, if this book has done nothing else, I hope it has shown that they should never be able to get away with that trick again. Conservatives and progressives have substantively opposed visions of the Constitution, but the difference does not turn on activism or restraint. The difference turns on whether the Constitution is seen to embody values of statist traditionalism or progressive democracy.

Whatever the politics surrounding this or that nomination, the progressive forces will be much stronger in making their case if they do so against the background of a swelling national movement for democratic constitutional change. This movement will lay down the bright-line principles of "common conceptual cohesion," in Bob Moses' terms, that will define a democratic ethos for the new century.[45] This will be our best hope—politically, intellectually and institutionally—to counteract the awesome agenda-setting power of a conservative White House, a conservative Congress, a conservative Supreme Court, and a conservative corporate sector.

For active justice to be done in America, we need to have people in motion in vibrant democratic institutions where everyone can be seen and heard. Yet the Supreme Court is systematically obstructing the channels of democracy. The people need to intervene to break the repetitive cycles of political exclusion and social injustice. It is time to reassert our political sovereignty and reclaim our rightful democratic destiny as the true authors of America.

NOTES

Chapter One: The Supreme Court and America's Democracy Deficit

1. John Dewey, *Education Today* 358 (1940).
2. Stephen Breyer, *Our Democratic Constitution*, 77 *N.Y.U. L. Rev.* 245 (2002).
3. 531 U.S. 98 (2000).
4. 509 U.S. 630 (1993).
5. 115 S. Ct. 2475 (1995).
6. 118 S. Ct. 1633 (1988).
7. *See* United States v. Morrison, 529 U.S. 598, 609 (2000) (invalidating statute in part as exceeding Congress' Commerce Clause powers).
8. *See* United States v. Lopez, 514 U.S. 549, 561 (1995) (striking down statute as exceeding Congress' Commerce Clause powers).
9. *See* City of Boerne v. Flores, 521 U.S. 507, 532–33 (1997) (striking down law as exceeding Congress' enforcement powers under the Fourteenth Amendment).
10. *See* Printz v. United States, 521 U.S. 898, 933–34 (1997) (holding law unconstitutional as an impermissible commandeering of state officials for a federal program).
11. *See* Alden v. Maine, 527 U.S. 706, 758–59 (1999) (invalidating as an abrogation of state sovereign immunity Fair Labor Standards Act provision authorizing private actions against states in state courts).
12. *See* New York v. United States, 505 U.S. 144, 169–70 (1992) (finding unconstitutional in part a law requiring states to regulate radioactive waste according to Congress's instructions or to take title to the waste).
13. *See* Kimel v. Fla. Bd. of Regents, 528 U.S. 62, 72–3 (2000) (holding ADEA cannot remove Eleventh Amendment immunity from the states).
14. *See* Lujan v. Defenders of Wildlife, 504 U.S. 555 (1992) (finding environmental groups lacked constitutional standing).
15. *See* Board of Trustees of Univ. of Ala. v. Garrett, 531 U.S. 356, 372–73 (2001) (holding that legislative history of Americans with Disabilities Act did not show pattern of discrimination by states against disabled, thus denying Congress' power to override Eleventh Amendment immunity of states from money damage suits under Title I).
16. 17 U.S. (4 Wheat) 316 (1819).
17. *Id.* at 404–5.
18. *Id.* (Emphasis in the original).
19. *See also* Seth P. Waxman, *Defending Congress*, 79 *N.C. L. Rev.* 1073, 1075 (2001) (pointing out that since 1995, the Court has invalidated 26 federal laws, an extraordinary number).
20. 530 U.S. 290 (2000).
21. *See* John T. Noonan, Jr., *Narrowing the Nation's Power: The Supreme Court Sides with the States*, (University of California Press, 2002) for a masterful critique of the Rehnquist Court's unconvincing federalism.

22. See Richmond v. Croson, 488 U.S. 469 (1989).

23. *See, e.g.*, Nat'l Foreign Trade Council v. Natsios, 181 F.3d 38 (1999), *cert. granted*, 528 U.S. 1018 (1999) (striking down Massachusetts's decision not to do business with companies operating in Burma as an interference with the federal government's foreign policy powers).

24. *See* William P. Marshall, "Conservatives and the Seven Sins of Judicial Activism," forthcoming in the *University of Colorado Law Review.* (Copy on file with the author.)

25. *See* Text of 96 Congressmen's Declaration on Integration, *N.Y. Times*, Mar. 12, 1956, at 19 (criticizing Brown as impermissible judicial activism).

26. *See* Bernard Schwartz, *Superchief: Earl Warren and His Supreme Court: A Judicial Biography* 250, 280–81 (1983).

27. *See* Planned Parenthood, 505 U.S. at 997 (Scalia, J., dissenting) ("the Imperial Judiciary lives!").

28. *See generally* Neil A. Lewis, Judicial Nominees Stir Partisan Fight, *Seattle Times*, Apr. 7, 2002, at A13 (reporting President Bush's statement that he wanted a Republican-controlled Senate so he could put conservatives on the bench); Statement of Orrin G. Hatch, Ideology and Judicial Nominations, Cong. Testimony 2001 WL 21756492 (June 13, 2001) (expounding on the importance of judicial restraint).

29. *See, e.g.*, Abraham Lincoln, The Dred Scott Decision: Speech at Springfield, Illinois (June 26, 1857), in *Abraham Lincoln: His Speeches and Writings* 352 (Roy P. Bosler ed., 1946) (describing the decision as "erroneous" and made with "apparent partisan bias").

30. *See* Wright, *supra* note 4, at 154.

31. *See, e.g.*, Nathan Miller, *FDR: An Intimate History* 392 (1983); Franklin D. Roosevelt, *The Public Papers and Addresses of Franklin D. Roosevelt* (Samuel I. Rosenman ed., 1941).

32. *See* 77 *N.Y.U. L. Rev.* 245, 247 (2002).

33. Richard A. Posner, *Breaking the Deadlock* 25 (2001).

34. *Id.*

35. Judge Posner repeatedly and unabashedly used the word "philistine" to describe the attitudes of the American public in a visit to American University on December 10, 2001. The word reappears and functions in the same way in a draft of his important forthcoming work on democracy (copy on file with author).

36. *Id.* at 25.

37. *The Declaration of Independence* para. 2 (U.S. 1776).

38. Arthur M. Schlesinger, Jr., *The Age of Jackson* 6 (1953) (quoting a letter from Justice Story to Sarah Waldo Story (Mar. 7, 1829)), in *1 Life and Letters of Joseph Story* 562, 563 (William W. Story ed., 1851).

39. *Bush*, 531 U.S. at 104.

40. *See* Alexander v. Daley, 90 F. Supp. 2.d 35, 72 (D.D.C. 2000).

41. See International Covenant on Civil and Political Rights, Mar. 23, 1976, art. 25 6 I.L.M. 368 (recognizing inalienable rights to participate in one's own government).

42. For a penetrating overview of America's closed electoral system, see Steven Hill, *Fixing Elections: The Failure of America's Winner Take All Politics* (2002).

43. Since passage of the Presidential Election Campaign Fund Act and Presidential Primary Matching Payment Account Act in 1974, the Democratic and Republican parties have been given more than $1 billion in taxpayer checkoff funds. In 2000, the major party general election figure was $67.56 million, although George W. Bush, the Republican nominee, became the first major party candidate in history to bypass this apparently modest sum in favor of the greener pastures of Republican hard-money collection. Meantime, both the Democratic and Republican parties receive millions of dollars every year through the National Democratic Institute to carry the message of (closed two-party?) democracy to other nations.
44. *See* Jamin B. Raskin & John Bonifaz, Equal Protection and the Wealth Primary, 11 *Yale L. & Pol'y Rev.* 273 (1993).

Chapter Two: The Court Supreme

1. *See* Bush v. Gore, 531 U.S. 98, 121 (2000) (reversing Florida's Supreme Court decision).
2. *See* Gore v. Harris, 772 So. 2d 1243 (Fla. 2000), *rev'd sub nom.* Bush v. Gore, 531 U.S. 98 (2000) (indicating that while the manual recount of select counties was perfectly lawful, a statewide recount was more fair).
3. *Bush*, 531 U.S. at 119.
4. *Id.* at 106.
5. *Id.* at 110.
6. *Id.*
7. 506 U.S. 224 (1993).
8. *Id.* at 227.
9. *Id.* at 225.
10. 468 U.S. 737 (1984).
11. *Id.*
12. *Id.* at 755–56.
13. *See Bush*, 531 U.S. 98 (Making Bush's assumed injury all the more absurd, we do not even know who the handful of hypothetically injured voters actually voted for. One must assume that the potential difference in treatment of pregnant-chad ballots would have affected people of different presidential choices equally. If anything, of course, the "injured" voters were far more likely to be minorities, and therefore Gore supporters, since the more heavily minority counties had the highest rates of ballot spoilation.
14. *Id.*
15. *Id.* at 144–53 (Stevens, J., dissenting).
16. Bush v. Gore, 531 U.S. 1046, 121 S. Ct. 512, 513 (2000) (Stevens, J., dissenting).
17. *Id.* (Scalia, J. concurring).
18. *See id.* (Stevens, J., dissenting) (preventing the completion of the recount cast a cloud on the legitimacy of the election).
19. *See* Allen v. Wright, 468 U.S. 737 (1984).
20. *See* N.Y. Times Co. v. Sullivan, 376 U.S. 254 (1964).
21. 520 U.S. 681 (1997).

22. *See* Washington v. Davis, 426 U.S. 229 (1976) (requiring African-American plaintiffs challenging a civil service test that disproportionately failed minorities to prove that the test was deliberately designed to have that effect); McCleskey v. Kemp, 481 U.S. 279 (1987) (upholding against Equal Protection attack the death penalty in Georgia).

23. Phillip Garner and Enrico Spolare, *Why Chads? Determinants of Voting Equipment Use in the United States,* Working Paper No. 2001–26 (Brown Univ., June 2001).

24. Bush v. Gore, 531 U.S. at 147 (Breyer, J., dissenting).

25. 383 U.S. 663 (1966).

26. Bush v. Gore, 531 U.S. at 146 (Breyer, J. and Souter, J., dissenting).

27. *Id.* at 127 (Stevens, J., dissenting).

28. *Id.*

29. Bush v. Gore, 531 U.S. 98, 109 (2000).

30. U.S. Const. art. II.

31. Adams v. Clinton, 531 U.S. 941 (2000).

32. Alexander v. Daley, 90 F. Supp. 2d 35 (D.D.C. 2000).

33. 446 U.S. 55 (1980).

34. 446 U.S. at 66 (emphasis added).

35. *McKleskey,* 481 U.S. 279 (1987).

36. San Antonio Indep. Sch. Dist. v. Rodriguez, 411 U.S. 1 (1973).

37. Jerry Z. Muller, in *Conservatism: An Anthology of Social and Political Thought From David Hume to the Present* 16 (Jerry Z. Muller ed., 1997).

38. Edmund Burke, "An Appeal from the New to the Old Whigs (1791)," in Daniel Ritchie, ed., Edmund Burke: Further Reflections on the Revolution in France 163.

39. 773 So. 2d 519 (Fla. 2000).

40. *Id.*

41. *See* Max Boot, "Law Professors v. the Supreme Court," *Wall St. J.,* Aug. 13, 2001, at A13 (responding to my article in the March 2001, Washington Monthly, "Bandits in Black Robes").

42. 60 U.S. 393 (1856).

43. *Id.*

44. *Id.* at 400; *See also* Laurence H. Tribe, *American Constitutional Law* 549 (1988) (stating that Dred Scott is "often recalled for its politically disastrous dictum and wholly gratuitous announcement by Chief Justice Taney that the Missouri Compromise was unconstitutional. The decision's greatest constitutional significance, however, lay in its holding that African-Americans could not bring suit in federal court or become United States citizens").

45. *Dred Scott,* 60 U.S. 393 (1856).

46. *Id.*

47. *Id.*

48. *Id.* at 404–5.

49. *See id.* at 532–34.

50. Alan Dershowitz, *Supreme Injustice* 110 (Oxford University 2001).

51. Randall Kennedy, "Contempt of Court," *American Prospect*, Jan 1–15, 2001, at 15.
52. Vincent Bugliosi, "None Dare Call It Treason," *The Nation*, Feb. 5, 2001, at 1,3.
53. *New Republic*, Dec. 25, 2000, at 18.
54. Anthony G. Amsterdam, "The Law Is Left Twisting in the Wind," *L.A. Times*, Dec. 17, 2000, at M5.
55. *See e.g.* Laurie Asseo, "Justices, Scholars Discuss Politics Role in Law," Associated Press, Dec. 15, 2000, *available at*: http://archive.nandotimes.com/election2000/story/0,3977,500289744-500458954-503032703-0-nandotimes,00.html
56. Judith N. Shklar, *Ordinary Vices* 86 (1984).
57. Thomas Paine, *Common Sense*, in Collected Writings 6 (1995).
58. Thomas Paine, "The Forester's Letter II," *id.* at 65.
59. Democracy Now, "As Supreme Court Decides Presidency, Chief Justice Rehnquist is Accused of Past Harassment of Black Voters at the Polls," (Dec. 12, 2000) *available at* http://www.webactive.com/pacifica/demnow /dn20001212.html (discussing how, at his 1986 Senate confirmation hearings on his promotion to Chief Justice, numerous witnesses testified that Rehnquist in 1962 aggressively questioned minority voters on their way to vote in Arizona about their suffrage qualifications).
60. Herbert Wechsler, "Toward Neutral Principles of Constitutional Law," 73 *Harv. L. Rev.* 1 (1959).
61. Antonio Damasio, *The Feeling of What Happens: Body and Emotion in the Making of Consciousness* 41 (Harcourt, 1999).

Chapter Three: Reading Democracy Out

1. Bush v. Gore, 531 U.S. 98, 104 (2000).
2. *See* Reynolds v. Sims, 377 U.S. 533 (1964); Wesberry v. Sanders, 376 U.S. 1 (1964).
3. Roe v. Wade 410 U.S. 113 (1973).
4. Loving v. Virginia 388 U.S. 1 (1967) (invalidating Virginia's miscegenation statute and finding that marriage "is one of the basic civil rights of man, fundamental to our very existence and survival"); Zablocki v. Redhail 434 U.S. 374 (1978) (categorizing the decision to marry as among the personal decisions protected by the right to privacy).
5. New Jersey v. T.L.O, 469 U.S. 809 (1984) (holding that school searches need only meet a reasonable suspicion standard and do not require warrants).
6. U.S. v. Brigoni-Ponce, 422 U.S. 873 (1975) (holding that border searches require only reasonable suspicion).
7. U.S. Const., amend. XV, §1.
8. U.S. Const., amend. XIX, §1.
9. U.S. Const., amend. XXIII, §1.
10. U.S. Const., amend. XXIV, §1.
11. U.S. Const., amend. XXVI, §1.

12. Bush v. Gore, 531 U.S. at 104 (2000).

13. *NAACP Public Hearings on the Florida Vote* (CSPAN television broadcast, Nov. 11, 2000).

14. Election 2000 National Results, *available at* http://www.cnn.com/ ELECTION/2000/results.

15. CALTECH MIT Voting Technology Project, "Voting: What Is, What Could Be" (Jul. 2001).

16. Alexander v. Daley, 90 F. Supp. 2d 35 (D.D.C. 2000), *aff'd by* 531 U.S. 941.

17. *Id.*

18. *Id.* at 36. (I acted as co-counsel on the case, originally titled *Alexander v. Daley*, along with Assistant D.C. Corporation Counsel Walter Smith and Covington and Burling attorneys Tom Williamson, Evan Schultz and Charles Miller.)

19. *Id.* at 37.

20. *Id.* at 35–7.

21. *Id.* at 38.

22. *Id.* at 38.

23. *Id.* at 39.

24. *See* Adams v. Clinton, 90 F. Supp. 2d 35 (D.D.C. 2000) (dissenting Judge Louis Oberdorfer reviewing plaintiff's argument).

25. *See id.* at 45.

26. 376 U.S. 1 (1964).

27. *Id.* at 17–18.

28. Reynolds v. Sims, 377 U.S. 533, 567–68 (1964).

29. *See id.*

30. 531 U.S. 940 (2000).

31. Evans v. Cornman, 398 U.S. 419 (1970).

32. *See* Article I, Section 8, Clause 17 (Congress has power "To exercise exclusive Legislation in all Cases whatsoever, over such District (not exceeding Ten Miles square) as may, by Cession of particular states, and the Acceptance of Congress, become the Seat of Government of the United States …").

33. Jamin B. Raskin, "Is This America? The District of Columbia and the Right to Vote," 34 Harv. CR.-CL.L.Rev. 39 (1999).

34. *See* Bolling v. Sharpe, 347 U.S. 497 (1954).

35. Alexander v. Daley, 90 F. Supp. 2d. 35, 66 (emphasis added).

36. Harper v. Virginia Board of Elections, 383 U.S. 633, 665 (1966).

37. Alexander v. Daley, 90 F. Supp. 2d 35 at 48.

38. McPherson v. Blacker, 146 U.S. 1, 35 (1892).

39. Alexander v. Mineta, 531 U.S. 940 (2000).

40. U.S. Const., amend. XXIII, §1 ("The District constituting the seat of Government of the United States shall appoint in such a manner as the Congress may direct: A number of Senators and Representatives in Congress to which the District would be entitled if it were a State, but in no event more than the least populous state; they shall be in addition to those appointed by the States, but they shall be considered for the purposes of the election of President and Vice President, to be electors appointed by a state; and they

shall meet in the District and perform such duties as provided by the twelfth article of the amendment.")

41. Bureau of the Census, *Statistical Abstract of the United States* 822 (table 1355) (113th Ed., 1993).

42. Iguarta de la Rosa v. United States, 32 F.3d 8, 9 (1st Cir. 1994).

43. *See* U.S. Const., art I. §8, cl.1; David M. Helfeld, "The Constitutional and Legal Feasibility of the Presidential Vote for Puerto Rico," in Fred C. Scribner, Jr., *Six Special Studies Requested for the Ad Hoc Advisory Group on the Presidential Vote for Puerto Rico* 87, 103–4 (U.S. Government Printing Office, 1971).

44. *See* U.S. v. Valentine, 288 F. Supp. 957, 979 (D. Puerto Rico 1968) (holding that the Selective Service Act, which makes every male citizen of the United States liable for service in the armed forces, applies to Territorial residents who are United States citizens).

45. *See* Simms v. Simms, 175 U.S. 162, 168 (1899) (holding that "in the Territories of the United States, Congress has the entire dominion and sovereignty . . . and has full legislative power over all subjects upon which the legislature of a State might legislate within that state . . ").

46. *See* Amber L. Cottle, Comment, "Silent Citizens: United States Territorial Residents and the Right to Vote in Presidential Elections," *U. Chi. Legal F.* 315, 315–17 (1995).

47. Angel Ricardo Oquendo, "Puerto Rican National Identity and United States Pluralism," in *Foreign in a Domestic Sense*, ed. Christina Duffy Burnett and Burke Marshall (2001), at 315.

48. Xavier Romeu v. Cohen, 265 F.3d 118, 127 (2001) (citing Igarta II, 229 F.3d at 85–90 (Torruela, J., concurring).

49. Rafael E. Declet, Jr., "The Mandate under International Law for a Self-Executing Plebiscite on Puerto Rico's Political Status, and the Right of U.S.-Resident Puerto Ricans to Participate," 28 *Syracuse J. Int'l L. & Com.* 19, 41 (2001).

50. *Id.* (*citing* "Special Committee on Decolonization Hears Petitioners on the Question of Puerto Rico, United Nations Press Release GA/COL/2970, June 19, 1997).

51. *Id.*

52. The Sentencing Project, *Losing the Vote: The Impact of Felony Disenfranchisement Laws in the United States* 1 (Human Rights Watch, 1998).

53. In Virginia, for example, ex-felons must convince the Governor through the Parole Board to remove their political disabilities. According to the Sentencing Project and Human Rights Watch, which issued an excellent report on the subject, while there are more than 200,000 ex-convicts in Virginia, only 404—far less than 1 percent—won back their right to vote in 1996 and 1997. *Id.* at 5. In Mississippi, an ex-con needs a gubernatorial executive order or a bill passed by two-thirds of members in each house and a gubernatorial signature. *See id.* Good luck.

54. Loic Wacquant, "Deadly Symbiosis," *Boston Review* 23, April/May 2002.

55. *Id.* at 1.

56. The Sentencing Project, *Felony Disenfranchisement Laws in the United States,*

available at http://www.sentencingproject.org/brief.htm (last visited October 22, 2001).

57. *Id.*

58. *Id.*

59. *Id.*

60. *See e.g.*, Testimony of Peter Wagner, assistant director of the Prison Policy Initiative, before the New York State Legislative Task Force, March 14, 2000, *available at* http://prisonpolicy.org/importing.

61. Jonathan Tilove, "Minority Prison Inmates Skew Local Populations as States Redistrict," Newhouse News Service, March 12, 2002.

62. *Id.*

63. Richardson v. Ramirez, 418 U.S. 24, 54 (1974).

64. *Id.*

65. Michael Les Benedict, "Constitutional History and Constitutional Theory: Reflections on Ackerman, Reconstruction, and the Transformation of the American Constitution," 108 *Yale L. J.* 2011 (1999).

66. Judith N. Shklar, Redeeming American Political Theory 175, Stanley Hoffman and Dennis F. Thomson eds. (Univ. Chi. Press, 1998).

67. U.S. Const., art. III, §3.

68. Jones v. Alfred H. Mayer Co., 392 U.S. 409 (1968).

69. Richard A. Easterlin, "The Globalization of Human Development," 570 *Annals Am. Acad. Pol. & Soc. Sci.* 32 (July 2000).

70. Robert P. Moses & Charles Cobb Jr., *Radical Equations: Math Literacy and Civil Rights*, 91 (2001).

71. *See* Robert McKay, Reapportionment: Success Story of the Warren Court, 67 *Mich. L. Rev.* 233 (1968).

72. Reynolds v. Sims 377 U.S. 533, 558 (1964).

73. *See* Burdick v. Takushi, 504 U.S. 428 (1992).

74. *See* Timmons v. Twin Cities–Area New Party, 520 U.S. 351 (1997).

75. Bush v. Gore, 531 U.S. 98, 104 (2000) ("The individual has no federal constitutional right to vote ...").

76. oncampus.richmond/http.//www.oncampus.richmond.edu/~jjones// confinder/const.htm (provides index to all the constitutions of the world).

77. *Id.*

78. S. Afr. Const., Ch. I, sec. 1.

79. S. Afr. Const., Ch. II, sec. 19.

80. Universal Declaration of Human Rights, art. 21 GA Res 217(III), UN GAOR, 3d Sess., Supp. No. 14, UN Doc. A/810 (1948).

81. International Covenant on Civil and Political Rights, art. 25(b), Dec. 16, 1966, 999 U.N.T.S. 171 (entered ubti firce Mar. 23, 1976).

82. *See* American Declaration of Rights and Duties of Man, May 2, 1948, Res XXX. Final Act, Ninth Int'l Conference of American States, Bogota, Columbia, March 30–May 2, 1948, at 38, OAS Off. Rec. OEA/Ser.L/v/II.23/Doc.32/Rev.6; Charter of the Organization of American States, April 30, 1948, 2 U.S.T. 2394, U.N.T.S. 48.

83. Bush v. Gore, 531 U.S. 98, 109 (2000).

84. Alexander Keyssar, *The Right to Vote: The Contested History of Democracy in the United States*, 23 (Basic Books, 2000).

85. Election 2000 National Results, *available at* http://www.cnn.com/ELECTION/2000.

86. Fred L. Israel, *Student's Atlas of American Presidential Elections 1789–1996*, 84–85 (1997).

87. Maine and Nebraska each award one elector per congressional district to the presidential candidate who carries it and two electors to the statewide winner. Some have suggested that this system would be a fine and more politically plausible alternative to abolition. But there is nothing in this system which guarantees ultimate majority rule at the national level and it is likely to reproduce the political effects of Republican-tilting legislative gerrymanders in the states. At any rate, it is doubtful that heavily Democratic or Republican presidential states with corresponding state legislative majorities would consent to abandon their winner-take-all dominance in presidential elections.

88. *See* Alexis Simendinger, James A. Barnes and Carl M. Cannon, "Pondering a Popular Vote," 32 Nat'l J. 3650, 3653 (2000).

89. See http://www.fec.gov/elections.html.

90. Our presidential voting rate for 2000 was lower than presidential turnout in dozens of nations, from Algeria, Argentina, Armenia and Australia to Finland, Iceland, India, and Italy through Venezuela and Zambia. *See* Federal Election Commission, *available at* http://www.fec.gov/votregis/InternatTO.htm.

91. Christopher Hitchens, "Don't Blame Nader for Democrat's Problems," *Wall St. J.* Nov. 15, 2000.

92. *See e.g.*, www.voteswap.com (listing all voter match sites).

93. Jamin Raskin, "How to Save Al Gore's Bacon: Gore and Nader Can Both Win," *Slate*, October 25, 2000.

94. I learned at a conference that I organized after the election that someone else had hit upon the same idea before me: a wonderful person named Steve Yoder, who designed a website, www.voteexchange.org, but had no way to publicize it. His site received very little traffic until the movement exploded a few weeks later.

95. Brad Worley, "Raskin's Revolution: Copycats and Naysayers" in "Nader's Traders vs. State Regulators: Examining the Controversy over Internet Vote Swapping in the 2000 Presidential Election," 2 *North Carolina Journal of Law and Technology* 32, 38–40 (2001).

96. Letter on file with author.

97. Letter on file with author.

98. Cal. Elec. Code, section 18521 (2001).

99. Cal. Elec. Code, section 18522 (2001).

100. Letter on file with author.

101. Letter on file with author.

102. Letter on file with author.

103. Sam Smith, "Anti-Nader Dirty Trick Called Illegal," *Progressive Review*, October 31, 2000.

104. *Id.*

105. From www.Nadertrader.org/speakup (last visited Jan. 16, 2001).

106. *Id.*

107. *Id.*

108. There is very little scholarly literature on this point, but Professor Akhil Reed Ahmar made the point cogently in a *New York Times* op-ed during the heat of controversy over the 2000 presidential election when he wrote that "the college was designed at the founding of the country to help one group—white Southern males—and this year, it has apparently done just that." Akhil Ree Amar, The Electoral College, Unfair from Day One, *New York Times*, November 9, 2000.

109. U.S. Const., art. II, sec. 1, cl. 2.

110. U.S. Const., art. I, sec. 2, cl. 3.

111. U.S. Const., art. II, sec. 1, cl. 2.

112. *Id.*

113. U.S. Const., amend. XII.

114. *See* Rob Lopresti, "Which U.S. Presidents Owned Slaves," (Sept. 21, 2001), *available at* http://www.nas.com/~lopresti/ps.htm.

115. Matthew M. Hoffman, "The Illegitimate President: Minority Vote Dilution and the Electoral College," 105 *Yale L. J.* 935, 942 (1996).

116. *See id* at 950–1 for a fascinating discussion of Collins's strategy for Thurmond's presidential campaign.

117. *Id.* at 956 (quoting "Six Electors Bar Kennedy Support," *N.Y. Times*, Dec. 11, 1960, at 56).

118. Governor George Wallace, Address at the University of Alabama (June 1963) (quoted in Harvard Sitkoff, *The Struggle for Black Equality, 1954–1992*, at 145 (1993)).

119. *See* David A. Bositis, *The Black Vote in 2000*, The Joint Center for Political and Economic Studies 2 (December 2000).

120. *See* Judith Best, *The Case against Direct Election of the President: A Defense of the Electoral College* (Cornell University Press, 1975); Judith A. Best, *The Choice of the People? Debating the Electoral College* (Rowman & Littlefield 1996); Martin Diamond, *The Electoral College and the American Idea of Democracy* (American Institute for Public Policy Research 1977) (defending the Electoral College).

121. U.S. Const., amends. XIII, XIV, XV.

122. U.S. Const., amend. XVII.

123. U.S. Const., amend. XIX.

124. Judith N. Shklar, *Redeeming American Political Theory* 175, Stanley Hoffmann and Dennis F. Thompson eds. (Univ. Chi. Press 1998) (quoting Thomas Jefferson).

125. Quoted in *id.* at 138.

126. *See* John F. Banzhaf III, "*One Man, 3.312 Votes: A Mathematical Analysis of the Electoral College*," 13 *Vill. L. Rev.* 304 (1968).

127. *Id.* at 307.

128. *Id.* at 313.

129. *See, e.g.*, Lawrence D. Longley and James D. Dana, Jr., "The Electoral College's Biases in the 1992 Election—and Beyond," in The Electoral College and Direct Election of the President: Hearing Before the Subcommittee on

the Constitution of the Committee on the Judiciary on S.J. Res. 297, S.J. Res. 302, and S.J. Res. 312, 102nd Cong. 38, 43 (1992); George Rabinowitz and Stuart Elaine McDonald, "The Power of the States in U.S. Presidential Elections," 80 *Am. Pol. Sci. Rev.* 65, 75–78 (1986).

130. *See* John F. Banzhaf III, *ibid.*
131. Delaware v. New York, 385 U.S. 895 (1966).
132. *See id.*
133. *See id.*
134. U.S. Const., amend. XVII.
135. *See* John F. Banzhaf III, *ibid.*
136. *See* John Nichols, *Jews for Buchanan* (Free Press, 2001).

Chapter Four: Unequal Protection

1. Bob Moses and Charles Cobb, *Radical Equations* 41 (2001).
2. *Id.* at 41–42 (emphasis added in the first set of italics).
3. The useful taxonomy of first- and second-generation discriminatory tactics comes from Chandler Davidson, "The Recent Evolution of Voting Rights Law Affecting Racial and Language Minorities," 22–37 in Chandler Davidson and Bernard Grofman, ed., *Quiet Revolution in the South,* (Princeton Univ. Press, 1994).
4. James E. Alt, "The Impact of the Voting Rights Act on Black and White Voter Registration in the South," in Davidson and Grofman, 374, Table 12.1.
5. For an excellent overview of the history of the Voting Rights Act, see Davidson and Grofman, *Quiet Revolution,* at 21–37.
6. 446 U.S. 55 (1980).
7. 42 U.S.C. 1973.
8. *See* Bernard Grofman, et al., *Minority Representation and the Quest for Voting Equality,* 42–47 (1992).
9. Justice Brennan stated that three factors were critical to finding a claim of unlawful vote dilution under the Act. First, there must be a minority population present "sufficiently large and geographically compact to constitute a majority of a single-member district." Second, such group must be "politically cohesive," in that it votes generally as a group. Third, "the white majority" must vote "sufficiently as a bloc to enable it . . . usually to defeat the minority's preferred candidate." Thornburg v. Gingles, 478 U.S. 30, 50–51 (1986).
10. Grofman, Handley, and Niemi at 50.
11. Frank R. Parker, "The Constitutionality of Racial Redistricting," 3 *D.C. L. Rev.* 1, 1–3 (1995).
12. *Id.*
13. *Id.*
14. Grofman, Handley, and Niemi, 132.
15. 509 U.S. 630 (1993).
16. *See* Jim Sleeper, Rigging the Vote by Race, *Wall St. J.,* Aug. 4, 1992 at A14;

America's 'Segremanders," *Wall St. J.*, April 2, 1992, at A14; Against "Political Apartheid," *Wall St. J.*, June 30, 1993.

17. 509 U.S. 630 at 641–42.
18. *Id.* at 642.
19. *Id.* at 649.
20. *Id.* at 647.
21. *Id.* at 650.
22. *Id.* at 644.
23. *Id.* at 642.
24. Abrams v. Johnson, 117 S. Ct. 1925, 1935 (1997) (stating that the "twisted shapes of [Georgia's] Second and Eleventh districts again bear witness to racial motivation").
25. *Shaw*, 509 U.S. at 635.
26. *Abrams*, 117 S. Ct. at 1935 (stating: "[T]he Eleventh has an iguana-like shape betraying the same invidious purpose we condemned in *Miller*").
27. *Shaw*, 509 U.S. at 635.
28. *Id.*
29. 115 S. Ct. 2475 (1995).
30. *Id.* at 2488.
31. *See* Jamin Raskin, "The Supreme Court's Racial Double Standard: Unequal Protection in Politics and the Scholarship that Defends It," 14 *J. L. & Pol.* 591, 641–42 (1998) (quoting Richard H. Pildes, "Principled Limitations on Racial and Partisan Redistricting," 106 *Yale L. J.* 2505, 2510 (1997)).
32. The Court allows race as a consideration in drawing districts as long as it is not the *primary* consideration. *See* Bush v. Vera, 116 S. Ct. 1941, 1948 (1996) ("The evidence amply supports the District Court's conclusions that racially motivated gerrymandering had a *qualitatively greater* influence on the drawing of district lines than politically motivated gerrymandering") (emphasis added).
33. 116 S. Ct. 1620 (1996).
34. *Id.* at 1628.
35. *Id.*
36. Even Professor Pildes, who has worked to rationalize *Shaw* jurisprudence, has written that "[o]rdinary observers, for example, might recoil at the shape of many or most congressional districts today." Richard H. Pildes and Richard G. Niemi, "Expressive Harms, 'Bizarre Districts,' and Voting Rights: Evaluating Election-District Appearances after *Shaw v. Reno*," 92 *Mich. L. Rev.* 483, 537 (1993).
37. *See, e.g., Bush*, 116 S. Ct. at 1960–61.
38. *See id.* at 1950 (affirming lower court's holding that districts 18 and 29 were unconstitutional); Vera v. Richards, 861 F. Supp. 1304, 1309, 1310, 1345 (S.D. Tex. 1994) (considering challenge to 24 Texas congressional districts, including districts 3 and 6, and holding only districts 18, 29, and 30 unconstitutional), *aff'd sub nom.*, Bush v. Vera, 116 S. Ct. 1941 (1996).
39. *See, e.g.*, Smith v. Beasley, 946 F. Supp. 1174, 1208 (D.S.C. 1996).
40. *See id.*
41. *See id.* at 1207.

42. *See id.*
43. Miller v. Johnson, 515 U.S. 900, 938 (1995) (Ginsburg, J., dissenting, joined by Stevens, Souter, and Breyer, JJ.) (quoting Busbee v. Smith, 549 F. Supp. 494, 501 (D.D.C. 1982)).
44. 384 U.S. 73 (1966).
45. *See id.* at 89 n16.
46. 412 U.S. 735 (1973).
47. *Id.* at 738.
48. 117 S. Ct. 1925 (1997).
49. *Id.* at 1933.
50. 116 S. Ct. 1941 (1996).
51. *See id.* at 1950.
52. *Id.* at 1952.
53. *See id.* at 1954 (quoting Vera v. Richards, 861 F. Supp. 1304, 1334 (S.D. Tex. 1994)).
54. *See id.* at 1974–75 (Stevens, J., dissenting).
55. *Id.* at 1975.
56. *Id.* at 1976 (Stevens, J., dissenting).
57. *Id.* at 1981.
58. *Id.* at 1981 n17.
59. *Id.* at 1955–56.
60. Vera v. Richards, 861 F. Supp. 1304, 1318 (S.D. Tex. 1994) (citation omitted), *aff'd sub nom.*, Bush v. Vera, 116 S. Ct. 1941 (1996).
61. *See Bush*, 116 S. Ct. at 1954.
62. Justice Stevens, in his dissent to *Bush*, recognized the force of this point. *See id.* at 1975 n2. He stated:

    > Because I believe that political gerrymanders are more objectionable than the "racial gerrymanders" perceived by the Court in recent cases, I am not entirely unsympathetic to the Court's holding. I believe, however, that the evils of political gerrymandering should be confronted directly, rather than through the race-specific approach that the Court has taken in recent years.

    Id. (citations omitted). Justice Stevens later expanded on this theme:

    > Legislatures and elected representatives have a responsibility to behave in a way that incorporates the "elements of legitimacy and neutrality that must always characterize the performance of the sovereign's duty to govern impartially." That responsibility is not discharged when legislatures permit and even encourage incumbents to use their positions as public servants to protect themselves and their parties rather than the interests of their constituents.

    Id. at 1992 (Stevens, J., dissenting) (quoting City of Cleburne v. Cleburne Living Ctr., 473 U.S. 432, 452 (1985) (citations omitted)).
63. James A. Gardner, "The Uses and Abuses of Incumbency: *People v. Ohrenstein* and the Limits of Inherent Legislative Power," 60 *Fordham L. Rev.* 217, 221 (1991).
64. 319 U.S. 624 (1943).
65. *See* Kristen Silverberg, "The Illegitimacy of the Incumbent Gerrymander," 74 Tex. L. Rev. 913 (1996).

66. *Id.* at 929.
67. Cheryl Harris has argued that whiteness "signifies and is deployed as identity, status, and property, sometimes singularly, sometimes in tandem." Cheryl I. Harris, "Whiteness as Property," 106 *Harv. L. Rev.* 1707, 1725 (1993) (discussing the evolution and assimilation of whiteness into the very foundations of American property law). Harris also argues, with great force, that today the "protection of a property interest in whiteness is achieved by embracing the norm of colorblindness. . . . Thus, at the very historical moment that race is infused with a perspective that reshapes it, through race-conscious remediation, into a potential weapon against subordination, official rules articulated in law deny that race matters." *Id.* at 1768.
68. 426 U.S. 229 (1976).
69. *See id.* at 240.
70. *See id.* at 230–31.
71. *See id.* at 239 (stating that, "Our cases have not embraced the proposition that a law or other official act, without regard to whether it reflects a racially discriminatory purpose, is unconstitutional").
72. *Id.* at 240.
73. 446 U.S. 55 (1980).
74. *Id.* at 66 (emphasis added).
75. *See Shaw*, 509 U.S. at 650 (1993).
76. *See* Allen v. Wright, 468 U.S. 737, 739 (1984).
77. *Id.* at 755–56.
78. *Id.* at 754.
79. *See* Shaw v. Reno, 509 U.S. 630, 649–50 (1993).
80. Federal Election Campaign Act of 1971, Pub. L. No. 92–225, 86 Stat. 3 (codified as amended in sections of 2 U.S.C., 18 U.S.C., & 47 U.S.C.).
81. Indeed, in Albanese v. Federal Election Comm., 884 F. Supp. 685, 693 (E.D.N.Y. 1995), a federal district judge in New York denied standing to a congressional candidate and a group of working class voters who alleged that the system of private financing of federal campaigns discriminated against them on the basis of wealth and class. Still, there are legal challenges to the private campaign finance regime multiplying on Equal Protection grounds. *See, e.g.,* NAACP v. Jones, No. 96–56455, 1997 U.S. App. LEXIS 35152, at *7 (9th Cir. Dec. 16, 1997). These cases have far more merit than challenges to majority-minority districts. After all, some racial and ethnic groups will, by definition, almost always have to be in the minority, but there is a clear alternative to the system of private campaign financing: public funding. *See generally* Jamin Raskin and John Bonifaz, "Equal Protection and the Wealth Primary," 11 *Yale L. & Pol'y Rev.* 273 (1993) (arguing current campaign financing violates Equal Protection).
82. *See, e.g., Shaw*, 509 U.S. at 647.
83. 512 U.S. 874 (1994).
84. *Id.* at 905 (Thomas, J., concurring in the judgment) (emphasis added).
85. 347 U.S. 483 (1954).
86. *See id.* at 486n1.
87. *See Shaw*, 509 U.S. at 659–666 (White, J., dissenting).

88. *See* A. Leon Higginbotham et al., "*Shaw v. Reno*: A Mirage of Good Intentions with Devastating Racial Consequences," 62 *Fordham L. Rev.* 1593, 1621–24 (1994).

89. *See* McCleskey v. Kemp, 481 U.S. 279, 320 (1987) (Brennan, J., dissenting); Jamin B. Raskin, "Affirmative Action and Racial Reaction," 38 *How. L. J.* 521, 530 (1995).

90. *See* City of Memphis v. Greene, 451 U.S. 100, 102–4 (1981); David Kairys, *With Liberty and Justice for Some* 130–36 (1993).

91. *See* Erika L. Johnson, "A Menace to Society: The Use of Criminal Profiles and Its Effect on Black Males," 38 *How. L. J.* 629, 629 (1995); Randall S. Susskind, "Race, Reasonable Articulable Suspicion, and Seizure," 31 *Am. Crim. L. Rev.* 327, 338, 347 (1994).

92. *See* Missouri v. Jenkins, 495 U.S. 33 (1990) (reversing court-ordered property tax increase to fund school desegregation measures); Milliken v. Bradley, 433 U.S. 267 (1977) (striking interdistrict desegregation plans).

93. Abrams v. Johnson, 117 S. Ct. 1925, 1937 (1997) (quoting Johnson v. Miller, 922 F. Supp. 1556, 1568 (S.D. Ga. 1995)).

94. This is true not only as a matter of voting rights but also housing rights. *See* Village of Arlington Heights v. Metropolitan Hous. Dev. Corp., 429 U.S. 252 (1977).

95. *Shaw*, 509 U.S. at 647.

96. *Id.* at 648.

97. *Id.*

98. *Id.*

99. *See Shaw* at 666 (White, J., dissenting).

100. Leslie Bender and Daan Braveman, *Power, Privilege and Law* 22–23 (1995) (excerpting Peggy McIntosh, *White Privilege and Male Privilege: A Personal Account of Coming to See Correspondences through Work in Women's Studies*, Wellesley College for Research on Women Working Paper No. 189 [1988]).

101. *See* Martha R. Mahoney, "Segregation, Whiteness and Transformation," 143 *U. Pa. L. Rev.* 1659, 1660 (1995) ("Since race is a phenomenon always in formation, then whiteness—like other racial constructions—is subject to contest and change. 'Whiteness' is historically located, malleable, contingent, and capable of being transformed").

102. Abigal Thernstrom, "Redistricting Civil Rights Groups, GOP Partners in Quota Conspiracy," *Phoenix Gazette*, Oct. 3, 1991, at A13.

103. "GOP Clash on Redistricting: Some Say the Plan Is a Back-Door Endorsement of Racial Quotas," *S.F. Chron.*, May 10, 1991, at A11.

104. *Shaw*, 509 U.S. at 642.

105. Chandler Davidson, "The Recent Evolution of Voting Rights Law Affecting Racial and Language Minorities," 24 in Davidson and Grofman, *Quiet Revolution in the South: The Impact of the Voting Rights Act 1965–1990* (1994).

106. *See* Plessy v. Ferguson, 163 U.S. 537, 550 (1896).

107. *Id.*

108. This draining of progressive content from constitutional ideals set a pattern in conservative jurisprudence that Justice Scalia keeps alive today. He would define Due Process liberty with respect only to rights that have been

"traditionally protected by our society," which is why he and other conservatives believe gay people do not have the same rights of privacy other Americans have.

109. For a more measured statement of the same idea, see Pamela Karlan and Daryl J. Levinson, "Why Voting is Different," 84 *Cal. L. Rev.*, 1201, 1207 (1996) (stating: "[R]ace itself is as traditional as districting principles come.").

110. Jamin B. Raskin, "From 'Colorblind' White Supremacy to American Multiculturalism," 19 *Harv. J. L. & Pub. Pol'y* 743, 743 (1996).

111. 512 U.S. 874 (1994) (Thomas, J., concurring in the judgment, joined by Scalia, J.).

112. *Id.* at 905–6.

113. Richmond v. Croson, 488 U.S. 469 (1989).

114. Adarand Constructors, Inc. v. Pena, 515 U.S. 200 (1995).

115. *See Missouri*, 495 U.S. 33 (reversing court-ordered property tax increase to fund school desegregation); *and Milliken*, 433 U.S. 267 (striking interdistrict desegregation plans).

116. Eric Foner, *Reconstruction: America's Unfinished Revolution 1863–1877*, 69 (1988).

117. *Id.*

118. 163 U.S. 537 (1896).

119. *Id.* at 559.

120. *Id.* at 555–56.

121. *Id.* at 562.

122. *See* Randall Kennedy, "Persuasion and Distrust: A Comment on the Affirmative Action Debate," 99 *Harvard L. Rev.* 1327, 1335–36 (1986) ("the concept of race-blindness was simply a proxy for the fundamental demand that racial subjugation be eradicated. This demand. . .focused upon the *condition* of racial subjugation; its target was not only procedures that overtly excluded Negroes on the basis of race, but also the self-perpetuating dynamics of subordination that had survived the demise of American apartheid. The opponents of affirmative action have stripped the historical context from the demand for race-blind law") (citation omitted).

123. Harlan's dissent at 559.

124. Jeffrey Rosen, "*Kiryas Joel* and *Shaw v. Reno*: A Text-Bound Interpretivist Approach," 26 *Cumb. L. Rev.* 387, 402 (1995–96).

125. *See id.* (quoting 377 U.S. 533, 595 (Harlan, J., dissenting)).

126. *See, e.g., Shaw*, 509 U.S. at 642.

127. As James Blacksher observes: "In a real sense, redistricting is the recurring expression of the people's freedom by renewing their consent, through their representatives, to the fundamental terms upon which the government will be formed." James V. Blacksher, "Dred Scott's Unknown Freedom: The Redistricting Cases as Badges of Slavery," 3a *How L. J.* 633, 635 (1996).

128. *See The Federalist* No. 52 (Alexander Hamilton or James Madison). "As it is essential to liberty that the government in general should have a common interest with the people, so it is particularly essential that the branch of it under consideration [the House of Representatives] should have an immediate dependence on, and an intimate sympathy with, the people." *Id.*

129. *See* West Virginia Bd. of Educ. v. Barnette, 319 U.S. 624, 642 (1943) (stating: "If there is any fixed star in our constitutional constellation, it is that no official, high or petty, can prescribe what shall be orthodox in politics."); *see also* Denver Area Educ. Telecom. Consortium v. FCC, 116 S. Ct. 2374, 2405 (1996) (Kennedy, J., concurring in part, and dissenting in part). Justice Kennedy stated:

> In the realm of speech and expression, the First Amendment envisions the citizen shaping the government, not the reverse; it removes "governmental restraints from the arena of public discussion, putting the decision as to what views shall be voiced into the hands of each of us, in the hope that use of such freedom will ultimately produce a more capable citizenry and a more perfect polity."

Id. (quoting Cohen v. California, 403 U.S. 15, 24 (1971)).

130. *See Shaw*, 509 U.S. at 642–45.

131. 60 U.S. (19 How.) 393 (1856).

132. 163 U.S. 537, 543–44 (1896). The Court stated:

> A statute which implies merely a legal distinction between the white and colored races ... has no tendency to destroy the legal equality of the two races.... The object of the [Fourteenth] amendment [*sic*] was undoubtedly to enforce the absolute equality of the two races before the law, but, in the nature of things, it could not have been intended to abolish distinctions based upon color, or to enforce social, as distinguished from political, equality, or a commingling of the two races upon terms unsatisfactory to either.

133. *See Shaw*, 509 U.S. at 641–42, 657.

134. *See, e.g.*, Holder v. Hall, 512 U.S. 874, 905–6 (1994).

135. This idea has been a major theme running through the work of Derrick Bell, and I have been influenced by it. *See* Derrick A. Bell, *And We Are Not Saved: The Elusive Quest for Racial Justice* (1987).

136. *See Miller*, 515 U.S. at 919.

137. Stephen J. Malone, "Recognizing Communities of Interest in a Legislative Apportionment Plan," 83 *Va. L. Rev.* 461, 492 (1997). This meticulous article explains how to accomplish this task.

138. *See* Hunt v. Cromartie, 532 U.S. 234 (2001) (Justice O'Connor joining the Court's moderates and liberals in overruling a district court judgment that the North Carolina legislature improperly used race as the predominant factor in drawing districts, finding instead a satisfactory political and partisan explanation for the districts).

Chapter Five: America's Signature Exclusion:

1. CNN/Gallup/ *USA Today* poll conducted July 16–18, 1999; surveyed 1,028 adults; margin of error plus or minus 3 percent.

2. For a more detailed doctrinal development of this argument, see Jamin Raskin and John Bonifaz, "Equal Protection and the Wealth Primary," 11 *Yale Law & Policy Review* 273, 273 (1993).

3. 319 U.S. 624 (1943).

4. *Id.* at 641.

5. *Id.* at 642.

6. *Texas v. Johnson*, 491 U.S. 397, 414 (1989).

7. *See* Jürgen Habermas, *Between Facts and Norms: Contributions to a Discourse Theory of Law and Democracy* 457, William Rehg trans. (MIT Press 1996).

8. Jürgen Habermas, *Legitimation Crisis* 36–37, Thomas McCarthy trans. (Boston: Beacon Press, 1975) (1973).

9. U.S. Term Limits v. Thornton, 514 U.S. 779, 779 (1995).

10. *Id.* at 829 (stating that the sole purpose for the rule was to achieve a result forbidden by the Federal Constitution).

11. *Id.* at 784.

12. Article I, sec. 2, cl. 2 provides: "No person shall be a Representative who shall not have attained to the Age of twenty five Years, and been seven Years a Citizen of the United States, and who shall not, when elected, be an inhabitant of that State in which he shall be chosen." Article I, sec. 3, cl. 3 states: "No person shall be a Senator who shall not have attained to the Age of thirty Years, and been nine Years a Citizen of the United States, and who shall not, when elected, be an Inhabitant of that State for which he shall be chosen."

13. *U.S. Term Limits*, 514 U.S. at 78 (declaring forcefully that "if the qualifications set forth in the text of the Constitution are to be changed, that text must be amended").

14. *Id.* at 783 (quoting Powell v. McCormack, 395 U.S. 486, 547 (1969)).

15. 17 U.S. (4 Wheat.) 316, 404–5 (1819).

16. 395 U.S. 486 (1969) (concluding that the Constitution prohibits the House from excluding any duly elected person who meets all the constitutionally prescribed requirements).

17. *Id.* at 490 (noting that a special subcommittee had concluded that Powell had deceived House authorities as to travel expenses).

18. *See U.S. Term Limits*, 514 U.S. at 790 (construing *Powell*, 395 U.S. at 533–34). The Court in Powell relied on the story of John Wilkes, whom the British House of Commons allowed to assume his duly elected seat in Parliament, despite Parliament's refusal to seat him because of Wilkes' prior conviction for seditious libel. The House of Commons said that Parliament's exclusion of Wilkes was "subversive of the rights. . .of the electors." 395 U.S. at 528.

19. The Federalist No. 60, at 394 (Alexander Hamilton) (Random House ed., 1937).

20. *Powell*, 395 U.S. at 540–41.

21. *U.S. Term Limits*, 514 U.S. at 793 (quoting Powell, 395 U.S. at 548).

22. *Id.* at 794.

23. *Id.*

24. *Id.* at 795 (quoting Powell, 395 U.S. at 540–41).

25. *U.S. Term Limits*, 514 U.S. at 795 (adopting a sentiment first expressed by Wilkes in his argument before Parliament and later relied on by the Court in *Powell*).

26. *Id.* at 820–21.

27. *Id.* at 831.

28. *Id.*

29. Cook v. Gralike, 531 U.S. 510, 510 (2001).

30. *See id.* at 525–26 (holding that the ballot information did not reflect an attempt to regulate the procedural mechanism of the election but rather to "dictate electoral outcomes.").

31. *Id.* at 514–15.

32. *Id.* at 525.

33. *See, e.g.,* Gould v. Grubb, 14 Cal. 3d 661 (1975) (the California Supreme Court invalidating a state law placing incumbents first on the ballot).

34. *See, e.g.,* Timmons v. Twin Cities Area New Party, 520 U.S. 351, 367 (1997) ("The Constitution permits the Minnesota Legislature to decide that political stability is best served through a healthy two-party system.")

35. Maurice Duverger, "Factors in a Two-Party and Multiparty System" in *Party Politics and Pressure Groups,* 23–32 (New York: Thomas Y. Crowell, 1972).

36. *Timmons* 520 U.S. at 9.

37. *See* Black and Black, "Perot Wins! The Election That Could Have Been," 4(2) *Public Perspective* 15–16 (1993).

38. Richard Hofstadter, *The Idea of A Party System: The Rise of Legitimate Opposition in the United States,* 1780–1840, 40 (1969).

39. *The Life and Selected Writings of Thomas Jefferson,* Adrienne Koch et al. eds. (1988).

40. George Washington, Farewell Address, September 19, 1796, p.17.

41. *See* David Cole, "First Amendment Anti-Trust: The End of Laissez-Faire in Campaign Finance," 9 *Yale L. & Pol'y Rev.* 236 (1991) (for an excellent statement on the need for a First Amendment anti-trust principle).

42. *See* N.Y. Times v. Sullivan, 376 U.S. 191, 270 (1964).

43. Burson v. Freeman, 504 U.S. 191, 200 (1992).

44. *Id.*

45. *Id.* at 204–5.

46. *See, e.g.,* Peter Argersinger, "From Party Tickets to Secret Ballots: The Evolution of the Electoral Process in Maryland During the Gilded Age," 82 *Maryland Historical Magazine* 214 (Fall 1987).

47. *See* Richard Winger, "History of U.S. Ballot Access Law for New and Minor Parties," 1 The Encyclopedia of Third Parties in America 72 (Armonk, N.Y.: M.E. Sharpe, 2000).

48. *See id.*

49. *See* Brief of Appellant, Maryland Green Party v. Maryland Board of Elections (September Term, 2001, No. 00075).

50. "During that time, fearing that Socialists or Communists would become significant political rivals, the major parties enacted legislation intended to deny them that opportunity." The Appleseed Center for Electoral Reform and the Harvard Legislative Research Bureau, "A Model Act for the Democratization of Ballot Access," 36 *Harv. J. on Legis.* 451, 452 (1999).

51. *Id.* (citing Joshua Rosenkrantz, Voter Choice '96: A 50-State Report Card on the Presidential Elections 4 [1996]).

52. *Id.* at 453.

53. A federal court in 1970 did order that the name of the American Party's candidate for governor that year be placed on the ballot (*see* Barnhart v.

Mandel, 311 F. Supp. 814 (D.Md. 1970)) and one ex-Democrat, Hyman Pressman, won ballot status as an Independent in 1966 to give liberals a chance to vote against the conservative Democratic nominee George Mahoney and Republican Spiro Agnew. As far as alternatives to the two-party system go, that is it.

54. Green Party brief in *Maryland Green Party v. Maryland Board of Elections*, Case no. t-2000-657880t.

55. Colegrove v. Green, 328 US 549, 556 (Justice Frankfurter stating the "courts ought not to enter this political thicket").

56. 403 U.S. 431 (1971).

57. *Id.* at 434–35 (quoting Williams v. Rhodes, 393 U.S. 23 at 24).

58. *Id.* at 438.

59. *Id.*

60. *Id.* at 438–39.

61. *Id.* at 440.

62. *Id.* at 438.

63. *Id.* at 442.

64. Richard Winger, "The Supreme Court and the Burial of Ballot Access: A Critical Review of *Jenness v. Fortson*," 1 *Election Law Journal* 235, 235 (2002).

65. *U.S. Term Limits* at 831.

66. *Id.* at 438–39.

67. *Id.* at 440.

68. *Id.* at 438.

69. *Id.* at 442.

70. *See supra* n64 at 242.

71. Munro v. Socialist Workers Party, 479 U.S. 189, 194–195 (1986).

72. *See supra* note 64 at 243.

73. *See id.*

74. *Munro* at 195.

75. *See supra* 64 at 236.

76. 520 U.S. 351 (1997).

77. *Id.* at 356.

78. Burdick v. Talenshi, 504 US 428, 438 (1992).

79. Minn. Stat. Sec. 204B.04, subd. 2.

80. 73 F.3d 196, 198 (8th Cir., 1996).

81. 520 U.S. 351 (1997).

82. *Id.* at 359.

83. *Id.* at 364.

84. *Id.* at 365.

85. *Id.* at 366.

86. *Id.* at 366–67 (emphasis added).

87. 460 U.S. 780 (1983).

88. "No state shall . . . grant any Title of Nobility." U.S. Const., art. I, sec. 10, cl. 1.

Chapter Six: "Arrogant Orwellian Bureaucrats"

1. Abraham Lincoln, Gettysburg Address, Gettysburg, Pennsylvania, November 19, 1863).

2. Harold Holzer, *The Lincoln-Douglas Debates* 2 (HarperCollins, 1993).

3. See *id.* at 24, noting the pervasive belief that "Lincoln shrewdly used the debates mainly to position himself for the presidency two years later."

4. Although it now claims to be "nonpartisan," the CPD was launched in 1987 by the Democratic and Republican National Committees as an explicitly "bipartisan" private corporation to sponsor "general election presidential and vice-presidential debates . . . by the national Republican and Democratic Committees between their respective nominees." Jamin Raskin, "The Debate Gerrymander," 77 *Tex. L. Rev.*, 1943, 1982 (1999).

5. Joint Memorandum of Agreement on Presidential Candidate Joint Appearances signed by Paul G. Kirk, Jr. and Frank J. Fahrenkopf, Jr. (Nov. 26, 1985).

6. CanadaVotes, "A Guide to This Year's Federal Elections" (February 9, 1997) *available at* http://www.southam.com/national/fed97 (visited July 2, 2001), stating that Canada has always had inclusive "all-candidate debates."

7. PR Newswire, "Todito.Com to Webcast Mexican Presidential Debate" (April 24, 2000), *available at* findarticles.com/m4PRN/2000_April_24/66163853/pl/article/html (visited June 21, 2001)

8. U.S. Const., amend. XII ("if no person have such majority, then from the persons having the highest numbers not exceeding three on the list of those voted for as President, the House of Representatives shall choose immediately, by ballot, the President.")

9. Arkansas Educational Television Commission v. Forbes, 118 S. Ct. 1633 (1988).

10. This was the memorable name of the case, given to it by Ralph Forbes, before the court changed it to Forbes v. Arkansas Educational Television Network (93 F.3d 497(8th Cir. 1996)).

11. Forbes v. Arkansas Educational Television Commission, 93 F.3d 497 (8th Cir. 1996).

12. *Id.* at 504.

13. *Id.* at 504–5.

14. *Forbes*, 523 U.S. at 675.

15. *Id.* at 680.

16. *Forbes*, 523 U.S. at 682.

17. *Id.*

18. Harper v. Virginia Bd. of Elections, 383 U.S. 663, 666 (1966); Bullock v. Carter, 405 U.S. 134, 143 (1972).

19. *Rosenberger v. Rectors and Visitors of University of Virginia*, 115 S. Ct. 2510 (1995).

20. Similarly, in *Lamb's Chapel v. Moriches*, 508 U.S. 384 (1993), where the Court struck down a school system's practice of opening its facilities after hours to all groups except religious ones, there was nothing in the record to suggest that the Center Moriches school system had personal or political hostility towards

the religious groups that it was excluding. Nonetheless, the Court found the practice viewpoint-discriminatory.

21. *Rosenburger* 115 S. Ct. at 2518.
22. Press release on file with the author.
23. News from the Democratic and Republican National Committees (Feb. 18, 1987), on file with the Texas Law Review.
24. 11 C.F.R. sec. 11.13(c) (1996).
25. For a fuller examination of the legal twists and turns in *Perot '96 v. Federal Election Commission*, 1996 WL 566762 (D.D.C.), see Jamin B. Raskin, "The Debate Gerrymander," 77 Texas Law Review 1943, 1976–1987.
26. *See* Perot '96 v. Federal Election Commission, 1996 WL 566762 (D.D.C.) at 3.
27. This is a great quadrennial conference where the campaign managers tell the truth about everything they were lying about during the campaign.
28. *Campaign for President: The Managers Look at '96,* 170, Harvard Univ. Inst. of Pol., ed. (1997).
29. *Id.* at 171.
30. *Id.* at 162.
31. *Id.* at 162.
32. FEC Statement of Reasons MURs 4481 and 4473, (February 24, 1998).
33. *Id.* at 8.
34. See *id.* at 8, n.7.
35. *Id.* at 9.
36. Ralph Nader, *Crashing the Party* 221 (St. Martin's Press 2002).
37. *Id.*
38. In Forbes's case, this was the explanation of AETN's executive director, who testified in court that: "He didn't have popular support and didn't have a chance to win the election."
39. Texas v. Johnson, 491 U.S. 397, 414 (1989).
40. Buckley v. Valeo, 424 U.S. 1, 15 (1976), quoting Monitor Patriot Co. v. Roy, 401 U.S. 265, 272 (1971).
41. The one possible exception to this principle might be that the Secret Service, in preparing to protect the future President, should probably be allowed to husband its resources by extending protection only to those presidential candidates it deems most likely to win. This should be done in a nonpartisan and viewpoint-neutral way and in as low-key a fashion as possible so as not to skew the public perception of the candidates. Given that Secret Service protection does not extend to candidates at lower levels of office, this is a very slender exception.
42. Indeed, most candidates excluded from debates would probably prefer the chance to debate and voice their ideas face-to-face with their opponents and then receive a "not viable" tag on the ballot than to be declared "not viable" earlier on and excluded from the debates but not be so designated on the ballot. Getting the chance to debate creates the potential for a political breakthrough in the campaign. A lot of voters would also instinctively recoil at the blatant manipulation of the ballot effectuated by placing "(not viable)" next to the candidate's name.
43. The government may presently guarantee the seriousness of certified

candidates by placing minimal conditions on access to the ballot. Whatever the merits of this system, seriousness for ballot access purposes is defined with respect to a person's willingness to devote time and energy to gathering signatures rather than the person's likelihood of actually winning the election. See Chapter Five for a detailed discussion of this problem.

44. Clerk of the U.S. House of Representatives, *Statistics of the Presidential and Congressional Election of November 3, 1992*, at 5 (1993).

45. *Id.*

46. *Congressional Quarterly's Guide to U.S. Elections* 978–1321 (3d ed. 1994) (John L. Moore, ed).

47. *See id.*

48. Federal Election Commission Financial Data for House General Election Campaigns through Dec. 31, 1992, at 22.

49. *See* Clerk of the U.S. House of Representatives, *Statistics of the Presidential and Congressional Elections of November 3, 1992*, at 5 (1993).

50. "Governor's Run for White House Heads Arkansas' Slate on Nov. 3," Associated Press, Oct. 24, 1992.

51. Federal Election Commission Financial Data for House General Election Campaigns Through Dec. 31, 1992 at 22.

52. *See* "Media Notes," *Washington Post* at D1 (October 28, 1996).

53. *See* "Behind Closed Doors," *Indianapolis Star* at B3 (September 29, 1996).

54. *See* "Media Notes," *supra.*

55. *See* Norman J. Orenstein et al., *Vital Statistics on Congress 1995–96*, at 60 (1996), calculation based on statistics from 1976–1996, inclusively.

56. *See id.* at 3–4.

57. The Eighth Circuit was right to find that "political viability" is "so susceptible of variation in individual opinion" as to "provide no secure basis for the exercise of governmental power consistent with the First Amendment." Forbes v. Arkansas Educ. Television Comm. 93 F. 3d 497, 504 (8th Cir. 1996). The whole point of a political campaign period is to allow candidates—through popular appeals, organizing and debates—to change public opinion.

58. The Appleseed Citizen's Task Force on Fair Debates, *A Blueprint for Fair and Open Presidential Debates in 2000*, at 4 (2000).

59. *See* "Moody and Checota in Close Race for Senate Nomination," *Milwaukee J.* at A1 (August 16, 1992).

60. *See* "Landslide for Feingold," *Milwaukee Sentinel* at 1A (September 9, 1992).

61. Arianna Huffington, *How to Overthrow the Government* at 82 (Regan Books, 2000).

62. This idea has support in Supreme Court case law. *See, e.g.,* Illinois Elections Bd. v. Socialist Workers' Party, 440 U.S. 173, 186 (1979), "[An] election campaign is a means of disseminating ideas as well as attaining political office."

63. *See* J. David Gillespie, *Politics at the Periphery* at 27 (1993).

64. *See* Michael Kelly, "The President's Past," *New York Times* at F20 (July 31, 1994).

65. *See* Michael deCourcy Hinds, "A Victory over Illness Plays Well in Politics," *New York Times* at A18 (Feb. 20, 1994).

66. *See* Michael deCourcy Hinds, "The 1992 Campaign: Pennsylvania," *New York Times* at A15 (February 21, 1992).

67. *See* Gordon Black, "The End of the Two Party Era?" *Polling Report*, September 18, 1995. "The two parties have today lost the firm allegiance of a majority of the American electorate. Nearly 40% of the electorate is fully Independent in its preferences and less than 30% is strongly attached to either of the two parties combined"; Emmet T. Flood and William G. Mayer, "Third-Party and Independent Candidates: How They Get on the Ballot, How They Get Nominated," in *In Pursuit of the White House* 317, William G. Mayer ed. (1995), noting "long-term decay of party allegiances within the national electorate."

68. Micah L. Sifry, *Spoiling for a Fight: Third Party Politics in America* 3 (2002, Routledge). *See* John C. Berg, "Cracks in the U.S. Two-Party System," at 41, Presented at the Annual Meeting of the New England Political Science Association, Suffolk University, May 3–4, 1996, showing rapidly growing numbers of Independent and minor-party House candidates placing second in general elections and receiving more than 5 percent of the vote; *Third Party Prospects*, CQ Research, Congressional Quarterly, Inc. at 1139 (December 22, 1995) ("The disposition to vote for an Independent candidate is higher than it has ever been in the past. While it is difficult to make the choice, it is getting easier") (quoting Andrew Kohut, director of Times Mirror Center for the People and the Press).

69. Micah L. Sifry, *ibid.*

70. *Forbes* at 14, internal citations omitted.

71. Brief for the Petitioner in *Forbes* at 29.

72. This figure, along with all the others, was calculated from election returns reported in *Congressional Quarterly Almanac* and *Congressional Quarterly Weekly Report* for each of the respective election years from 1948 to 1996. Even if we look at the period of 1986 to 1996, a time of growth in minor party activity, the Supreme Court's parade of horribles looks silly. In 1986, there were 91 Independents or minor-party candidates; in 1988, there were 154; in 1990, there were 170; in 1992, there were 458; in 1994, there were 256; and in 1996, the peak year last century for minor-party House candidacies, there were 487, or just barely more than one per district on average. *Id.*

73. As an amicus in Forbes v. Arkansas Educational Television Network, CPD made a similar argument that presidential debates would become less manageable if the lock of the two-party system were broken. *See* Brief of *Amicus Curiae* CPD at 4. But in 1996, only three presidential candidates were eligible to receive public funding in the general election, which is the only federal statutory definition of seriousness we have. *See* Ron Scherer, "The Perot Factor: Maverick May Mine Voter Discontent," *The Christian Science Monitor* at 3 (August 20, 1996), noting Perot's, Clinton's and Dole's receipt of federal campaign funds. In addition, only four presidential candidates secured ballot status in all fifty states and the District of Columbia; *see* Mimi Hall, "Not to Forget the 18 Other Candidates," *USA Today*, November 5, 1996, at 8A, and only six candidates made it onto the ballot in sufficient states to be able theoretically to collect a majority of votes in the Electoral College. *See* Donald P. Baker, "Third-Party 'Musketeers' Duel on TV," *Washington Post* at A20

(October 23, 1996). If a government broadcaster were to sponsor a presidential debate (none presently do), it would have any of these stringent yet viewpoint-neutral tests available to it.

74. *See, for example,* Bill Lambrecht, "The Democratic Presidential Hopefuls to Use Debate to Kick Off Campaign," *St. Louis Post-Dispatch* at 1B (December 14, 1991).

75. *See* Lloyd Grove, "GOP Presidential Hopefuls Prepare for Premiere Debate," *Washington Post* at A5 (Oct. 27, 1987).

76. *Cohen v. California,* 403 U.S. 15 (1971).

77. *Buckley v. Valeo,* 424 U.S. 1, 48–49 (1976).

78. *Rosenberger,* 515 U.S. 819, 835 (1995).

79. This is the clear and correct implication of *Hurley v. Irish-American Gay, Lesbian & Bisexual Group of Boston, Inc.,* 515 U.S. 557 (1995) (upholding the right of a St. Patrick's Day Committee to exclude an unwanted contingent of gay and lesbian marchers from its parade).

80. Participants included former congressman and presidential candidate John Anderson; John Bonifaz, executive director of the National Voting Rights Institute; Joan Claybrook, president of Public Citizen; Steve Cobble, the former political director of the National Rainbow Coalition; Ron Hayduk, assistant professor of political science at Touro College; author and activist Ariana Huffington; Rob Richie, executive director of the Center for Voting and Democracy; attorney Jonathan Soros; Ed Still, the director of the Voting Rights Project of the Lawyers' Committee for Civil Rights Under Law; M. Dane Waters, president of the Initiative and Referendum Institute; and Richard Winger, editor of the *Ballot Access News.*

Chapter Seven: Schooling for Democracy

1. *See* Plyler v. Doe, 457 U.S. 202 (1982) (finding that Texas could not exclude the children of undocumented persons from public schools).

2. Brown v. Board of Educ., 347 U.S. 483, 493 (1954).

3. John Dewey, *Democracy and Education* 360 (MacMillan, 1961) (1916).

4. 347 U.S. 483 (1954).

5. 393 U.S. 503 (1969).

6. 319 U.S. 624.

7. *Id.*

8. *Id.* at 641.

9. *Id.* at 642.

10. *Id.*

11. *Id.* at 505–6.

12. *Id.* at 506.

13. 393 U.S. 503.

14. *Id.* at 509.

15. *Id.*

16. *Id.* at 511.

17. *Id.* at 508.

18. *Id.* at 512.
19. John Dewey, *ibid.*
20. *Id.* at 358.
21. *Id.* at 305.
22. *Id.* at 360.
23. Bethel v. Fraser, 478 U.S. 675 (1986).
24. *Id.* at 687.
25. *Id.* at 693 (quoting 393 U.S. 503, 509 (1969)).
26. *Id.* at 679.
27. *Id.*
28. 478 U.S. 675, 681 (1986).
29. 478 U.S. at 685.
30. *Id.* at 690 (Marshall, J., dissenting).
31. *Id.* at 687–90 (Brennan, J., dissenting).
32. 484 U.S. 260 (1988).
33. *Id.*
34. *Id.* at 263.
35. *Id.*
36. *Id.* at 271.
37. *Id.* at 273.
38. *Id.* at 277–91 (Brennan, J., Marshall, J. and Blackmun, J., dissenting).
39. *Id.* (Brennan, J., Marshall, J. and Blackmun, J., dissenting).
40. *Id.* at 283 (Brennan, J., Marshall, J. and Blackmun, J., dissenting).
41. *Id.* at 283–84 (Brennan, J., Marshall, J. and Blackmun, J., dissenting).
42. *Id.* at 285–86 (Brennan, J., Marshall, J. and Blackmun, J., dissenting).
43. "'Hazlewood School District v. Kuhlmeier' A Complete Guide to the Supreme Court Decision," Student Press Law Center (1992).
44. 162 Mass. 510, 39 N.E. 113 (Mass. 1895).
45. Brown v. Board of Education, 347 U.S. 483, 495 (1954).
46. 163 U.S. 537 (1896).
47. *Id.* at 538.
48. *Id.* at 544.
49. *Id.* at 550.
50. *Id.* (emphasis added).
51. *Id.* 550–51.
52. 163 U.S. 537.
53. *Id.* at 551.
54. *Id.*
55. *Id.*
56. *Id.* at 551–52.
57. 60 U.S. 393, 407 (1856).
58. 163 U.S. at 559 (Harlan, J., dissenting).
59. *See* Leland B. Ware, "Setting the Stage for Brown: The Development and Implementation of the NAACP's School Desegregation Campaign, 1930–1950," 52 *Mercer L. Rev.* 631 (2001); *and also* Mark V. Tushnet, *The*

NAACP: Legal Strategy Against Segregation (Chapel Hill: The University of North Carolina Press, 1987).
60. 347 U.S. 483 (1954).
61. 347 U.S. at 494.
62. *Id.* at 494.
63. *See* Washington v. Davis, 426 U.S. 229, 239 (1976) (holding that a civil service exam that resulted in a racially disproportionate failure rate was not unlawful unless plaintiffs could show that the purpose for having the test was to discriminate against African Americans).
64. 358 U.S. 1, 16 (1958).
65. 418 U.S. 717 (1974).
66. *Id.*
67. *Id.*
68. *Id.*
69. *Id.* at 769 (White, J., Douglas, J., Brennan, J. and Marshall, J., dissenting).
70. *Id.* (White, J., Douglas, J., Brennan, J. and Marshall, J., dissenting).
71. *Id.* at 806 (White, J., Douglas, J., Brennan, J. and Marshall, J., dissenting).
72. 411 U.S. 1 (1973).
73. *Id.*
74. 411 U.S. at 12.
75. *Id.* at 12–13.
76. *Id.*
77. 411 U.S. 1.
78. *Id.* at 40.
79. 411 U.S. 1 (1973).
80. *Id.* at 23.
81. *Id.* at 35.
82. *Id.*
83. *Id.* at 36.
84. *Id.* at 62–133 (1973) (Brennan, J., Marshall, J. and White, J., dissenting).
85. *Id.* at 63 (Brennan, J., dissenting).
86. *Id.* at 71 (Marshall, J., dissenting).
87. *Id.* at 112 (Marshall, J., dissenting).
88. Gary Orfield and John T. Yun, "Resegregation in American Schools," The Civil Rights Project, Harvard University (June 1999).
89. 503 U.S. 467 (1992).
90. *Id.* at 474.
91. *Id.* at 490.
92. *Id.* at 496.
93. *Id.* at 506 (Scalia, J., dissenting).
94. 115 S. Ct. 2038 (1995).
95. *Id.* at 2050–51.
96. *Id.* at 2051–55.
97. *Id.* at 2062 (Thomas, J., concurring).
98. *Id.* (Thomas, J., concurring).

99. *Id.* (Thomas, J., concurring).
100. *Id.* (emphasis added).
101. Rosenberger v. University of Virginia, 515 U.S. 819, 823 (1995).

Chapter Eight: Democracy and the Corporation

1. First Nat'l Bank of Boston v. Bellotti, 435 U.S. 765, 809–10 (1978) (White, J., dissenting).
2. Dartmouth College v. Woodward, 17 U.S. 518 (1819).
3. *Id.*
4. *Id.*
5. *Id.*
6. Marsh v. Alabama, 326 U.S. 501 (1946).
7. *Id.*
8. Grace Marsh, "Our Fight for the Right to Preach," *Awake!* 226, 228, April 22, 1998.
9. *Marsh,* 326 U.S. at 502–3.
10. *Id.* at 501.
11. *Id.*
12. *Id.*
13. *Id.*
14. *Id.* at 504.
15. *Id.* at 505.
16. *Id.*
17. *Id.* at 506.
18. *Id.*
19. *Id.* at 503.
20. *Id.* at 507.
21. *Id.* at 508.
22. *Id.* at 509.
23. *Id.* at 511 (Reed, J., dissenting).
24. Amalgated Food Employees Union v. Logan Valley Plaza, Inc., 391 U.S. 308 (1968).
25. *Id.*
26. *Id.*
27. *Id.* at 318.
28. *Id.* at 319–20.
29. Lloyd Corp. v. Tanner, 407 U.S. 551 (1972).
30. *Id.*
31. *Id.* at 556 (quoting Amalgamated Food Employees Union v. Logan Valley Plaza, 391 U.S. 308, 319 (1968)).
32. *Id.* at 560.
33. *Id.* at 564.
34. Lloyd Corp. v. Tanner, 407 U.S. 551, 568 (1972).
35. *Id.* at 565.

36. *Id.*
37. Marsh v. Alabama, 326 U.S. 501 (1946).
38. *See Lloyd Corp.,* 407 U.S. at 565.
39. Hudgens v. NLRB, 424 U.S. 507 (1976).
40. *Id.* at 518.
41. *Id.* at 510.
42. *Id.* at 539.
43. *See* Pruneyard Shopping Center v. Robins, 447 U.S. 74 (1980) (rejecting First Amendment and Taking Clause attacks by shopping-mall owners on the California Supreme Court's determination that the state constitution allowed political speech in shopping centers); New Jersey Coalition Against War in the Middle East v. J.M.B. Realty Corporation, 138 N.J. 326 (1994) (holding that regional and community shopping centers must allow leafleting on public issues consistent with reasonable regulation); *see also* Batchelder v. Allied Stores Int'l Inc., 388 Mass. 83 (1983) and Bock v. Westminster Mall Co., 819 P.2d 55 (Colo. 1991).
44. Robert Nozick, *Anarchy, State and Utopia* (New York: Basic Books, 1974), 26.
45. *Id.* at x.
46. See Eric Foner, The Story of American Freedom (New York: Norton: 1998).
47. Lochner v. New York,198 U.S. 45 (1905).
48. West Coast Hotel v. Parrish, 300 U.S. 379 (1937); *see also* Nebbia v. New York, 291 U.S. 502 (1934).
49. *Lochner,* 198 U.S. at 45.
50. *Id.* at 57.
51. *Id.* at 61.
52. For an excellent article on how the Thirteenth Amendment changed our notions of liberty and contrasting notions of "Republican Free Labor" and "Commodity Free Labor," *see* James Gray Pope, "Labor and the Constitution: From Abolition to Deindustrialization," 65 *Texas L. Rev.* 1071, 1100–1111 (1987); *see also* J. Auerbach, *Labor and Liberty* (1966).
53. Clara Bingham and Laura Leedy Gansler, *Class Action* (Doubleday, 2002); Jenson v. Eveleth Taconite Co., 130 F.3d 1287 (8th Cir. 1997).
54. *See* Suzanne Sangree, "Title VII Prohibitions Against Hostile Environment Sexual Harassment and the First Amendment: No Collision in Sight," 47 *Rutgers L. Rev.* 461 (1995).
55. *See* Eugene Volokh, "Freedom of Speech and Workplace Harassment," 39 *UCLA L. Rev.* 1791 (1992); Eugene Volokh, "What Speech Does 'Hostile Environment' Harassment Law Restrict?" 85 *Geo. L. J.* 627 (1997).
56. *See* Deborah Epstein, "Can a 'Dumb Ass Woman' Achieve Equality in the Workplace? Running the Gauntlet of Hostile Environment Harassing Speech," 84 *Geo. L. J.* 399 (1996); Deborah Epstein, "Free Speech At Work: Verbal Harassment as Gender-Based Discriminatory (Mis)Treatment," 85 *Geo. L.J.* 649 (1997).
57. NLRB v. Jones and Laughlin Steel Corp., 301 U.S. 1 (1937).
58. First Nat'l Bank of Boston v. Bellotti, 435 U.S. 765 (1978).
59. *Id.* at 768 (quoting Mass. Gen. Laws Ann. Ch. 55 sec. 8 [West 1977]).
60. *See id.*

61. Buckley v. Valeo, 424 U.S. 1 (1976).
62. 435 U.S. at 776.
63. *Id.* at 776–77.
64. *Id.*
65. *Id.* at 788–89 (quoting United States v. Automobile Workers, 352 U.S. 567, 570 [1957]).
66. *Id.* at 789.
67. *Id.*
68. First Nat'l Bank of Boston v. Bellotti, 435 U.S. 765, 789–90 (1978).
69. *See id.*
70. *Id.* at 790.
71. *Id.*
72. *Id.* at 787.
73. *Id.* at 793.
74. *Id.* at 793–94.
75. *Id.* at 794.
76. *Id.* at 795.
77. *Id.* at 803 (White, J., dissenting).
78. *Id.* at 809 (White, J., dissenting).
79. *Id.* (White, J., dissenting).
80. *Id.* at 809–10 (White, J., dissenting) (emphasis added).
81. *Id.* at 823 (Rehnquist, C.J., dissenting).
82. *Id.* at 823 (Rehnquist, C.J., dissenting) (quoting Dartmouth College v. Woodward, 17 U.S. 518, 636 (1819).
83. *Id.* at 826 (Rehnquist, C.J., dissenting).
84. Tillman Act, ch. 420, 34 Stat. 864 (1907).
85. First Nat'l Bank of Boston v. Bellotti, 435 U.S. 765 (1978).
86. Buckley v. Valeo, 424 U.S. 1 (1976).
87. *Id.* at 48.
88. Adam Winkler, *Corporate Contribution Bans and the Separation of Ownership and Control in the Early Twentieth Century*, 1–3 (2000).
89. *Id.*
90. *Id.*
91. *Id.*
92. *Id.*
93. Quoted in 31 Upton Sinclair, *The Brass Check: A Study of American Journalism* (1919), 31.
94. Winkler at 47.
95. "The Week," 81 *The Nation* 475, 475 (1905).
96. "The Week," 81 *The Nation* 434, 435 (1905).
97. *See* Robert Borosage, "Enron Conservatives," *The Nation*, May 4, 2002.
98. *See* "The Great Recusal," *The American Prospect*, February 25, 2002, at 2.
99. *See* Center for Responsive Politics, "Enron and Anderson: The Issue," *available* at http://www.opensecrets.org/news/enron/index.asp (last visited April 30, 2002).

100. *See id.*

101. Tillman Act, ch. 420, 34 Stat. 864 (1907).

102. First Nat'l Bank of Boston v. Bellotti, 435 U.S. 765 (1978).

103. Buckley v. Valeo, 424 U.S. 1 (1976).

104. Anderson v. City of Boston, 376 Mass. 178 (1978).

105. *Id.* at 192.

106. *Id.*

107. *Id.* at 196.

108. *Id.*; *see also* First Nat'l Bank of Boston v. Bellotti, 435 U.S. 765 (1978).

109. National Labor Relations Act of 1935 (Wagner Act), Pub. L. No. 198, 49 Stat. 449 (codified as amended at 29 U.S.C. sec. 151–69).

110. NLRB v. Jones and Laughlin Steel Corp., 301 U.S. 1 (1937).

111. Jamin Raskin, Book Review, "Reviving the Democratic Vision of Labor Law," 42 *Hastings L.J.* 1067 (1991).

112. 29 U.S.C. sec. 158(c).

113. NLRB v. Gissel Packing Co., 395 U.S. 575, 620 (1969).

114. *Id.* at 617.

Chapter Nine: Unflagging Patriotism

1. *As I Please 1943–1945, The Collected Essays, Journalism and Letters of George Orwell,* 361 (New York 1968).

2. *Id.* at 362.

3. *Id.* (emphasis in original). Nationalism revolves most frequently around the nation-state, but Orwell wanted to use the term also to describe the dogmatic mind-set and authoritarian power-worship of monistic political ideologies such as Communism, fascism, Nazism, pacifism, Trotskyism, and politicized religion.

4. *See* George Will, "Onward and Upward," the *Washington Post,* March 12, 2002, at A21. Will, for example, obviously celebrates the very same "nationalism" that Orwell denounced:

    > Soon after Sept. 11, Wal-Mart's shelves held Little Patriots Diapers, spangled with little blue stars. Americans are not only virtuosos of marketing, they are famously patriotic. Nationalistic, too. Patriotism is love of one's country; nationalism is the assertion of national superiority. Nationalism is the rejection of cultural relativism, the basis of "multiculturalism." Hence nationalism is anathema to the avant garde.

5. Professor Judith N. Shklar described a "liberalism of fear" that built in structural checks and balances to prevent the abusive usurpation of power and laid down carefully defined civil liberties to build a shield against official cruelty. See Judith N. Shklar, *The Liberalism of Fear* (1989) and *Ordinary Vices* (1984).

6. Jürgen Habermas, "Struggles for Recognition in the Democratic Constitutional State," in Jürgen Habermas, *The Inclusion of the Other: Studies in Political Theory* 225–26, 203–36 (Ciarin Cronin & Pablo DeGrieff, eds., Ciarin Cronin, trans. 1998).

7. See generally Jed Rubenfeld, *Freedom & Time* (2001), for a lucid and

authoritative statement about the importance of the Constitution being written.

8. Dr. Martin Luther King, Jr., "I See The Promised Land" (April 3, 1968). Speech available at: http://www.creighton.edu/ulk/speeches/promised.html. I have italicized the word "for" since Dr. King gave it special emphasis in the delivery of his speech.

9. *Id.*

10. Texas v. Johnson, 491 U.S. 397 (1989).

11. *See* S.J. Res. 7 (March 13, 2001); H. Res. 36 (March 13, 2001, passed July 17, 2001).

12. *See* 4 U.S.C sec. 8(k) ("The flag, when it is in such condition that it is no longer a fitting emblem for display, should be destroyed in a dignified way, preferably by burning.")

13. 18 U.S.C. sec. 700(b).

14. See Roland Barthes, *Mythologies*, 109–156 (Jonathan Cape Ltd. trans. 17th prtg. 1985).

15. This story has been told in fascinating detail by Robert Goldstein, *Saving Old Glory* 1 (Westview Press 1995). (Hereafter *Saving Old Glory.*)

16. Judith Shklar, *American Citizenship: The Quest for Inclusion* 53 (1991).

17. *See generally, Saving Old Glory.*

18. *Id* at 41. The first flag desecration bill passed by the House of Representatives in 1890 was designed to stop flag desecration by business advertisers but its failure in the Senate in the face of business opposition forced the early movement to turn to state legislatures for action.

19. Halter v. Nebraska, 205 U.S. 34 (1907).

20. *Saving Old Glory* at 14.

21. *Id.* at 92. Goldstein writes that: "by 1920, flag protection etiquette in practice primarily focused on suppressing political dissent."

22. *Id.* at 74.

23. West Virginia v. Barnette, 319 U.S. 624 (1943).

24. 1971 article in *Art in America* (cited in *Saving Old Glory, supra,* n15).

25. *Saving Old Glory* at 169.

26. *Id.* at 165.

27. *Id.* at 154–55.

28. Joyce v. United States, 454 F.2d 971 (1971).

29. *Id.* at 981–82.

30. *Id.* at 977–78.

31. *Saving Old Glory* at 19.

32. *Id.* at 23.

33. Minersville Sch. Dist. v. Gobitis, 310 U.S. 586 (1940); West Virginia v. Barnette, 319 U.S. 624 (1943).

34. 319 U.S. at 627.

35. *Id.* at 629 (stating that the Jehovah's Witnesses teach that "the obligation imposed by law of God is superior to that of laws enacted by temporal government," and citing their literalist interpretation of Exodus, chapter 20, verses 4 and 5: "Thou shalt not make unto thee any graven image, or any like-

ness of anything that is in heaven above, or that is in the earth beneath, or that is in the water under the earth; thou shalt not bow down thyself to them nor serve them.").

36. *Id.* at 633.
37. *Id.* at 633–34.
38. 310 U.S. 586 (1940).
39. 319 U.S. at 640.
40. *Id.* at 641.
41. *Id.* at 642.
42. *Id.*
43. Street v. New York, 394 U.S. 576 (1969).
44. *Id.* at 579.
45. *Id.* at 576.
46. Texas v. Johnson, 491 U.S. 397 (1989).
47. *Id.* at 400n1 (citing Tex. Penal Code Ann. Sec. 42.09(b) (1989)).
48. *Id.* at 406.
49. United States v. O'Brien, 391 U.S. 367, 376 (1968).
50. 491 U.S. at 407.
51. Texas v. Johnson, 491 U.S. 397, 414–17 (1989).
52. *Id.* at 422 (Rehnquist, C.J., dissenting).
53. *Id.* at 429 (Rehnquist, C.J., dissenting).
54. *Id.* at 437 (Stevens, J., dissenting) (emphasis added).
55. *Id.* at 436 (Stevens, J., dissenting).
56. H.R. 2978, 101st Congress (1989).
57. United States v. Eichman, 496 U.S. 310 (1990).
58. *Id.* at 317.
59. H. Res. 36, 107th Congress (2001).
60. *See* "Amending the Constitution to Protect the Flag," Statement of Richard Parker, Professor of Law, Harvard Law School, Before the Subcommittee on the Constitution, Federalism, and Property Rights of the Committee on the Judiciary, United States Senate, June 6, 1995.
61. *American Heritage Dictionary* 357 (1981).
62. 4 U.S.C. sec. 8(k).
63. Indeed, many patriotic American citizens and entities sponsor annual flag-burning bonfires on Flag Day. The Dixie Flag Company in Austin, Texas, has one which, according to its owner Pete Van DePuutte, consists of nine consecutive hours of flag-burning.
64. Supporters sometimes object that this is a misreading since the Flag Amendment bans physical flag desecration from the political right, left and center alike. Yet, from a free-speech vantage point, banning *all* speech considered unpatriotic by government does not cure the censorship, it just expands it. As Justice Kennedy pointed out in 1995 in his majority opinion in Rosenberger v. Rector & Visitors of the University of Virginia, the idea that "debate is not skewed so long as multiple voices are silenced is simply wrong; the debate is skewed in multiple ways." 515 U.S. 819, 831–32 (1995).
65. 4 U.S.C. sec. 8(i)

66. 4 U.S.C. sec. 8(d), (j).
67. 4 U.S.C. sec. 8(i).
68. *Saving Old Glory* at 23. A correspondent to the Letters to the Editor page of the *New York Times* on October 5, 1904, made the cogent and widely felt point that the flag was the "property of the whole people, not any one party."
69. 4 U.S.C. sec. 8(g) (emphasis added).
70. 18 U.S.C. sec. 700(b).
71. *Saving Old Glory* at 112.
72. 18 U.S.C. sec. 700(b).
73. In Jones v. Mayer, 392 U.S. 409, 439 (1968), the Court ruled that the Thirteenth Amendment "clothed Congress with the power to pass all laws necessary and proper for abolishing all badges and incidents of slavery."
74. Mary R. Dearing, "Veterans in Politics," *The Story of the G.A.R.* 410 (1952). For that matter, why not ban the swastika, which represents genocide and fascism, and which millions of people lost their lives fighting against? Why not the hammer and sickle? Why not ban pornography, which to many Americans sends a message equally vicious and dehumanizing as a flag on fire? We should not open the door to regulation of offensive and hateful expression in this way, for there is no logical place to close it.
75. West Virginia v. Barnette, 319 U.S. 624, 641 (1943).

Chapter Ten: Democracy Rising

1. Thomas Paine, *Collected Writings* 85 (1995).
2. 446 U.S. 55 (1980); 42 U.S.C.S. sec. 1973.
3. 491 U.S. 164 (1989) (holding that the ban on race discrimination in the making and enforcement of contracts "does not apply to conduct which occurs after the formation of the contract").
4. 494 U.S. 872 (1990).
5. 521 U.S. 507 (1997).
6. *Id.* at 520.
7. *Id.* at 536. ("When [the] Court has interpreted the Constitution, it has acted within the province of the Judicial Branch, which embraces the duty to say what the law is. When the political branches of the Government act against the background of a judicial interpretation of the Constitution already issued, it must be understood that in later cases and controversies the Court will treat its precedents with the respect due them under settled principles, including stare decisis, and contrary expectations must be disappointed.")
8. *U.S. v. Virginia,* 518 U.S. 515 (1996).
9. *Harper v. Virginia Board of Elections,* 383 U.S. 663 (1966).
10. *Id.* at 669 (emphasis in original).
11. Kathleen M. Sullivan, "What's Wrong with Constitutional Amendments?" in *Readings for American Government: Power and Purpose* 14, ed. David T. Canon, John J. Coleman and Kenneth R. Mayer (W.W. Norton, 2002).
12. *See* discussion of proposed amendments in *Great and Extraordinary Occasions:*

Developing Guidelines for Constitutional Change (The Constitution Project, 1999).

13. *McCulloch v. Maryland*, 17 U.S. 316 (Wheat. 1819).
14. This is the aspect of power that theorist John Gaventa considers "second dimension" because it concerns the structuring of background rules to produce particular kinds of political outcomes. Gaventa contrasts this with "first dimension" exercises of power which involve A more directly causing B to do something B would rather not do. The "third dimension" of power relates to the deployment of power through ideology and culture. See John Gaventa, "Power and Participation," in *Power and Powerlessness: Quiescence and Rebellion in an Appalachian Valley* (1980). I am indebted to Professor Gerald Frug for assigning Gaventa's essay as homework in my Local Government Law class when I was in law school. It had a profound effect on me.
15. See Steven Hill, *Fixing Elections: The Failure of America's Winner Take All Politics* (2002), for a lucid and authoritative argument for proportional representation.
16. Democracy insists that the people be able to choose freely their own leaders, and equal opportunity demands that each citizen has a chance to experience political leadership. Madison had something like this in mind when he wrote about the congressional Qualifications Clauses in *The Federalist*: "Who are to be the objects of popular choice? Every citizen whose merit may recommend him to the esteem and confidence of his country. No qualification of wealth, of birth, of religious faith, or of civil profession is permitted to fetter the judgment or disappoint the inclination of the people." Madison, *The Federalist* No. 57 at 351
17. Speeches given during presidential campaign, 1991–1992.
18. J.S. Mill, *Representative Government* (1861).
19. "Congressional Redistricting: How to Rig an Election," *The Economist*, April 27, 2002.
20. *Id.*
21. A thorough and nuanced argument for proportional representation appears in Robert Richie and Steven Hill, *Reflecting All of Us: The Case for Proportional Representation* (1999).
22. 462 U.S. 725 (1983).
23. Act of December 14, 1967, Pub. L. No. 90–196, 81 Stat. 581. The first statutory requirement for single-member districts was embodied in an 1842 statute (5 Stat. 491) which provided that representatives "should be elected by districts composed of contiguous territory equal in number to the number of representatives to which said state may be entitled, no one district electing more than one representative." An 1850 apportionment statute (9 Stat. 433) got rid of the single-member district requirement and Congress continued to see-saw on the issue.
24. See Steven Hill, *Fixing Elections: The Failure of America's Winner Take All Politics* 35 (2002).
25. *See* op-ed by Clint Bolick, *Wall Street Journal*, April 30, 1993.
26. For extensive statistical evidence about racially polarized white-bloc voting in the South, see Grofman, Handley and Niemi, *Minority Representation and the*

Quest for Voting Equality; Chandler Davidson and Bernard Grofman, *Quiet Revolution in the South: The Impact of the Voting Rights Act 1965–1990.*

27. Davidson and Grofman at 338.

28. Lani Guinier and Gerald Torres, *The Miner's Canary: Enlisting Race, Resisting Power, Transforming Democracy* (2002). *See also* Douglas Amy, *Real Choices, New Voices: The Case for Proportional Representation Elections in the United States,* Columbia Univ. Press, 1995.

29. Guinier and Torres at 252.

30. *Id.* at 253.

31. 424 U.S. 1 (1976).

32. Jamin Raskin and John Bonifaz, "Equal Protection and the Wealth Primary," 11 *Yale Law and Policy Review* 273 (1993).

33. The free market in campaign contributions and expenditures is passionate dogma among libertarians and conservatives today. *See e.g.,* Bradley A. Smith, *Unfree Speech, The Folly of Campaign Finance Reform* (Princeton Univ. Press, 2001).

34. See Terry v. Adams, 345 U.S. 461, 474 (1953) (Frankfurter, J., concurring) (stating that an all-white private club's endorsement process in which elected officials participated amounted to "a wholly successful effort to withdraw significance from the State-prescribed primary. . . ."

35. Bullock v. Carter, 405 U.S. 134, 143 (1972).

36. *Id.*

37. Raskin and Bonifaz, "The Constitutional Imperative of Democratically Financed Elections," 94 *Colum. L. Rev.* 1160 (1994).

38. Information available from the Arizona Clean Elections Institute at www. azclean.org.

39. 424 U.S. at 57n65 ("Congress may engage in public financing of election campaigns and may condition acceptance of public funds on an agreement by the candidate to abide by specified expenditure limitations.").

40. Jamin Raskin, "Legal Aliens, Local Citizens: The Historical, Constitutional and Theoretical Meanings of Alien Suffrage," 141 *U.P.A. L. Rev.* 1391 (1991).

41. For those interested in a much more detailed treatment of the issue, *see id.,* from which this discussion is drawn.

42. 112 S. Ct. 2791 (1992).

43. *Id.* at 2874.

44. Michael H. v. Gerald D., 491 U.S. 110, 123 (1989).

45. Robert P. Moses and Charles Cobb Jr., *Radical Equations: Math Literacy and Civil Rights* 91 (2001).

Blacksher, James, 258n. 127
Bond, Julian, 226
Bonifaz, Joan, 234
Bonifaz, John, 236, 267n. 80
Bork, Judge Robert, 241
Bradbury, Bill, 52–53
Brady Handgun Violence Prevention Act, 4
Brennan, Justice, 71, 253n. 9; corporate free
  speech and, 189; desegregation and, 160,
  162; First Amendment and, 92, 152, 153;
  Texas v. Johnson and, 210–11
Breyer, Justice Stephen, 2, 7, 23; *Bush v. Gore*
  and, 15, 18, 19
Brown v. Board of Education, 6, 82, 146,
  154, 157–65
Brown, Janet, 132
Brown, Jerry, 138
Brown, Justice Henry Billings, 85, 155–57
Bryan ,William Jennings, 208
Buchanan, Pat, 54
Buckley v. Valeo: First Amendment and, 139,
  186; limits on campaign spending and,
  139, 186, 189–90, 193, 234, 237
Budweiser, 142
Bugliosi, Vincent, 26, 28
Bullock v. Carter, 235
Burdick v. Takushi, 41, 112–13
Burger Court, the: desegregation fatigue and,
  160; education and, 146, 151
Burger, Chief Justice Warren, 109, 151–52
Burke, Edmund, 23
Burns v. Richardson, 78
Bush v. Gore, 56; Article II and, 13, 20; con-
  servative judicial supremacy and, 11; *Dred
  Scott* decision and, 24–25; Due Process
  and, 17–18; Equal Protection violation
  and, 12, 14–16, 17, 19, 21, 44, 231; Fif-
  teenth Amendment and, 22; Florida vote
  recount and, 11–12, 14–20, 24–26; Fourteenth Amendment and, 22, 89; Rehnquist Court decision on, 3, 8–10, 11–29,
  91; rule-of-law principles and, 25; Twelfth
  Amendment and, 13
Bush v. Vera, 76, 77, 79–80
Bush, President George H. W., 27, 119, 125,
  212
Bush, President George W., 245n. 42; 2000
  presidential election and, 45, 47–48, 52,
  53, 59; corporate interests and, 192; electoral college votes and, 38, 45–46; Equal
  Protection claim of, 14–16, 17, 19, 61;
  judicial activism and, 6; Supreme Court
  justices and, 20, 27, 241
Bush-Gore Debates, 118, 140; corporate

sponsorship of, 129–32 (*see also* CPD;
  presidential debates)
Byrd, Senator Harry F., 58

California: Elections Code, 51; free speech
  in, 179
campaign financing (*see also* McCain-Feingold legislation): Clean Elections, 236;
  contribution limitations and, 236; corporations and, 186–94; electoral politics and,
  234–38; Equal Protection and, 235, 256n.
  81; hard money, 192, 236, 245n. 42;
  limits on, 139, 193; matching funds, 236;
  private, 82, 234–38, 256n. 81; public, 98,
  235–37, 256n. 81, 278n. 39; reform, 229,
  235–36; soft money, 125, 129, 192–93;
  special interests and, 235
candidates: access to public airwaves, 237
  (see also *Arkansas Educational Television
  Commission v. Forbes*); black, 85; campaign financing for (*see* campaign financing); constitutional rights of, 121–24;
  Democratic, 133–36; discrimination
  against, 28, 44, 101–104, 118, 120; filing
  fees for, 123; incumbent, 93–95; independent (*see* independent candidates); major-
  party, 45, 109, 111, 114, 119, 139;
  minor-party, 72 (*see also* independent candidates; third–party candidates), 97,
  104–106, 108–109, 266nn. 68; minority-
  preferred, 76; presidential, 62; Republi-
  can, 52, 133–36; right to debate, 132–37;
  Socialist Workers Party, 105, 136; third-
  party (*see* third-party candidates); viable,
  133–36; write-in, 93, 95, 105
Cardille, Jeff, 50
Carter, President Jimmy, 33
Casey, 6
Casey, Robert, 136
Catania, David, 233
Cato Insititue, 181
Center for Voting and Democracy, 66, 230,
  267n. 80
Checota, Joe, 136
Christian Coaltion, 129
Citizens': Flag Alliance, 203, 213, 217; Task
  Force on Fair Debate, 140
City of Boerne v. Flores, 224
City of Mobile v. Bolden, 21–22
civil rights, 58, 82, 87; laws, 71; shrinking
  of, 223
Civil Rights Act of 1964: Title VII, 184–85
Civil Rights movement, 41, 45, 58, 69,
  225–26; American flag and, 206 (*see also*
  flag); public schools and, 145 (*see also*